A QUEST FOR TEARS
SURVIVING TRAUMATIC BRAIN INJURY

Seán Dwyer

A QUEST FOR TEARS
SURVIVING TRAUMATIC BRAIN INJURY

Seán Dwyer

Penchant Press International
Bellingham, Washington
United States of America

The thoughts, opinions, and experiences described in this book are those of the author, who is not a medical professional. Those seeking medical attention should confer with a licensed medical professional.

Penchant Press International
PO Box 1333
Blaine, WA 98231
USA

Penchantpressinternational.com

ISBN 978-0-97249606-3
LCCN 2018912104

A Quest for Tears: Surviving Traumatic Brain Injury
Seán Dwyer 1st ed.

sean@seandwyerauthor.com

For my wife, Maureen,
for making this story possible.

For my father, Jack Dwyer,
for supporting every goal I set for myself.

For Patty Shadrix,
Who raised me as her own, with unconditional love.

For Robyn Bennett Underwood,
for shaping me into a writer.

For Cami Ostman,
for shaping my words into this text.

The only disability is one's refusal to adapt.
~ Dr. Sean Stephenson

Contents

Part 2: Convalescence.

Part 4: Quest Dismissed.

Introduction

Who am I? Prior to being rear-ended at high speed, I was *that* guy, a polyglot who was especially a whiz at Spanish, a well-respected college educator, a creative writer with two novels and a nonfiction book under his belt, someone at ease with the written word as both a reader and a writer, a prolific songwriter, someone blessed with an excellent memory and a wide range of interests and knowledge, an avid networker and supporter of my talented writer colleagues, and a person compassionate enough to cry at the misfortunes of others.

Now, I'm *that* guy, the one who listens to audiobooks because reading makes him dizzy and nauseated and brings on sudden deep fatigue, the one who goes to bed at 7pm and sleeps 10 hours and then naps for two hours in the afternoon, the one who really does wear sunglasses at night and on cloudy days, the one who would have remembered your name two years ago but can't quite keep hold of it now, the one who can't write fiction because he can't slip into the milieu where his characters live, the one who studies research on recovery from Traumatic Brain Injury to the exclusion of almost all previous intellectual pursuits. The one who hasn't shed a single tear for any reason, tragic or joyful, for more than three years.

I am writing nearly four years after a car accident that gave me a concussion and ligament damage in my neck. I missed six months of work as a university professor, and I would have done well to stay home another year, if I could have. Returning to work, though, gave me concrete ways to measure my deficits and my progress in recovering my faculties. The stimuli I have faced are slowly turning my deficits into surpluses. And no one sees much indication of my struggle except for my continuous use of the darkest sunglasses I can find.

Traumatic Brain Injuries (TBI) are a medical mystery. You can't see them, so for many people, they don't exist.

Medical professionals can predict their course and duration about as well as seismologists can predict earthquakes. Diligent researchers have found ways to mitigate the short-term damage they cause, but TBIs foster long-term damage as well, and that damage is unpredictable, ranging from none to early-onset dementia. A TBI is, for many people, a time bomb that ticks for decades.

The invisibility of a TBI (without expensive imaging) underscores the need for everyone involved in a head-bumping mishap and its aftermath to be hyper-aware of the possible complications of Post-Concussion Syndrome. Once the patient gets over the need to sleep in a dark room for a couple of days, headaches, light sensitivity, confusion, and other seemingly minor annoyances may continue. Everyone gets headaches and forgets words, so these reactions to a concussion are likely to be dismissed as a minor glitch or annoyance.

You may find yourself on one side or the other of that perceptual barrier; you may be the person who hears "you don't look injured," or the person who forgets that your friend or loved one isn't quite the same and needs your help, or a teacher who doesn't even know that the sleepy, distracted kid in your class fell on the playground last week and never told anyone she hit her head.

And yet, for the TBI Survivor who loses enough of an intellectual edge to feel the cognitive deficit, every day is a struggle to keep pace with the treadmill of life, to find workarounds allowing for an appearance of normality, and to avoid collapse under the weight of the battle. Some of us sleep too much, and others suffer terrible insomnia, but we all feel the same fatigue. Some of us find effective ways to mask the headaches, and some of us don't. Some of us find our work affected by various cognitive issues, and others may work in jobs that allow them to fake it until they make it.

The likely readers of this book are Traumatic Brain Injury Survivors, their caregivers and friends, educators who work with young people, and medical professionals who seek the perspective of a Survivor. My goal is to share my physical and emotional experiences, challenges I have faced since I reemerged in society, my own classroom experiences with TBI Survivors, and a discussion of resources with good recovery tips and promising research.

One new facet of life that I already experience is a strong desire to advocate for you—the TBI Survivor, caregiver, family member, teacher, or doctor—who comes into the TBI world. I have already blown a lot of frustration out of my soul through talks with my wife, Maureen, Facebook posts, and monthly meetings of the Brain Injury Alliance of Washington. I am not writing this book to vent. I am writing it to create another road map (some exist already), another perspective, another tool for you to use in your recovery.

I hope you find the narrative useful and interesting, and that you glean a number of insights into your struggle, or that of someone you love, because my journey will apply to a surprising degree to the experience of many people who are recovering. Our brains are wondrous entities, capable of great plasticity and cleverness in the rebuilding process. Because we are all built more or less the same, our brains will tend to adopt the same techniques for repair. That makes my journey valuable to you, and yours to me.

Therefore, I want you to see me as a resource for your personal journey. You will find an Information section after my story, in an effort to give you access to resources you may need. Any questions you can't get answered from my book or other sources are welcome via my website. I'll use them to build a FAQ for the benefit of other Survivors and their allies. As a community, we can provide information and comfort to each other in this difficult time.

Thanks for joining me on my TBI journey. May your burden be lighter as we walk the path together.

Part 1: Accident-Aftermath.

Impact.
January 29, 2015 3:42pm

I'm driving from Fairhaven, on the south side of Bellingham, Washington, toward downtown. My route takes me up a two-lane road that hugs a condo-topped bluff on my right and overlooks a steep drop to Bellingham Bay on the left. To my right, ground cover, green even in January, holds the earth in place. To my left, the expanse of the Bay, dotted with a variety of watercraft, sparkles in the waning sunlight. Northbound, I have the sun at my back, low in the sky, not bothersome in my rearview mirror.

On this stretch of road, named the Boulevard, I drive through an empty pedestrian crosswalk. I round a curve and approach a Crosswalk Ahead sign, which alerts me to a second crosswalk, its sign shrouded in shrubbery.

Standing at the right side of the road are two college-age men who are waiting to cross. A glance in the rearview mirror tells me no one is on my tail, so I slow and stop. One of the men nods his thanks and steps into the crosswalk. He focuses on something behind me, and his eyes widen. He pushes his friend away from the road and leaps back onto the sidewalk. My gut does a flip.

I prepare for a possible impact. It won't help to watch the mirror. I put the stick in neutral and nestle into my seat, trying to relax to lessen any injury if I get bumped. I don't have time to put my car back in gear and race forward. A thought flashes through my mind: I may lose my Honda Civic's third bumper in twelve years. I listen for the screech of tires; I spend five long seconds praying that the driver behind me will stop.

The tires never screech. Maybe the approaching car stopped. I wait for the pedestrians to step into the road again. I hear a *bang!* right behind me that sounds like the lid of an empty Dumpster dropping, echoing. My seat slams into my back and head. I prepare to fly forward, and I wince at the thought of getting a face full of air-bag powder. Instead, my seat gives way, and I fall flat on my back. My legs fly up, my right shin scraping the dash. It burns, but a moment later I forget it when my seat catapults me skyward. The shoulder belt squeezes the air from my lungs, but it doesn't support my head. I feel it snap forward on my neck, my chin bouncing off my sternum.

I find myself lying against my seat, which is at a 45-degree angle from the horizontal. I hear gravel on the roadway, louder than it should be. My eyes focus, and I look up through my moon roof at the trees that overhang the sidewalk. The Civic rolls for a few seconds, and it eases to a stop with a gentle rasping sound from the rear end. The engine is purring, and I want to turn it off in case the gas tank is ruptured and the car is going to blow up. I can't reach the keys from my position. I wiggle my toes. They rub against my socks, and relief washes over me.

I lean forward on my left arm, and a searing pain throws me back onto the seat. My arm might be broken. I roll to my right, get painless leverage, and push myself more upright. I put the stick in gear. I reach for the keys, but my steadfast engine sounds so sweet that I hesitate to shut it off. I don't know how long it will be before my baby returns from the repair shop.

I give in and turn the key. The mirror from the sun visor has fallen intact into my lap. I pick it up with my good hand and place it in a cup holder. I don't want it to break. I don't need seven years of bad luck. My phone is still lying on the passenger seat. I grab it and dial 911 in case no one else calls.

911 Operator: What's your emergency?
Me: [Is it an emergency?] I just got rear-ended.
911: Is anyone injured?
Me: [Am I?] I am, some. I don't know about the

other car.

911: Do you need an ambulance?

Me: My left arm is really sore, and my neck isn't so great.

911: What is your location?

A woman appears and opens my door. She asks if I'm okay and tells me she is a nurse practitioner. Then running footsteps, growing louder, signal the arrival of a dark-haired man. His eyes wide, he asks, "Are you okay?"

I raise a finger to ask them for a moment to finish the call. I try to describe my location to the operator. She doesn't understand where I am, but finally I get through to her. I drop the phone to the seat and look to my left. Pain jolts my neck.

"I think I'm okay," I say. I turn to put my legs on the ground, but a wave of vertigo makes me lie back. "Maybe I'll rest a moment."

I take a few deep breaths, figuring I really have no need to hurry. The vertigo passes, and I hear sirens.

Aftermath.
January 29, 2015 4pm

I pull out my phone. I have 10 percent battery life left, and I kick myself for not having a charge when I need it. I'm getting ready to dial my wife, Maureen, at work when flashing lights draw my gaze to an ambulance that is inching past traffic from the south. It pulls up in front of the Civic. Two overall-clad men jump out and trot over to me.

"Did you call us?" They invite me to climb into the back of the ambulance.

I grunt and groan my way out of the car. I pull myself upright with my right hand. Traffic is stopped in both directions. There's a cop on a motorcycle, his little lights blinking a blinding, bright blue and red, blocking the southbound lane. In front of my car is a southbound SUV that I might have hit if I had crossed the center line. The driver of the Toyota Land Cruiser that hit me has gone back to his SUV. His grille is smashed on the passenger's side. A dark liquid has pooled in the long space between our vehicles. I don't understand why he is so far back.

I shuffle up to the ambulance. The steps are tall, and it hurts to climb in. I sit, and an EMT prepares to wrap a blood-pressure cuff around my left arm.

"That's the arm I hurt. It's really sore." They ask about any other injuries, and I mention my neck and show them my right shin. The BP cuff goes on my right arm, and they clip a sensor to my right index finger. Blood oxygen and pulse rate.

One EMT fiddles with my neck. I ask if I can call my wife of five months, because I am going to need a ride home. They agree to it, so I dial Maureen.

"Hi sweetie, is there any way you can leave work? My car is disabled on the Boulevard." An EMT raises his eyebrows at my description of the scenario. I wonder if he wonders if my brain is working right. I know what I'm doing, trying to keep her from worrying if she's stuck at work.

"We're interviewing for a receptionist. I have to stay until 5. I'm sorry."

"That's OK. I'll find someone else to give me a ride. I'll be fine."

The skeptical EMT says, "Well, your vital signs are good. If we transport you, you have to pay for the trip. So, we can release you. But you should get yourself checked out."

I know I won't be paying for this accident, so I should let them transport me. I'll get in to see someone at the ER much faster that way. But I think they don't want the hassle of delivering me, so I thank them and step slowly from the ambulance, trying to avoid jostling my left arm. It's on fire, sending jolts of pain to my head and down to my fingertips. I check my phone battery again. Just 7 percent left. I try to think of who could come for me. I mull over some names of people who are surely working, and then it hits me: I can ask my steadfast friend Cami. She's going to run the writers' meeting I'm headed to. It's a couple of hours till the meeting, but if she's going to the Pickford Theatre early, she can swing by for me. Bonus: she has a 2001 Civic as well, and until mine is fixed, the only way I'll be able to ride in one is to hop into hers.

I dial her number. "Hi Seán. How are you?"

"Well, OK, but my car is dead, and I'm wondering if I can get a lift from you to the meeting."

"I'm tied up for now, but I can come for you closer to meeting time. Where are you?"

"Not far from Downtown. On the Boulevard. But I'll go ahead and check for another ride. Actually, I got rear-ended, so I'll probably walk there after I talk to the cop. See you at 6." Battery is down to 3 percent.

I see two young men huddled together on the sidewalk. I walk over to them.

"Are you the guys I stopped for?" They nod.

"Thanks for sticking around. Did you talk to him?"

"We told the officer you stopped for us."

I walk toward the BPD motorcycle, which is sitting a few feet behind the Civic, and now I address the officer. "I'm the guy who got hit."

"Yes, you are." I hand him my license. I turn and face the back of the Civic for the first time.

"Oh."

"Yeah, you got nailed pretty good."

I see the Land Cruiser in the distance. "Did he back up?"

"No. You rolled 136 feet." I look beyond the Land Cruiser and see the Crosswalk sign in the distance.

"Wow." It feels as if I rolled maybe twenty feet. My car has jumped onto the sidewalk, and I didn't even notice when it hopped the curb. I try to ponder how my perception could be so far off, but no explanation comes to me. The officer takes the other driver's statement. He was talking to his wife, and when he looked back forward, I was stopped. He didn't have time to hit the brakes, but he veered a foot or so to the left. As an afterthought, he said that the sun in his rearview mirror made it harder to see me.

The officer snaps shut his notebook and hands me my license. I'm free to wander. I shuffle back toward the Land Cruiser with the driver. He joins his wife on the sidewalk. A child, probably ten years old, looks distressed.

"It's OK," the driver says. "This is why we have insurance."

"I'm fine," I tell the kid. "This is no big deal. They'll fix my car, and your dad's car, and that will be it."

"He's worried that it will cost us a lot of money," the driver tells me in a stage whisper.

"Nah," I reply. I'm wearing a thin leather jacket, and it's not really cold, but I'm shivering. Each shiver sends a jolt through my throbbing arm. The intense pain makes me stamp my feet, and I admire how tough I am, because I'm not crying. My eyes aren't even watering the slightest bit.

My phone finally dies, so I get the driver to take a photo of the back of the car and text it to me. "This will be something to show my kids," I say.

I turn around again, and Maureen is talking to the officer.

"Oh, hi," I say to her. She looks me up and down. "I thought you were at work," I continue.

"I couldn't stop thinking about you disabled on the side of the road, so I asked if I could go. Why didn't you tell me you got hit?"

"I didn't want you to worry. I'm OK."

"Are you sure?" I hear a quaver in her voice. Maureen is long and lithe, with shoulder-length brown hair, brown eyes and, generally, a sunny smile. I see no smile now.

"Yah. Well, my arm hurts, and my neck, and my head, and my leg. But I'm basically all right."

"When we get done here, let's see about getting you to a clinic."

I grimace, but I say, "That's probably good. I keep thinking about how Natasha Richardson bumped her head and died a couple of days later." Maureen looks away.

The cop stops southbound traffic again, and a tow truck pulls into the spot where the ambulance had sat. The towtruck driver and I inspect the car. It's crumpled to where there is no trunk left. The back window has shattered, and someone swept the glass into three tidy piles between the crosswalk and the Civic's final resting place.

"You took quite a hit," the towtruck driver says.

"I'm glad I didn't fill the gas tank this morning."

"That would have been a waste of money."

"Now that I'm looking at it, I'm not sure they'll be able to fix it."

"Oh, no, it's totaled. I'll haul it up to Ferndale, and you can come get your stuff out of it, but you won't be driving this one again."

"Oh, man, I spent $700 on a tune-up last week. And I bought new headlights."

"That's a drag. But here's one cool thing. You'll get a rental car, and we handle rentals for State Farm. Right now, we have a sweet Dodge Charger. Ask for that when you come for your rental."

"Nice!" It does sound like fun. And right now, a bigger car sounds good to me. I've always thought smart cars were cute, but I'm swearing off the idea of driving one as of now.

The driver starts prepping the Civic for its final ride. He straps my seat belt around the steering wheel. Maureen quickly take a series of photos from all sides of the car, including an interior shot, and then he drags my baby onto a flatbed and chains it down.

He pulls away, and I make a small wave at the crumpled rear end of the car I've driven since 2003. 227,000 miles, and I had just made up my mind to drive it to the 300,000-mile rollover. And here I am, carless, one-armed, with a sore neck and a headache. The adrenaline begins to wear off, and suddenly, my life sucks.

Maureen and I walk to her CR-V, parked off the road facing southbound. We climb in. Next up is dealing with State Farm. As cars whiz by us, Maureen helps me get the paperwork moving. It takes quite a while to get the claim open. (My claim number has a 5 and an S next to each other, and that really makes life hard at times.) She calls several walk-in clinics. They are all closed, as the delay in getting the claim number means it's now after 5pm. The only option I have is to go to the emergency room, if I want to get checked out. I don't want to make her sit in the ER for ages; the one time we went, we watched an ill, elderly man sit for a couple of hours, and we watched a stabbing victim, blood soaking though her shirt, come in and sit for too long as well. I can call the doctor in the morning.

Maureen looks wary of my decision to wait for treatment, but she doesn't push hard. We decide we need to eat dinner before we settle in for the night. She drives about a mile to Busara, a Thai place in a shopping center.

She goes in to get takeout. I have charged my phone a bit, so while I sit in the dark, I call a school colleague, Joan, and ask her to have our department chair, Paqui, call me. I tell Joan I won't be in Friday, and that's about all I can say. Maureen comes out with food, and we head home.

The decision to go home rather than to the emergency room isn't one I make lightly, nor is it the safest approach to my situation. My headache could be a symptom of a brain bleed that would also threaten my life.

Somehow, I don't care. It would be a drag to die that way, but I want to lie down. The ER will just send me home with pain meds anyway. I can keep tabs on my headache, and Maureen will as well. Should I sleep? Should I try to stay awake all night? I hope I can sleep before my incipient headache really comes on. That way, Maureen can rest before work tomorrow.

Maureen sets me up on the couch with my food and two Tylenol®. I don't even remember walking from her car to the living room. I'm just sitting, food in a bowl on my lap, with Sophie sitting next to me. Sophie is a Sphynx, a beige hairless cat of great elegance and dignity. She usually climbs onto my shoulder and snuggles under my chin, but right now, she curls up beside me. Maureen disappears.

Between bites, I pull the photo out of my text message. I'm feeling a bit of dark humor in the situation, because the car is destroyed, but I'm going to be fine in a day or two. I post to Facebook: "I'm fine, but I'm going to post a photo shortly of what happened to me this afternoon." I wait a couple of minutes, so people see my warning first, then I upload the photo of my car, again with reassurances of my well-being. This photo generates more than 100 comments in an hour or less. The well-wishing brings me comfort, but I really just want to share my amazement that I walked away from a car that now resembles a ball of crumpled tinfoil.

Then I check the Whatcom Scanner Report to see if I made the cut. They did report my accident. I comment that I'm sorry for tying up the road.

The Red Wheelbarrow Writers meeting has started. I call Cami to tell her I won't be able to make it. I ask her to give my regrets to the writers I was supposed to see that evening. I somehow forgot about the meeting, with all the insurance talk. I might have been able to get Maureen to drop me off downtown, but now, I'm feeling more pain, and it's just as well that I'm not trying to participate in the conversation.

I already had planned to call my son John, because it's his birthday. At this point, I don't know if I'll sound healthy or wobbly, so I opt to text him my message, with my car's photo to serve as my excuse. Then I do call my sister Cindy, because she is the nerve center of the family news network. I won't have to call anyone else. The evening's work gets wrapped up when Paqui calls me.

"I won't be able to come in tomorrow. My neck and arm hurt too much."

"I think you're going to need more time off than that. I suggest you take two weeks, because that way you can claim long-term medical leave, and both you and your subs will be paid for the time."

"Oh! Well, I don't like to miss class, but I am pretty sore."

We settle on a two-week leave. Maureen, whose job involves the nuances of insurance and medical legalities, tells me she will take care of discussions with Human Resources and the insurance company. Under the best of circumstances, I don't like insurance paperwork, and today I feel especially grateful for her support, because the pain in my head has ratcheted itself up a couple of notches, and I can't imagine leaning on my left arm to fill out paperwork with my right hand.

My other sons, Tom and Steve, call when they see my Facebook post. I assure them that I'm well, just a bit sore, and they trust my response.

First Night.
January 29-30, 2015

I've eaten my Thai food. I've taken two Tylenol® for my head and a Flexeril® left over from a time I wrenched my back two years ago. I've notified my next of kin. It's bedtime. I put on shorts and a t-shirt, in case I go to the ER after all. Maureen says she will lie down with me, so she can keep an eye on my condition.

Getting to bed is another chore. The Tylenol® isn't cutting my neck spasms, and my back, from shoulders to glutes, is swelling and stiffening. I shuffle to the bathroom and pee. I inspect my urine carefully for blood. I realize that I have multiple headaches; I have one throbbing atop my spine, a dull ache in my forehead, and a sharp, knifelike jab on the crown of my head. I inspect my pupils in the mirror. They're even.

I sit on the edge of the king bed. The pillows lie flat, promising no support. My head has to drop a long way to reach them. I pivot sideways and start to lean toward the mattress. My head flops back, and I gasp when my neck muscles rebel. I sit up, lace my hands behind my head for support, and lower my back to the bed. Once the mattress stops jiggling, the worst neck spasms abate, and I can breathe.

Maureen slips an ice pack under my neck, and I relax into it. I close my eyes, and when a jolt of pain wakes me, I discover that Sophie has curled up in my armpit, and Maureen is breathing softly.

Every time I close my eyes, time jumps forward until I move and wake up in agony. I dream of the impact, I startle, and pain wakes me. My usual culprits for developing insomnia—my to-do list for the next day, story ideas, earworms—have vacated the premises. For now, I see the silence in my brain as a blessing, because I keep falling asleep after the shooting pains that wake me.

I sleep from 9:43pm until 3:22am. My Up exercise band/sleep tracker tells me so. Three hours of deep sleep, ten minutes awake at 2:40, 44 minutes of insomnia, and another good stretch of sleep between 4:06am and 6:18. I obsess over my sleep cycle because I know I'll need sleep to heal.

First Morning.
January 30, 2015, 6:30am

I give up on sleeping at 6:30 when Maureen's alarm goes off. I say hi, so she knows she can turn on the overhead light. I try to turn my head to face her, but my neck blasts laser rays of pain in every direction. I settle for giving her a side-eye and a smile she may not be able to see.

The sun won't rise for another hour, so the room is really dark. I usually cover my eyes with my hand to avoid shocking them when the light comes on, but today I forget to do so. Maureen flips the switch, and the overhead light blooms like a nuclear flash. I close my eyes against the incoming waves, but they have already shattered the calm my brain had finally achieved. My forehead and the back of my skull respond by clamping down in a cramp like a brain freeze from ice cream. I wonder if she installed brighter bulbs; I have no recollection of the room being so bright last night.

Light leaks through my scrunched-up eyelids, but the brain pain passes anyway. I take a couple of deep breaths to move it along quicker.

"Are you sore?" Maureen asks. I take stock.

"Everywhere."

"I could bring you a couple of Aleve®."

"Nah. I need to get up anyway. I want to get my rental car early." Maureen has set up a list of times I need drivers, and several people have volunteered to take me places as needed.

"When is Tele coming?" I ask. Tele is a fisherwoman in Alaska during the summer, but she's in Bellingham now, finishing her memoir about life on a boat. She volunteered to take me to get my rental car.

"She said to let her know when you want to go."

"After the Aleve® kicks in, and before it kicks out."

"So, nine?"

With Step One planned, Maureen leaves to prepare for work. She looks back at me from the doorway.

"I wish there was some way I could stay home today," she says. I know she means it, and I know it's a really bad idea, because her role at the nonprofit where she works is one of the essential positions.

"I'll be out of the house anyway, getting the car and seeing the doctor. I'll let you know if I run into problems."

The Flexeril® I took last night has stopped working. I have neck spasms again, but my legs still feel leaden from the medicine. I hope some coffee will clear the cobwebs. I move my elbows into position to sit up, but my left arm gives me a harsh reminder that it took the brunt of the force of the collision. I'll need an x-ray to see what is wrong. I place my left arm across my body and push up with my right elbow.

My chest rises, but my head stays put. There's some new pain, but the problem is that my neck is just too weak to lift the weight. I touch the sides of my neck. Either I caught the mumps overnight, or I have swelled from the whiplash to the point that I can't reach around my neck with my two hands.

If I can't lift my head, how am I going to get out of bed? I roll slowly onto my right side, swivel until my feet touch the floor, then pick up my head with my right hand. I still can't gain a sitting position, so I complete my roll and wind up looking down at the mattress, knees on the floor as if I were praying. I decide a prayer won't hurt anything, so I ask for the pain to end. I handle the situation with the same stoicism I presented at the accident scene, when my arm hurt so much.

Now I can lift my head with both hands, as I would a bowling ball. Once I'm upright, I can push myself into a standing position. Step Two accomplished. As I walk toward the bedroom door, I take stock of my aches: All the usual pain, plus a deep ache in my right shin from what might be a bone bruise.

Sophie greets me in the hallway, stropping my ankles and rubbing her face on my bare feet. I start to bend over to pet her, but I stop at the 20-degree mark. I can't bend at the waist. I'm not sure I can get up if I kneel, so I just say hello and continue walking.

The kitchen has nine light fixtures on one switch, so the room seems to be ablaze when I approach it. My brutal headache turns the bright lights into death rays. It would be silly to wear sunglasses before sunrise, so I don't even bother to seek the pair I've put away during what is normally a dreary time of year.

Maureen is at the stove, and she turns and hands me a plate with a fried egg on it. I didn't expect this gesture, and I give her a hug. I sit at the table to eat my egg. As soon as I finish, I make a small pot of coffee and take my morning dose of Aleve®. I can't take Flexeril® for my neck and back, because I will need to drive my rental car home. I sit on the couch next to Maureen while she eats and watches TV. I close my eyes, because the headache exaggerates the colors and sounds, sending shock waves through my senses.

I stir and shower at 8:30. The water soothes my muscles, but not my arm. I can't dry myself completely. I dress for a mild, sunny day and kneel on the couch, looking out at the road to see when Tele arrives, the way I as a preschooler used to gaze at the street when it was time for my dad to arrive from work.

A small car pulls up, and I trudge out to it. I open the passenger door before I realize I haven't looked to make sure Tele is the driver. Fortunately, it's Tele and not one of Maureen's co-workers or such. I lower myself to the seat, strap myself in with just my right arm, and we're off. The towing/car rental outfit is ten miles up I-5, and I thank Tele for taking me that far out of her way.

"I'm glad to help," she says. Tele is a cheerful, open person whose small, slender frame belies a strength of will that allows her to fish for salmon all summer. She makes sure I know she is willing to help as needed, an offer I need to hear out loud in order to accept it.

At the Hertz rental counter in Ferndale, I banter with the office manager. I show her the photo of my car, and she gasps. She hands me the paperwork, and I remember that the towtruck operator told me about the Dodge Charger. I mention it to her, and she asks me if I want it. I'm trying to save gas and not take advantage of my insurance company, but she says the Charger comes in well under my daily rental allowance.

"What the heck?" I say. "Let's do it."

The Charger isn't at this location. It's at the Hertz lot at the airport, so she rents me a red Hyundai for the short drive to Bellingham International Airport. I sign the paperwork without scrutinizing it as I normally would, because my head still hurts when I try to think.

Tele walks to her car, and I walk to the rental. I forgot to thank her, so I walk over and tell her I'm grateful for her help. I sit in the Hyundai and pull out my phone.

There's so much to do. First, I call my doctor's office. When I ask for an appointment with Dr. Banjanin, the scheduler tells me he is out on a family emergency. Dr. Patterson is covering for him, and he can see me at 1:00. I accept, and I prepare to pull out of the lot. As I back up, I see that Tele has waited for me to drive off before starting her trip home. I feel dumb for not being more mindful of her needs.

I drive to the airport, but I get confused. I drive around the Hertz drop-off lot three times before I figure out where to park the Hyundai and drop off the keys. Once I slide the keys into the door slot, I head into the airport and rent the Charger. Everyone at the desk is a bit envious that I get to cruise town in that monster for a couple of weeks. I locate the car. It has a push-button ignition. Never having used such a thing, I press it, and the ignition grinds as if I had turned the key. It startles me, and I'm glad the car is in park.

The last time I drove a vehicle this big was when I rented a cargo van. I back out slowly, turn corners slowly, get to the road in front of the terminal, touch the accelerator, and find myself plastered to the seat. I learn the trick of keeping the acceleration steady by the time I reach the airport exit, and in this big car I feel less likely to be injured if I have another accident.

I don't even feel concern when drivers pull up behind me at traffic signals. There is so much metal between us that I can't imagine feeling anything if someone does bump me. Now I understand why Maureen, after being rear-ended, chose to buy an SUV to replace her small car. I don't know what I'll do about a replacement car yet. I just know I need to get one soon or risk being badgered by the insurance company.

The Doctor Is In... My Life.
January 30, 2015, 9:50am

At 9:50 I pull into our driveway, and my phone calendar dings to remind me that it's time to head down from my office to teach German. I pick up the phone, see the notification judging me, and my world goes silent. I love my job, and even though it would be physically taxing to push through the whiplash, back, and arm pain, I would rather be teaching than take off the next two weeks.

I look up and stare at the gate to the back fence. I decide I need to reflect on my situation for a few minutes. I enter the garage, grab a light lawn chair with my good hand, and drag it to the back corner of the yard. There are three low evergreen bushes there, as well as an open space where I can set out the chaise longue. Setup is a challenge, but finally I sit in the cool, sunny corner and stare at the evergreens.

The last time I hurt in so many places was when I got knocked off my bike by a speeding Harley when I was seven. I flew about 20 feet and landed on my head. I was unconscious for a couple of minutes at least, and I missed school for two weeks, just like this event. I had a concussion and lots of road rash then. A scar on my left knee and a thin spot where I scraped off my scalp attest to the damage.

Now, I wonder how my colleagues are going to manage teaching my classes as well as their own. One of the professors has a young child, and the extra workload simply won't be helpful. At least the two-week absence means they will be paid, without my having to cover their salary. It crosses my mind that I am fortunate to have medical and leave benefits.

With that thought, I rise and go into the house to call my insurance company. I find a voice mail from Maureen: She has already called for me. The other driver's company took full responsibility for the collision, and that company will mail me a check for my $500 deductible. My own company totals my Civic. I guess I knew in my heart that they wouldn't try to repair it, but hope remained that the steadfast engine, purring until the end, would have another set of body parts attached so it could cross the 300,000-mile mark in a couple of years.

It's not to be. A note tells me Maureen made me a salad for lunch, and while I eat I ponder the 200,000 miles I drove that car without incident. I take two more Aleve®, and I go to bed until it's time for my medical appointment. The bed feels like a rock slab under my body. I lie on my right side, not daring to turn onto my back, given how hard it was to get up this morning. I rest uneasily, and I can't fall asleep because I left the drapes open. Daylight is clawing at my eyelids. But it feels so good to be off my feet, with support for my head.

I didn't know what to expect, seeing a doctor who doesn't know me. I could describe Dr. Patterson as "patrician." Calm demeanor, knowledgeable, gentle. I tell him a bit about what happened, but for the second time, I pull out my phone and show the photo of the car. I don't have the words to do justice to my predicament. He checks my neck, my arm, my back (orders x-rays of all areas), and my leg (no evident bone chips, but I get an x-ray anyway). The images show no damage to the bones in my neck, my arm, or my leg. I'm pleased that my arm, now swollen and sporting a wraparound bruise from mid-biceps to mid-forearm, will not be encased in a cast. Not having a broken neck is a bonus. But I can't figure out how I injured my arm. I hit something really hard, like the door handle, or the frame between the doors.

Diagnosis: whiplash, upper and lower back sprains, leg contusion, soft-tissue damage to my arm. He says that, had I come in right after the accident, he would have ordered a CT scan to detect any brain bleed. I'm alive 22 hours later, which means the impact did not cause me to hemorrhage. It will be better not to add the dose of radiation from a CT to my brain.

Dr. Patterson prescribes more Flexeril®. I refuse opioids before he even brings up the subject. I'll stick to the Aleve® and make sure I eat when I take it so I don't burn up my stomach.

I drive to the pharmacy, prescription in hand. As I walk toward the drop-off window, I see one of my students. She is the most adept student in my first class, and I'm not sure she thinks highly of me.

"You weren't in class today," she says.

"I was in a car accident yesterday. I'll be out for a couple of weeks."

"You look fine."

I show her my arm and tell her I have a painful whiplash. She nods at the bruise, doesn't comment on my swollen neck. We part. I get my fresh pills and drag myself home.

Diagnosis.
January 30, 2015, 4:30pm

I may be too sore to teach for a couple of weeks, but I figure nothing will cheer me up as well as attending my regular Friday happy hour will. I've been meeting the same colleagues weekly for more than two years, and we are close enough that they all attended our wedding in August, 2014. Today, we're converging at 5pm at the Star Club, a funky new restaurant-bar set up in an historic building near downtown.

But first, a nap. I lie down at 2:30 because I simply can't stay awake. My body seems to be fighting to repair the sprains at a record pace. I close the drapes, making my back scream at me, because my headache demands darkness. I lie on my right side again. I can't lie on my left side. I would have trouble rolling onto my left side anyway.

I never nap for two hours, but just before I fall asleep, I decide to set an alarm for 4:30. If I get up by then, I can drive three miles to our gathering and be early or on time. I feel miserable enough that I'm looking forward to the company more than usual.

Suddenly, it's 4:30. I hit snooze instead of turning off the alarm, because I'm groggy. I fear I might fall asleep again before I can drag myself off the bed. As I've done twice today, I roll into an attitude of prayer beside the bed. I take another moment to pray for the pain, vertigo, and nausea to pass.

While I was asleep, Sophie came in to lie beside me. She stands and stretches while I gain my balance. She rubs her cheek against mine and purrs. I kiss her between her ears and lurch to my feet. I almost decide the effort is too great, but I am lonely and need the comfort of my friends.

I climb into the Charger and push the button. Again, the keyless ignition startles me. I won't be looking for that feature in a car. I back into the street, faster than I wanted to, but the power of this car takes some getting used to. Two lefts, and I'm on the road that will take me to the Star Club.

There is a string of three empty parking spots a block up the hill from the club on Holly Street, and I park in the easiest spot to exit when I go home. This Charger fits me like shoes that are three sizes too large. I have no spatial understanding of where the front and back of the car are as I drive. I would have walked several blocks to avoid trying to parallel park between two other cars.

The sun is setting just as I approach the Star Club. Even so, I don't take off my sunglasses. The entrance consists of eleven concrete steps that lead to heavy wooden doors. I lean on the metal pipe handrail on the right side and walk under a large white star centered in a limestone arch. The building reminds me of Indiana University, where many structures owe their stately nature to nearby limestone quarries. Another layer of melancholy settles over me. I would love to visit family in Indiana as I convalesce, but I can't imagine traveling while I'm in this much pain.

I grunt as I open the door. I can't use two hands, and my back demands more support than I can offer it. I catch my breath as I face the bar, then I turn to my right and head for the room where I'm most likely to find my friends.

Rather than a traditional dining room, I encounter a couch against the wall, with a coffee table in front of it and an armchair on either end. There are a couple of tall tables with bar chairs on the opposite wall. The overhead light on the ten-foot ceiling is no brighter than that of a typical bedroom. The walls are painted a deep maroon, the large window frames glossy white.

I step onto the thin hardwood slats of the floor, the heels of my dress shoes clacking, echoing. I peer at the couch. People are sitting there, but I can't figure out their faces. I move closer, hesitant to greet people who might not know me.

And then, a voice I recognize. Carmen calls to me, "Seán, it looks like you've already been drinking!" I recognize Linda's laugh, and I see that the third person on the couch is Carmen's husband. Now sure of my surroundings, I lower myself slowly into the soft armchair that faces away from the window.

We exchange greetings, and Carmen asks me how my week has been. I pull out my phone and show them the photo of my crushed car. Gasps, murmurs of concern, then Carmen says, "Wow, I take back my joke about drinking. How are you doing?"

Carmen is a mentor of mine, a warm-hearted, dark-haired woman who runs the curriculum-development program that connected all of us who come to these gatherings. Now, I see anxiety in her brown eyes.

"I'm sore, lots of headaches, my neck is swollen, but nothing is broken."

Others trickle in and join us, including my best friend on campus, Michael. He's a professor of Communication Science and Disorders, and he specializes in football head injuries. He also did me the favor of introducing me to a hometown friend of his, Michael Poore, a well-regarded novelist.

Carmen tells me to share my story again, but all I can do is find the photo and pass it around. Again, the reactions. This time, we're interrupted by a server. My friends order wine and food. I order a snack, but I tell the server I won't be drinking anything. I show her the photo.

"Because this happened," I add.

"Ooh, that's terrible," she replies. I agree with her that a glass of water would be good. She goes to place our order.

Michael is looking at me. After I make a couple of comments to add to the conversation, he says, "Seán, I think you might be concussed."

I stare into the space above his head. It makes sense. My headaches, the issues with light, lots of other things I feel but can't articulate. *It makes sense.*

"That makes sense," I finally reply. "It's a good thing I'm taking a couple of weeks off work."

I go home early, driving the Charger carefully in the dark, this time finally with my sunglasses off. But the oncoming headlights zap my brain, and I make up my mind that I won't drive without sunglasses, even at night.

Maureen is watching TV when I arrive. Sophie has jumped off her lap to run to the door, and she marks my ankles with her head. My right leg still aches.

"Michael says I have a concussion," I say across the room.

She pauses her program. "That's not surprising. Did he tell you what to do?"

"Stay in the dark, avoid screens for a few days, start exercising when I can."

"Let me know what you need."

Right now, I need to go to bed. I'll sort out the meaning of this idea in the morning.

Dealing and Wheeling.
January 31, 2015

Overnight a thought occurred to me, and as I lie in bed, I realize the idea is valid. I remembered a time in the 1980s when I had an at-fault accident and my insurance company pushed me to get my car fixed. I had to come up with $500 to cover my deductible, and at the time it was a nightmare. How much worse would it be to need to do a thorough search for a car now, and have my insurance company rush me into a purchase? Just imagining buying an unsatisfactory car has my gut clenching.

It's 7:30, minutes before dawn, but I can't just lie here and be forced to buy a car I'll hate, can I? I roll out of bed with slightly more grace than yesterday, thanks to the new Flexeril® that my doctor gave me. My neck complains less, but when I sit up, the room spins for a moment, and I blink a dozen times to get my bearings. I don't know if it's the medication or the newly minted concussion that, I remember now, Michael diagnosed last night.

I'm supposed to spend this weekend in the dark, and I promise myself I will do so, as soon as I find the car of my dreams. I lurch to my feet, lean on the wall until I get my balance, and pad down the hall in my boxers toward my office. As I pass the family room, I see Maureen in the kitchen. I wince when I look at her; the can lights in the kitchen are either all on or all off. The glare attacks as if Maureen were training a spotlight on me, the star of my own reality show, *A Concussed Life*. I look away and mutter a good morning. I want to sound cheery, but the explosion of light steals my words.

I enter my office and turn on the light and the computer for the first time since my accident. Once again, I wince at the brightness. Maureen follows me in and says something. I can't make out her words, because my ears have been ringing since the accident. She repeats herself, more loudly:

"Should you be on the computer?"

"Just for a little bit. I have to find a car."

"What car?"

"My new car. The insurance company won't let me keep the rental long, and then I'll need a car."

Before I look for a car, I look at my old one. I click on a photo of the smashed rear end and zoom in so it fills my 27" monitor. The image stuns me, as it has the dozen or so times I've looked at it on my phone. But now, I can see breathtaking detail of the damage: the caved-in trunk, the shattered rear window, the broken tail-light lens, the sheared-off bumper that exposes the inner workings of the device that helped save my life. I can still read the "I love Irish music" bumper sticker, and my license plate is nearly intact.

I point at the screen. "Watch this! Watch this! Can you believe it?"

No response. I turn slowly and look at Maureen. She says, "Is it a video?"

I'm confused. "No, just the picture."

"You were telling me to watch it, so I thought it was going to move."

"Did I say 'watch?' That's weird. In Spanish, I would use the same verb for 'watch' and 'look at.' I meant, 'Look at it.'" She comes over and looks at the enlarged photo. She gasps.

I close the photo and open a browser window. "OK, I'm going to find a car." Maureen wanders back to the kitchen, and Sophie joins me.

A month ago, I had to decide whether to keep the Civic and have minor maintenance done or replace it. I checked then to see how much a Certified Used Civic would cost me. The available cars, with mileages from 30,000 to 70,000, ranged from $15,000 to $21,000. They were all automatics, and I had been hoping to get another manual. My Civic had come with 29,000 miles and cost $12,000. I decided to give the car some TLC and keep it until I hit 300,000 miles.

Today, I do a search for used 4-door Civics with a manual transmission, and I get a hit. They have a black 5-speed for $16,999. It has 512 miles on the odometer. The number stuns me, so I call the dealership. The sales department doesn't open until 9, but the office people will tell them to hold the Civic for me.

I eat breakfast and drive the Dodge Charger over to Iowa Street, where most of the dealerships in town sit in a row. I see the familiar blue-and-white sign, and I turn in. I meander past the new cars, toward the back of the building, in search of the used cars. Finally, a man approaches me. I ask him where the used cars are.

"They're down the street, near the Toyota dealership," he says. That seems odd, because I had previously seen used Hondas on the same lot as the new cars. But I drive back onto Iowa and turn left. Then, I see another familiar blue-and-white sign. This is the Honda dealer, with a big H on the sign. I pull in, and when I look over at where I had gone first, I see an intertwined VW on their sign. Grateful that I didn't get talked into buying a new Jetta, I park and enter the salesroom.

A young man greets me at the door, and I tell him I'm interested in the 5-speed Civic. He tells me that an older woman had bought it, but it hurt her shoulder too much to shift, so she brought it back almost immediately. She paid the penalty for driving the car off the lot; I can buy it for the Kelly Blue Book used price.

The test drive shows me that I have chosen the right car. It fits my body the way the other Civic did. It has a rear camera, and there are a number of electronic advances that have become standard features since my 2001 Civic rolled off the assembly line. The one thing the car doesn't have is spikes sticking ten feet out the back of the bumper to keep people from rear-ending me. Back in a smaller car, I notice that I am wary each time I slow for a light. I look in the rearview mirror and beg the car behind me to slow down and stop.

I make it back to the dealership safely, and I sign off

on the paperwork. I somehow let myself be talked into a bunch of extras that I might regret later, but they amount to a couple of thousand dollars, and I leave the lot in the Dodge Charger, knowing that my new car will be prepped and ready to go in a day or so.

Mozart in the Dark.
February 1, 2015

Every muscle in my body has tightened up. I can't lie on my back or on my left side. When I lie on my right side, I place my head into a trough in my pillows that will keep my neck stationary. Yet what scares me is what's happening in my head.

It's more accurate to say I'm concerned about what is *not* happening in my head. Yesterday, I couldn't tell the difference between a VW sign and a Honda logo. Those pale-blue signs never confused me prior to my accident. I'm mixing up words. Maureen asked me if I put some leftovers from Saturday dinner in the fridge. I said I put them in the car, and then I pointed at the fridge when she looked confused. I don't have enough brain juice to be either amused or embarrassed by the glitches.

A big change has struck me on this Sunday morning. I have been musical all my life. I wrote my first piece of music when I was four. I get song ideas all the time. When I'm not actively listening to music, I always have a song running through my head. Earworms, they call that phenomenon. My usual cure is to listen to the song that's playing on repeat in my mind.

Now, I find myself lying on the bed in the darkened guest room so Maureen won't jostle me at night. She had to close the blinds for me. She had to cover me. I can't watch TV because the light gives me worse headaches. I set up my computer to play my favorite pop songs, but the sound pounds my ears the way light does my eyes, resembling a buzz saw ripping my eardrums apart.

So, I try Mozart. I have a lot of Mozart in my digital collection, and I keep a playlist of his compositions in chronological order. Recordings of his earliest works, from age five on, bother my head only a bit, yet they don't calm my system at all, as I expect.

And then, Mozart gets more complex. I usually see music, as well as hear it, and Mozart should look like what you see in a scene from *Fantasia*. But now all I perceive is bows hacking at strings, piano keys hammering wires, and horns blaring like sirens. I get up and turn off the music. The pain of rising is worth the blessed silence that ensues.

Except that it's too quiet in the room now. But how do I define quiet? A strong, mosquito-like tinnitus invades my head. My ears are ringing far more than the usual mild hum I experience after years of lawn-mowing and working in loud factories. Ambient noise usually drowns out my tinnitus, but I can't handle the melodic sounds that would mask it now.

How I define quiet: I have no earworm.

I don't know when I last had no sound, no thoughts, running like a ticker tape through my mind. But even when I try to imagine a conversation with myself, try to generate a memory of a song I find entertaining, nothing happens.

My hackles rise. I feel fear for the first time since the accident. I do get one thought: Maybe I didn't go to the ER because I was too brain-damaged to reason with myself. Over the sixty hours since my accident, my mental faculties have deteriorated to a great degree, slowly but consistently. At first, I didn't know why I was unable to think clearly; now, I know why. Will I reach a point when I once again don't know that I'm in a complete, perpetual fog?

I am scared, and I want to cry. But I don't cry, and I assume that means I'm not as scared in my subconscious as I am in my conscious mind. I think about discussing my thoughts with Maureen, but I get drowsy, and finally I fall into a dreamless morning nap. I need to rest up for some TV watching.

I agreed a week ago to attend a Super Bowl party at Anna's house. Our Seattle Seahawks are in the game for the second straight year, and Maureen and I don't watch enough TV to bother with a cable connection. Anna and her husband said I should come over for the game, so I will.

I haven't seen them since my accident, so I see surprise on Anna's face when I show up in a cervical collar and sunglasses. To explain my unusual gear, I display the photo of my car on the phone. Anna winces as she examines my car. I tell her I will get my replacement from the dealer on Tuesday, and I'm driving a Charger for now.

The game starts at 3:30. The TV is huge, probably 80 inches, and brutally bright, even with my shades. Before the opening kickoff, I've eaten potato chips and onion dip, a couple of finger sandwiches, and a variety of other items. I also consent to try a cocktail Anna prepared, since the Flexeril® has worn off. I can't remember what drink she made, but that's not because I drank too many of them to recall.

A few other friends are over, including a medical professional who is just short of being an MD. He notes the severity of my accident, but he doesn't seem concerned about my health. It's not his job, of course, and I don't pump him for free advice about how to manage my concussion or my whiplash.

The game doesn't go well for our side, and my brain rebels during the fourth quarter. I've mostly been listening to the grating sounds from the TV while glancing up from time to time to see the visuals. First, I get the knife-jab headache on top of my skull, just right of center, that has plagued me since Friday morning. Then comes a new pain, above my left eye. It begins with a tingle behind my forehead and then morphs into a throb. I already have the back-of-my-skull headache that I associate with my whiplash. Do I call this a trifecta of headaches?

As soon as time runs out on the Seahawks, I head home. Three headaches, an immobile neck, and light sensitivity make driving even a few miles a less-than-joyous experience. I don't have any mishaps, but once when I stop at a light, I see a car approaching from the rear, and

I cower in my seat until it stops a reasonable distance behind me.

I enter the house, pet Sophie, hug Maureen, and drop the Charger keys on the coffee table. I look at Maureen and shake my head. I'm done driving except when I absolutely must.

Life Goes On?
February 3, 2015, 8:00am

I should be resting, avoiding lights and movement, but some appointments, like those with governmental agencies, cannot be canceled easily. In December, I made an appointment with the TSA to be vetted for a NEXUS Pass. The NEXUS Pass allows one to cross the border into Canada without carrying a passport. More importantly, it allows one to use a fast-moving special lane at the border crossing. While most people wait up to an hour to get across the border, holders of a NEXUS Pass normally cruise through the line in less than five minutes.

I can't drive to the office in Blaine, Washington for my interview with the TSA, but it happens that a university colleague of mine has scheduled her NEXUS interview for today as well, so she is going to drive me to the border. We scheduled our interviews on the same day partly because my colleague, Joan, has some mobility issues, and I can help her walk to where she needs to be in this somewhat tense situation. Joan and I think that having a NEXUS Pass will make life much more simple. We never imagined back in December that she would end up helping me more than I am going to help her today.

Joan comes to my house to pick me up at 8 o'clock. This is one of the earliest times I have gotten up since my accident, and I am groggy. It's a sunny day, so I don my darkest sunglasses and ease myself into the passenger seat of her car. I am wearing my cervical collar, and I lean the seat back a couple of notches to ease the pressure on my neck. I close my eyes and try to relax. Even with my eyes closed, the light coming through my sunglasses and my eyelids burns my brain.

This is the first time Joan has seen me since my accident. I think she realizes that the accident was more severe than either of us expected. She is not used to seeing me lethargic, sluggish in my speech, stiff and bruised. I have known Joan since 1988, so she has many points of reference to compare the old Seán to the new one. She handles the experience of seeing me post-accident well, because she's stoic and not prone to panic.

We reach the modern, wood-and-stone building and present our paperwork at the front windows. We sit in hard plastic chairs and wait for our names to be called. It feels as if we were waiting at the DMV to get our drivers' licenses renewed, except with much higher stakes. I see no reason why I should not be allowed to have a NEXUS Pass, but if I don't pass the interview, I foresee many hours spent in line at the border, breathing exhaust from other cars and wishing I had decided not to go to Canada.

My head has begun to sag on my damaged neck, the weight of my skull compressing the discs between my cervical vertebrae. I took Flexeril® before we left, but the muscles in my neck are reacting to the pressure anyway. At last I hear my name. I struggle from my seat and walk over to the woman who called me. I know I look like a dork with my collar and sunglasses on. I remove the sunglasses despite the bright overhead lights because high-security areas are not a good place to cover one's face.

The woman directs me to a window where I face both an American and a Canadian Border Patrol official. They both examine my paperwork, and the American official has more questions for me than the Canadian officer does. I feel dull-witted as I dredge up the data he requests. This is the first time since my accident that I have had to deal with a government official, and I am beginning to realize what a challenge this type of situation must present to someone whose faculties are diminished by health issues or long-term substance use.

The most vulnerable Americans are the ones who spend the most time talking to the type of official whose job it is to pick apart medical claims and accident reports, as well as requests for housing and food. I am nearly overwhelmed by this vetting process, and it is really nothing compared to the scrutiny one undergoes to receive government benefits that involve money.

I suddenly feel a strong sense of horror that my diminished faculties will make me seem to be a bad bet for a NEXUS Pass. I start to sweat. I am sure the nystagmus that makes my eyes move back and forth without my being able to control them is noticeable to the official. I was born with this condition, but many people develop nystagmus when they are on certain drugs or after drinking too much alcohol.

Between the eye movement, my word-seeking, and my slow answers, I become more and more concerned that my concussion is going to doom my attempt to get this coveted card. If I am rejected, I will have to wait months, I believe, before I can apply again.

The questioning finally ends. I hold my breath. Both officials sign off on my application. I get my photo taken without my dark glasses and my cervical collar. I receive a temporary pass, and they tell me that my permanent pass will come in the mail. My anxiety level drops by half. I look for Joan. I see her at another window, going through her own grilling. I know she is more articulate today than I am, and that she will do fine.

She earns her pass as well, and soon we are on our way back to Bellingham. I recline the seat even more to take some of the pressure off my neck. Once I make it to my bed, I lie awake, wondering if I have any other such tasks awaiting me, official appointments I made prior to my accident, having no inkling that getting through these processes would be so debilitating and exhausting.

Cravings.
February 3, 2015, noon

My body talks to me a lot. That's why I take as little Aleve® as possible; my neck is so damaged that I fear I'll overextend my activity and injure myself more if I mask my pain. I want to know how much I hurt when I see doctors, because I am not going to spend my life numb just to be able to report that I have healed enough to be pain-free.

My arm talks to me. My neck and back talk to me. My right leg talks to me. Now that I've gotten the NEXUS trip out of the way, my stomach is talking to me. But this talk is unusual and unexpected. What my stomach is saying, at the request of my brain, is that it wants me to eat certain foods. I don't expect such a demand in the middle of winter, even on a sunny day when I have been up early and active. My system usually perks up and wants a change in diet when spring rolls around.

I've gone through unusual periods of cravings before. I don't know what my diet lacked at the time, but I went through a spell when I craved canned peas, the tiny sweet ones. I included a can of them, heated with margarine, with my dinner almost every night for a few weeks.

I've also known about the message behind some specific cravings. I once had a student who was in the military and was pregnant. She told me that, when she starched the collar on her uniform, she wanted to spray a handful of starch and eat it. I told her to check with her obstetrician, because she was anemic. She got a blood test, and she was indeed mildly anemic.

Today, I suddenly crave three items: blueberries, salmon, and walnuts. I have blueberries on hand, because I like them in oatmeal, but I've been too sore to cook oatmeal and haven't been eating blueberries by themselves. But today I make for lunch a fried egg and a bowl of cold cereal that combines well with the berries. I warm about fifty frozen berries in the microwave and drop them on the buckwheat flakes, covering them completely.

After I sleep off my lunch, I text Maureen to see if she might be going to the grocery store on her way home from work. She asks what I need, and I write, "Salmon and walnuts and more blueberries." Oh, my.

There's absolutely nothing I can do to entertain myself. I retreat to the dark, silent room. I make myself try to think about the cravings I am experiencing. I have my first glimmer of insight into a possible positive outcome to this accident. I see a future where I eat a better diet than I have been stuffing into my body without much thought for the past 54 years.

I may be a bit harsh with myself. Yes, I eat mayonnaise, hot dogs, and too few vegetables, but I do consider my meal choices. I weigh 142 pounds, and that's not bad for someone who has aged into the time frame where many people expand their girth dramatically. My total cholesterol has exceeded 200, so I take a statin. That's my only potentially diet-related health issue.

Now, I realize that I have gained additional years of life simply because this accident could have killed me. Therefore, it is probably a good idea for me to push myself to eat well and, when I heal, exercise more frequently and more vigorously than I have for the past twenty years or so.

I get the idea of creating a six-week menu that will cover all the nutrition bases in a healthy way, at least over the course of a week. I used to have a month of menus that ensured I would not get bored with one type of food. It gave me a handy way to organize my grocery shopping.

Now, if I add the nutrition component to the easy-shopping concept, I may find myself eating better than I ever have before.

It's too bad I can't work on this project now. I'm lucky to have had an idea. When I can sit up, view a computer screen, and think—all without pain—I'll put this plan in motion.

But first, I text Maureen and ask her to bring me some pints of ice cream and Hershey bars as well.

Old Man and the Bay.
February 3, 2015, 11:00pm

There is a dock in Fairhaven that leads down to Bellingham Bay at a steep grade. At the end, it connects to a boardwalk that crosses the water a considerable distance from the shore. I find myself shuffling down the dock on a gray day. As I walk, older local people using canes walk past me. I move aside so I don't slow down these pedestrians.

Why am I here, and why am I walking so slowly? It strikes me that my muscles have locked up in my back and neck, and I can't walk at a normal pace. That answers one question. As for the other, when I round the corner, I see a path off the boardwalk that leads to a craggy outcropping on the shore. Atop it sits a concrete building of an irregular shape. I plod to its entrance, and a man and a woman greet me at the door. The woman has dark hair. The man is balding, with brown hair. They look like therapists, though I don't know why I view them that way. What does a therapist look like?

The man tells me they are going to help me sort out the tangled mess in my brain, as well as fix my arm and my neck. They will help me laugh and cry again. That all sounds pretty good to me.

For now, the woman says, sleep. Sleep, and eat brain food.

I'm already asleep, so I slide back into my body and end this dream.

Bus to the Doctor.
February 4, 2015, 8:30am

Armed with new symptoms to present, I call in the morning and get another appointment with Dr. Patterson. Then comes the question about how I am going to get to his office, because I didn't think to ask for a ride from my friends. I now understand that I have no business being behind the wheel, so I won't be driving anytime soon.

I call my old friends at the Whatcom Transit Authority (WTA). I take a WTA bus every day from the Park and Ride to campus, but I have never taken one from the stop by our house. That bus goes all the way downtown, and then I would have to transfer to get to campus, far later than if I drive a mile and park.

I tell the employee who answers that I need to get to the hospital. My doctor's office is right across the street from the ER, so I don't need to define my route any better. She tells me that I need to catch the Lakeway bus to the downtown station, then take the Number 4 bus to the hospital. She also tells me when I need to reach the bus stop to arrive before my appointment. I'm set.

I have three hours to kill, so I go back to the darkened guest room to take a nap. I set two alarms to ensure that I'll wake up long enough to remember why I set an alarm in the first place.

Sure enough, I have trouble focusing after the first alarm goes off, but I manage to clear my head, and I don't fall asleep again. Getting out of bed is just as hard as ever. I don black track pants and a gray sweatshirt. I haven't showered, but I don't think anyone will be examining me up close. I toss on a Chicago Cubs cap, my lucky green one, and walk through the drizzle to the bus stop.

I have an annual bus pass because I use WTA as part of my commute, so I don't need to dig up a dollar for each trip. I swipe my card and ask the driver where I would catch the 4 bus.

"At the main station on Railroad Avenue," he explains. "You get off this bus and walk across the way to the bus that says '4 Hospital.'"

I thank him and take a seat. I'm used to riding a bus packed with students when I commute. This bus has maybe ten people on it, some teens, some people whose physical limitations might preclude driving.

Like me, I think for the first time. I realize that I've joined a new demographic.

The first time the bus slows to pick up a new passenger, the lurch propels me forward. I grab the seat in front of me with my right hand, but my left side continues its trajectory. I shift sideways and bump my arm on the seat. My head keeps moving after the sudden stop, forcing my fragile neck into another whiplash. I gasp out loud, nearly cursing my decision to take the bus.

I adjust my sitting position. I slide my butt forward, brace my knees on the seat in front, bend my right arm and grab the seat frame behind me, and lay my head on my arm. This position protects me for the most part from the herky-jerky bus movements, which are not the fault of the driver, but rather the nature of the bus-beast.

When we pull up at the station, my neck has swelled against the collar. I wonder if the cables have gotten tangled, as I can't turn my head at all without tendons twanging and vertebrae grating bone on bone.

On top of the new pains, I can't recall which bus I need to take. I remember asking the route on the phone, but the number has hidden itself from my usable memory. Once everyone is off the bus, I give up on remembering and walk up to the driver.

"I'm sorry, sir. Which bus did you say I need to take to get to the hospital?"

He replies in a soft voice, "Number 4. Right over there." He points at the bus that says "Hospital."

Why couldn't I just walk around until I found the "Hospital" bus? Because I didn't remember that the bus would say "Hospital." At least I can answer my own internal question. But God help me, I didn't *hear* myself answer the question, as I expected. I have no internal voice, just as I have no earworms. My brain has no soundtrack.

I thank the driver and add, "I'm sorry I didn't remember which bus I need. I was in a car accident on Thursday, and I hit my head." I pull out my phone and show the driver my photo. What I am thinking, but don't say, is "Please don't think I took the bus because I lost my license because of alcoholism or drug use, or that I've always been this slow."

I put away my phone and step off the bus. Trying to be discreet, I make the number 4 with the fingers on my right hand and start walking toward the "Hospital" bus. I walk past a few aged or homeless-looking people who are sitting on the benches between the rows of buses, and I wonder if they have as much trouble navigating the bus system as I am having.

I am living my distant future, forty years ahead of time.

As my intake says I'm reporting a concussion, the nurse turns off the lights. My eyes cool down, but I don't remove my dark glasses. When I close my eyes, they no longer burn.

There's an apologetic note in Dr. Patterson's voice when he says, "I didn't consider a concussion when you told me about the whiplash and the back injury. I'm glad you're staying away from light." He tells me I should expect up to two weeks of light sensitivity (photophobia) and headaches. When I return to work, the headaches should be gone.

Now he diagnoses me with a mild Traumatic Brain Injury. I wonder what a moderate TBI would be like, if this is mild. He says I should look for symptoms of Post-Concussion Syndrome. Still no brain scan, and I still refuse pain pills before he discusses pain. I wander back to the bus stop and catch my ride home without getting lost again.

When Maureen comes home, I tell her about Post-Concussion Syndrome. She looks it up for me and reads me the information from the Mayo Clinic website[1]. I watch her as she reads, and I detect the strain these symptoms cause her. She is always solicitous about my well-being, and while I cannot get inside her head (since I can't even get inside my own head), I have enough understanding to remind myself to try to depend more on my village of helpers and less on my wife, who works full-time and then takes care of me.

She finishes reading the litany of horrid symptoms. I don't know the difference between concussion symptoms and post-concussion ones, but I don't think the label matters. I am experiencing all the listed symptoms except insomnia. I need to heal, and I have two weeks to do it. *Tick, tick, tick,* says the clock in my head. It's the only sound my quiet brain makes.

---

[1] Information is available in the Appendix.

I've Got Some 'Splainin' to Do.
February 4, 2015, noon

My bus ride to the doctor sets off a cascade of thoughts and compensatory actions on my part. I am aware now that I don't think fast or clearly. Thinking slowly like this is a new experience for me. People I know already will detect the difference, and I will simply tell them that I had a concussion and am a bit slow for the time being.

But what about people I don't know? I don't want people I have just met to think I am slow-witted or easily confused. I need to come up with a clear, concise way to convey my changed status to new acquaintances.

The problem is that my thought process is not clear enough to produce a plan. I also feel that I cannot explain exactly what I want to say with mere words. Even with my faculties intact, I would not be able to describe adequately the circumstances that have left me feeling that my brain's function is substandard.

I resort finally to pulling out my phone, opening the photo gallery, and displaying the photo of my smashed car. At the same time, I say I was rear-ended at a crosswalk. The guy behind me did not see me and did not put on his brakes. The photo, in tandem with my verbal explanation, achieves my goal, which is to deflect attention from the deficits I feel in my interactions with people, or at least to explain them.

People who already know me have told me they are not noticing my struggles as much as I do. They do note that I talk a lot more and repeat myself frequently. Apart from minor hesitations between words or sentences, I seem to be presenting myself as normal most of the time. But when I can't think of a word, or when I lose track of what I was trying to say, I now have a habit of holding my head in my hands as I urge the words to come to the surface so I can say them. It is emotionally and sometimes physically painful to know what I want to say and not to be able to articulate it vocally. I am extremely fortunate that the injury has not slurred my speech, which would affect my job when I go back to teaching. Not being able to pronounce German or Spanish words well would hobble my career.

But while I am speaking clearly according to the perceptions of my conversation partners, my brain is overworking at its fastest pace in order to be able to generate my seemingly effortless speech. I am really struggling to generate the sounds to keep up with my thoughts. Genetically I have the Irish gift of gab and a quick wit. Yet the words that used to roll off my tongue now have to be pulled kicking and screaming from the word-producing area of my brain and guided past the "road closed" sign, sometimes along a circuitous detour.

On occasion, in moments that devastate me, the words fall off a cliff where a bridge should be, landing in the abyss, never to be uttered as was my intent.

Words won't come out of my mouth the way I want them to. I wonder if they will ever come out of my fingertips onto my written documents the way they used to.

For now, I'm afraid to know the answer to that question.

Legalese.
February 4, 2015, 3:00pm

As soon as my attorney friend Emily Rose Mowrey learned of my accident, she contacted me, first to see how I was feeling and what she could do to help me, then, based on the photo she saw of my car, to recommend that I make an appointment with a personal-injury attorney whom she trusts. Today is the day I have a meeting to assess my case with Paula McCandlis and Matt Conner.

We made this appointment so soon after my accident because it would help the attorneys if they saw how battered I am now. Their office is in Fairhaven, the artsy section of Bellingham. Emily has come with me, allowing Maureen some respite. We are ushered into a conference room, and I sit at a long wooden table under harsh lights. Coffee appears before me, the mug seated firmly on a wooden coaster. The room is so bright I don't look up to see who provided it. I try to find a comfortable sitting position, because I expect this meeting to last an hour or more.

Paula and Matt shake my hand and take a seat. I am wearing the darkest glasses I own, but the light is beating on my brain. Paula asks if the light is a problem, and I reply that I am doing fine. I do mention that the light burns my brain a bit, but I can handle it.

I describe what happened in the accident. I show them the photos we have of my car. I show them my left arm, which still has a lump the size of a golf ball. The wraparound bruise extends now from my upper biceps nearly to my wrist.

The gist of the meeting is that accidents like mine instantly age the victim 10 years, according to Paula. I certainly feel 10 years older. I have had a dream in which I was an old man, moving slowly, thinking slowly. I take a sip of my coffee because my throat has suddenly gone dry.

Paula asks, "Have you been rear-ended before?"

I reply, "Twice. I don't bother putting bumper stickers on my car any longer, because I always lose them when they replace my bumper."

Everyone chuckles, and Paula asks, "Have you filed a lawsuit in these cases?"

I tell her no, because I was never injured before. This accident is different. She is pleased that I won't appear to be a chronic user of the legal system.

I roll up my sleeve, and they take photos of my arm. Then I pull up my pant leg, and we document the scrape on my skin. I ask whether the malfunction of my seat back would merit including Honda in the lawsuit. We decide it's hard to sue a huge corporation, so we discard the idea as quickly as I brought it up.

At the end of it all, Paula decides that my case is serious enough that they will take on my lawsuit against the insurance company of the other driver. I guess it's a good thing that I have the best lawyer possible, but it's a bad thing that I'm injured enough to be worthy of this level of representation.

I sign off on the agreement to have them represent me. If nothing else, I no longer can take calls from either insurance company. While I like talking to the people at my agency, I don't really feel much like talking to anyone, especially not to people who can use my words against me.

Just a Concussion?
February 6, 2015

In the beginning, there were two concussions from one collision. They got together and said, "Let's stick around awhile." And so they did. And the owner of the brain they inhabited was not pleased.

But the owner of the brain had no say in their antics. And the concussions decided to have a child, Post-Concussion Syndrome (PCS). And PCS was one twisted little bugger, worming its way into the brain that used to be so vibrant, creative and efficient. And the owner of the brain was even less pleased.

I, being the owner of the brain, swing between optimism about small bits of progress and dismay at the slow pace of recovery. I have to say in fact that I am not really "recovering"; I am forming part of a wobbly foundation that will give me enough stability to begin to recover. After all, if I am sitting around, unable to read, unable to watch even black-and-white television, my eyes protected by the darkest shades I can find, can I say I'm recovering?

I have lived an eventful week since my accident. I have been busy with doctors, and I have slept a lot. Right now, I have a moment to contemplate my situation, and I wish I could distract myself from facing the reality of my brain injury.

If I am going to sit around because my neck is swollen like a sausage, or because of debilitating headaches, I may as well read something. But I can't. Listen to music? Not really. Do *anything* other than just sit? Not yet. I remind myself of a poster that some of my teachers had on their classroom walls. It was a drawing of a tall stool, and the text read:

"Sometimes I sits and thinks,
"And sometimes I just sits."

I just sit. On the couch with the TV off, at the table, eating in the dark, in the passenger seat of a car. I sit.

I had not been so vigorously active that I am bothered that I can't go climb a mountain or take a kayak out on the Bay. I am bothered that I am aware of my existence because of my brain, but that's all I get. My brain actively fights to close off blood vessels to the areas necessary to think, to read, to engage in any activity that exceeds breathing, eating, and peristalsis.

My vision of what is happening morphs from "these headaches will pass shortly" to "I will have headaches and light sensitivity while I work" to the stark reality: I have a Traumatic Brain Injury severe enough to impede my work, my driving, my social life.

My entire life.

Some of my actions, like word-seeking, using the wrong word, using too many words, I am partially aware of. I can't catch myself, and I often can't stop myself from repeating ideas or talking too much, but at least after the fact, I realize what I did. But I also am self-aware enough that I fear the specter of a condition called anosognosia, where a person believes he or she is perfectly well, when the reality is different. About 30% of people with a TBI experience anosognosia.

Do I know what I don't know? Am I locked inside a reality where I am giving myself credit for skills I do not have? I feel far away from my true self. It terrifies me that, at times, I could be in a coma, dreaming scenarios that simply do not exist. Some TBI Survivors experience confabulation, where they have conversations or experiences that they share with friends and family, events that do not exist. Essentially, they believe dreams they have and relate to them as if they happened. And their friends and family must sort out reality from dreams when they interact with that TBI Survivor.

I am scared that I will live in this Twilight Zone until my heart stops beating. And yet, I feel no actual emotion about my future.

Reading—Not Reading.
February 7, 2015

Morning in February used to mean waking up before dawn. Today, I realize I'm awake, but my eyes don't pop open. I see daylight filtering reddish through my eyelids. I have no idea what time it is, but since I have nothing to do, I put off the eventual, if not inevitable, task of climbing out of bed.

After a few minutes of the deadly silence that passes for thinking now, I realize I'm hungry. Breakfast is my job, since Maureen is at work. I open my eyes and see that Sophie has burrowed under her blanket next to me. As a hairless Sphynx who loves warmth, she normally would not let me sleep in her daytime nap spot. She has been a constant snuggler since the accident, lying on my shoulder, her head tucked under my chin, clearly understanding that she has some nursing to do. Today, she has chosen not to push me aside.

Am I hungry enough to bother getting up? My head says yes. The idea of oatmeal with blueberries or a scrambled egg with onion and flaked salmon appeals to my brain. I can't see myself going back to sleep. I get up and head toward the hall. I hear a double thump behind me; Sophie has jumped out of bed, deciding to follow me. I turn toward the kitchen and see that the light is on. I can't remember when Maureen last forgot to turn off the kitchen light. I look down and squint. I reach the switch and shut off the light. Blessed darkness calms my eyes.

"Good morning!"

I jump. Maureen has walked up behind me. She is smiling, and I reach for a hug.

"Good morning. What day is it?"

"Saturday. I made you breakfast." I see a plate next to the stove, another plate covering it in flying-saucer mode. I point at it. "Yes. You may need to warm it up. I scrambled you an egg and put salmon and onion in it."

"Oh, wow. I thought you were at work. You were so

quiet."

"I wanted you to get your rest."

I microwave the plate for twenty seconds and carry my meal to the table. I have coffee left over from yesterday in the carafe, and I leave my plate to retrieve a mugful.

"Do you want coffee?" Maureen asks.

"Dr. Patterson says I'm supposed to drink it to wake me up."

"Yes. Stay at the table with your plate so Sophie doesn't eat it. I'll get your coffee."

"Oh." Sophie is eating my salmon, so I nudge her face off the plate and sit. After a couple of attempts to sneak back to the food, she wanders off to the far end of the table to chirp at the birds at the feeder. I look to my right to watch them, but I can't hold my head at that angle. I settle for listening to Sophie's tiny "*wat wat wat*" sounds and the occasional squawk from a Steller's jay.

My egg doesn't last long. My appetite explodes at the first bite, and I'm halfway done when the microwave beeps and my coffee arrives. It doesn't have the rich aroma that TV commercials promise. It tastes fine, and I remember that it tasted good yesterday when I brewed it. I just can't smell it except right when it is brewing.

"It's Saturday?"

"Yes," Maureen replies. "Do you want your medicine?"

"I'll get heartburn if I don't take the Prevacid®." A cyan-and-pink capsule appears beside my plate, along with two pills and a glass of water.

"Could you do me a favor, if your head isn't hurting?" she asks.

"Anything."

"I wrote a report for work, and I need to turn it in Monday. Could you proof it?"

"Of course. Let me have it."

"Are you sure? It's six pages. Double-spaced, though."

I hold out my hand for the paper. She returns from her office and gives it to me. She shoos Sophie from my empty plate. A moment later, I hear it clank into the dishwasher, and I realize that Maureen has cleared the table for me. I set the paper on my placemat. Sophie lies on the top half of the document.

"Sweetie, no."

"What?" Maureen calls from the living room.

"No, talking to her."

"Her?"

"Yeah." I hope Maureen understands my inarticulate explanation. I stroke Sophie's back and lift her front paws out of the way. She wanders off. I grab a pen and follow my gaze with the point. I find a comma I don't like in the second paragraph, and another on the second page. Halfway down, a lightning bolt shoots through my head, right at the top, just to the right of center. A dull thud begins to beat on my left frontal lobe, just above my eyebrow. My stomach lurches.

"I can't do this," I moan. I rub my face with my hands and lay my head on the table to try to stop the vertigo that rushes over me. *What's going on?* It's cloudy outside, and I'm wearing my dark shades. It's not that my eyes are straining because it's too dark; the brightness level is at the maximum I can tolerate.

Maureen comes to the table and takes back her paper.

"I'm sorry. I didn't know it would hurt you to read it."

Ah. The actual task of reading more than one typed page is more than I can handle. Yet another limitation confirmed. Now that I've tried to read, I've failed.

What abilities *do* I have? I can talk. I'm really lucky that my ability to form clear words has not been compromised. I have trouble finding the right word fairly often, and at other times I don't get any word at all when I want a particular noun or verb, but I can compete with the best motor-mouths. A true Jabber-wocky.

Now I haul myself from the table to my day bed. I'm dizzy, and I'm too queasy to drink enough water to down a couple of Alevo®. My brain is as tired and foggy as if I had stayed up for three days. Before the jolt of pain struck

my forehead, I felt a curtain coming down over my consciousness, and I could see the little icon of my brain battery draining rapidly in my mind. It drains a lot faster
than my phone or laptop ever could.

Now I know that, when I try to process the written
word, I will hit an invisible wall with little advance warning. There are also times that I can barely communicate
my thoughts. My brain is as wrecked as my old Civic. Can
I fight back against this terrifying damage?

Plans for Seán 2.0.
February 8, 2015

I have those down times. They tend to occur at night, when I wonder what is a dream, and what is reality. But during the day, a different thought pattern emerges. I have urges to map out the future of Seán 2.0.

First, I have to define "Seán 2.0." I am using the naming system that computer-programming developers use for next-generation software upgrades. After all, I am a reboot, a rewriting of code within a potentially powerful computer. Seán 1.0 is gone, filed under O for Obsolete. I cannot ever again be exactly who I was pre-accident. That's not pessimism; that's a factual understanding that I have brain damage and probably have lost access to more cells in one minute than I have lost in the 54 years leading up to that impact.

Who, then, is Seán 2.0? I envision myself as someone who regains the ability to write and uses those skills to explain to the non-TBI world what TBI Survivors experience. I aspire to be a comfort to TBI Survivors who need to know that their journey is in line with that of others who have dealt with the same issues.

I hope to become a clearinghouse for information on TBI. Not so much as a primary source, but as a gatherer of sources, including my new hero, David A. Grant, whom I encountered through the Brainline.org website. He has amassed a huge amount of information for Survivors and their caregivers and other loved ones. He tells his own compelling tale of recovery in his memoir, *Metamorphosis, Surviving Brain Injury*. I want to be a lesser version of David, because I doubt that I can improve on his work.

Another part of me wants to make the United States realize just how fast our society moves. There is a maze of legalities and bureaucracy that even non-TBI people can screw up if they become inattentive to their mail or email.

For those who move more slowly in the cognitive

realm, be it from TBI or any form of brain issue, learning that there is a mountain of paperwork to fill out is often a nightmare. I have Maureen to write down what I dictate to her: Social Security number, health insurance number, accident claim number. Many people have no one to help them write these data, and they also face the daunting task of deciphering the legal issues related to the paperwork they received.

I have come up with a plan to create an office where people with compromised cognition can go to get help with paperwork. Not with following through, as there are agencies that will do those tasks. But simply explaining the meaning of the letters or forms, telling the person where to go to get any further help, and helping to direct the reply to the right person. I would call it the Paperwork Center. The volunteers who provide the assistance would put in just a couple of hours a month, and we would smooth out life for a large number of people.

Finally, I have the goal of improving my diet. It was five days ago when I came up with the idea of creating my diet plan, but I don't know when I will be able to focus enough to sketch it out.

Seán 2.0 has big plans. Seán 2.0's brain isn't ready to implement any of them.

A Lot of Help from My Friends.
February 10, 2015, 10:00am

Back to the doctor. I have a medical appointment this morning with a neuropsychologist, and I expect the consult to tax my brain and leave it foggy and painful. Even if I had to drive to the Marina, where the doctor has his office, I would need to take a bus home, because I would not be able to drive after the two hours of cognitive testing we will do today.

I wanted to be independent (that is, not a hassle for my friends), but the neck pain from the previous bus trip taught me a lesson in accommodation. I need to rein myself in, learn my limits, and respect them at all times. Staying within my limits means accepting rides from friends. At least it doesn't require me to accept rides from strangers.

People are rallying around me from all directions. Writer friends; friends I know through my favorite coffee shop, the Black Drop; the colleagues at Western Washington University who took over teaching my German classes; my neighbors. I can rely on this newly discovered safety net. On days like this, nearly two weeks after my accident, I need this caring village.

When Maureen put out on Facebook a request for help with transportation, socialization, and occasional meals, I didn't ponder how the request would look to others. We weren't asking for money, but we were asking for the most valuable intangible anyone possesses: time. I can give someone a five-dollar bill for gas, but I can't give back time. I can't even replace the time used on me by doing something in return, unless the donor wants to wait a few weeks for repayment.

And therein lies the true beauty of the gifts of time I have received. I know that everyone who chauffeurs me, takes me out for coffee, or brings food over is bestowing on me a kindness I can't begin to repay.

That's the wonderful thing about having the support of a village.

... And from My Four-legged Friend.

February 10, 2015, 10:30am

I have mentioned all the help I have received from human friends, but I would be remiss if I did not talk in more detail about the high level of support that I get from my four-legged house companion, Sophie. Sophie is a spry 12-year-old Sphynx cat. I met her when I met her mother, Maureen. Sophie took to me instantly, which I was told is unusual with men. I think she sensed that I meant well, and that I found her company delightful.

She has no hair and needs to be warm all the time. She has her bed and her blankets and does not necessarily need to hang out with a human for heat. Before my accident, Sophie enjoyed resting on my chest while I watched the occasional movie. But she also had other things to do. She would climb off me, then walk around the house inspecting everything, mewing at the birds out the window, and then eat and sleep away from us.

Since my accident, I sit on the couch a lot, and even though I don't watch television, she hangs out with me. We have a routine. When I sit down on the couch, she jumps up and sits next to me, and I cover her with her blanket. She purrs, and I rub her cheek. After a while, she steps slowly onto my chest, and I support her back end with one hand. She finds the perfect position for herself, which involves getting her head tucked just under one exact part of my chin. She doesn't hurt my neck, and she purrs some more, which soothes my brain. At other times, she sits beside me as if she were hovering over a sick patient. Cat purrs break down cancer cells in humans, and I hope her purrs promote brain healing in me.

If I have stubble on my cheek from not shaving, she scratches her head by rubbing against my cheek. I feel useful to her by providing her this joy, in return for the comfort she brings me by being ever present at my side.

She senses what I don't tell humans: that I need extra attention and a sense of security. Sophie gives me all the love she has available, and she asks nothing in return.

When I consider how Sophie used to behave around me, I can see that she has changed her routine in order to spend time tending to me. My human friends have gone out of their way to take me to doctors, and Maureen has done many errands for me that she should not have to do. But I am very surprised that a cat, an animal allegedly aloof and bossy, would become my best source of comfort during this health event.

Sophie's social IQ has always been high. She is stubborn about just a few things. If I leave bacon grease in a pan to cool and forget to cover it, overnight she will walk on the counter and stove, and I will see footprints in the bacon grease when I get up in the morning. During the day, she doesn't try to get onto the counter, because we have told her that she's not allowed to be there. In her cat mind, at night she can go anywhere, because we don't tell her not to go on the counter when it's dark. I understand her logic.

But no one told her that I needed her to care for me while I sit on the couch. She senses that I need her, really *need* her, and she has stepped up to do an admirable job of being my nurse. I presume that I will outlive Sophie, but she has earned an eternal space of love in my heart and soul.

Percentiles.
February 10, 2015, 11:00am

I am fortunate to be getting neuropsychiatric intervention so soon after my accident. Many people—construction workers, fruit harvesters, even high-school football players—are told to shake off that bonk on the head and get back in the game. Expect a few days of dizziness, some headaches, maybe a couple of other odd symptoms. These TBI Survivors dutifully return to their jobs or classrooms, and if they can still pound a nail accurately, or fill a basket with fruit, or get grades that will keep them eligible for the team, they often get no further care.

In part, my symptoms have been severe enough to keep me out of work, and also the nature of my work, interacting with geniuses at a fast pace, indicates that it's not good PR for a university to have a zombie shuffling around, saying "verb" when I mean "window," staring blankly when a student asks when I will return their exams.

I've missed work for nearly two weeks. Right after the accident I thought I would be going back on Friday, February 13, an ominous date for my return. But I'm just getting started with treatment for a TBI that is not letting up at all. Today's early baseline evaluation will tell this professional, Dr. Judd, and me how long and tortuous a road lies ahead before I can return to being a productive member of society.

I am grateful that I get to see my doctor, because every time I read too many words, perhaps a hundred, or cringe when someone turns on a 40-watt light, I want to know why, and how long it will be before my brain returns to normal. Just a couple of weeks into this waking nightmare, I am suffering from mental cabin fever. I need to sit around because of my messed-up neck, but people who have neck injuries and no brain injury are able to read, watch TV, and make short forays into the world.

I, in contrast, spend my life sleeping, and for a change

of pace, I sit. And I sit. And I sit. And I think how screwed-up this existence is. I want answers.

The "drive Seán to medical appointments" contingent has stepped up today, and when I get into Laura's white Civic, I look at my brand-new black Civic, which is collecting dust. I feel that I am causing Laura a big hassle by, well, being unable to drive. Laura is an incredibly talented author who has often accompanied my group of writers on day-long writing retreats. She should be writing, instead of carting me around.

I have been supporting my writing community in a particular way since I got involved with it in early 2013. I started seeking out places where a number of writers could get together and sit and work on our projects. I call these gatherings Write Outs. We have gone to a number of coffee shops, restaurants, libraries, and islands. When we are there, we write for about five hours, then we read what we produced that day. Laura and I have shared pieces at the end of our writing days, and she has thanked me for my efforts in finding places for writers to gather and be productive.

But Laura's gratitude can't possibly be great enough for me to deserve this ride in the middle of the morning to a doctor's office that is four miles from my house and maybe six miles from hers. She has had to pause in her daily routine, perhaps her writing, to get in the car and deliver me to the doctor. I resent my frailty on her behalf.

She accepts my thanks with a casual shrug. She says it's nothing, very easy for her to help me today. I try to accept her generosity with the grace it deserves. In fact, if my car had a mechanical problem and I needed a ride to a doctor, I would be grateful and capable of feeling good about the ride. The question arises: Why does this brain injury make me less deserving of a ride to the doctor? It makes no sense, but I suspect that my brain, the injured part of me, is ashamed of its infirmity.

Laura drives so as to make me feel safe and comfortable in her car. No jerky movements, no risks. And within ten minutes, I am at Dr. Judd's office, and Laura is relieved of duty. Someone else will pick me up.

I walk into the building whose number matches the one I wrote on a slip of paper. I wander around the first floor, and in a minute or so I find a directory. Dr. Judd's office is on the second floor. There is a broad staircase leading up, and I begin the climb, holding the railing firmly, as my kindergarten teacher, Mrs. Ballinger, taught me. The last thing I need now is to take a tumble on these stairs. My sudden-onset vertigo is reason enough to hang onto that wooden lifeline.

I check in and take a seat. Of course, there is paperwork I can barely complete without aggravating my symptoms. I feel conspicuous with the neck brace I'm wearing, but I'm not planning to shed it to please any of the other waiting-room denizens. Sooner than I expect, I get the call, and I meet Dr. Judd.

He is a genial man, expansive, welcoming. He has white hair and a beard, and he gives off an easygoing vibe that makes me feel good about his testing.

We chat a few minutes. We talk about Spanish, and he busts out a few sentences for me. He speaks Spanish well. I'm pleased that I understand him. I spoke Spanish with my department chair, Paqui, the night of my accident, but since my brain started being suffocated by the swelling and has kept me from functioning at full speed, I have not used my Spanish. It's a relief to hear and respond without effort in the language I love most.

After we discuss my symptoms, Dr. Judd has a protocol of tests he follows. The first tests involve word-color associations.

I can tell my assessment will be dire. I am a 90th percentile kind of guy. On my Graduate Record Exam, I topped out on English at the 99th percentile. I scored a perfect score on a later GRE English test. I don't do 80s.

But today, my scores on the word-color relationships, and on his other tests, settle firmly into the 30s. On the word-color associations, I struggle constantly to remember my task, which aspect of the words and colors to note for each situation. When I am asked to build stacks of wooden circles by moving the largest to the base and the smallest to the top, I need to think for an agonizing amount of time to get it right.

I am stunned.

Really, really shocked.

Forgive me, but this is the moment when I realize that my brain is fucked.

Thirtieth percentile? Really? Me? I am horrified. I don't let on. I accept the results with a modicum of curiosity, and I mention that I'm not used to such low scores. He nods his understanding, because he can see my innate intelligence. I ask myself where it has gone. Not my intelligence, perhaps, but my ability to translate that intelligence into action.

I stand 5'6", weighing 140 lbs. With my neck injury, especially at my age, I am not built for manual labor. If my brain is now better-suited for delivering pizza (a job I did for ten years) than for teaching college Spanish, so be it. But I am certainly going to mourn the loss of my career, of the most beautiful job I could ever imagine for myself. My brain has been my *only* real asset when it comes to employment. If I lose the ability to think as I did prior to this accident, I will be lost. My brain function is certainly not adequate to teach students who have managed to be accepted into the university where I teach.

I can barely avoid telling Dr. Judd that I am horrified at my percentiles. We discuss them calmly, and he has some suggestions. First, Ritalin, to get my brain moving. But he's not a prescribing doctor, so I will have to take his suggestion back to my current primary-care physician. And, blessed be this doctor, he agrees with Dr. Patterson that moderate amounts of coffee will be beneficial to my alertness at this point. I have mostly avoided caffeine (I enjoy tea and the occasional cup of coffee) until I got a neurological opinion. Now, I can make use of that stimulant on a regular basis.

I ask him about reading. He says I can try reading until I can't. That is, if I read some pages and work at it until my brain shuts down, I'll know my limits, and with luck my limits will increase. His optimism is encouraging, and it allows me to be less concerned about the terrible results of my testing. I'm less than three weeks into my post-accident phase, so I should be patient and give myself a couple of months to get back to reading.

A couple of months?

Once we have finished documenting how much my TBI has affected my cognition, I go outside, where one of my writer friends, Kathy, should be waiting for me.

Sure enough, Kathy is sitting in her large white SUV. She also has a small car she uses to carry books around, but I find her tank comforting for the ride home. She asks me how I'm doing, and I give her the optimistic version, that I'm in less pain, that my dark glasses make it possible for me to go outside without feeling agony, that I am more alert. We talk about the writing organization of which she is president and our upcoming meeting.

We reach my house, and I happen to notice a Toyota logo on her steering wheel.

"This is a Toyota?" I ask. She nods. "A Land Cruiser?" Another nod. I turn as far toward her as my neck brace allows. She looks at me, wondering why I asked.

"A Land Cruiser is what hit me."

Kathy's mouth drops open. "Oh my God. Ohhhh my God." She is speechless, apart from those epithets. Finally, she recovers from her shock. "That's terrible," she continues. "One day, I bumped a concrete post at the Bellwether Hotel, one of the short ones, at about five miles per hour. I knocked it over, and there was just a tiny scratch on my bumper. And this guy hit you how hard?"

"Close to fifty."

"Oh, my fucking God."

"His radiator busted from the impact."

She has no words. She tells me to count on her for any rides I need, and I toddle to the house, glad to be done with this adventure. My brain barely allows me to remember the code for the garage, but I get it right, and the door opens. Kathy waves and drives off.

Yeah, I got hit hard by a tank. Remembering the visual of the grille of the Land Cruiser that hit me, with antifreeze puddled on the asphalt of the Boulevard, I compare his damage to that in Kathy's story. Those concrete posts, built like fire hydrants but much heavier, would have crumpled my front bumper at five miles per hour. For my car to breach the bumper and take out the radiator of such a monster blows my mind, what there is left of it for today.

Good job, valiant little Civic, I think. If a hunk of metal is going to kill you, a final act of defiance, that of inflicting great damage to a nearly invincible opponent, shows what a true hero you were. God bless you, and God bless the people in Ohio who put you together so well.

Writer on Autopilot.
February 11, 2015

My activity today reminds me of a scene in the movie *Dawn of the Dead*, where the zombies go to a mall. A woman who is not a zombie asks another human why the zombies gather at the mall. The man replies that, before they became zombies, the mall was an important place to them. So where else would they go?

I belong to two large writing groups in Bellingham. One is Red Wheelbarrow Writers (RWB), a group that exists to keep writers connected and celebrate their progress in their writing. The other group, Whatcom Writers and Publishers (WWP), has monthly speakers who discuss various aspects of the writing and publishing industries. This evening is the monthly meeting of WWP. And I will be there because, like the zombies at the mall, this is the place I go at 5:30pm on the second Wednesday of every month.

I get a ride to the meeting, of course, which is held at Nicki's Bella Marina restaurant. We meet in their upstairs meeting room, which is usually lit with bright can lighting. I have my sunglasses on, and I navigate to a seat at the table farthest from the projector screen. I have two options now: I can walk around and greet the many people I know here, or I can sit and let the world go by. I opt for the former tactic.

People who are my Facebook friends are aware of my accident and injuries. Some are surprised to see me here so soon, but all are glad to see that I am on my feet and able to converse with them. As I so often do, I have taken out my phone, and I am showing the photo of my car to anyone who asks what happened. After all, if you see a friend wearing a cervical collar and sunglasses long after the sun has gone down, you probably are going to wonder if it's a new fashion statement or a sign that something has gone wrong in that person's life.

Once I make my rounds, I resume my seat and lean

against the wall to rest my head. Now I notice an issue I had not expected. In addition to the blindness and pain caused by the lighting, the conversation of 50 people going on around me does not sound like small conversations where I can pick out snippets of dialogue here and there. All I hear is a roar that reminds me of crashing surf or the wind accompanying a tornado. People describe the latter sound as resembling a freight train roaring by, and that's how the conversation mix sounds when it reaches my ears.

The combination of bright light and loud talk overwhelms me. I lay my head on my arms, which I have folded on top of the table. It feels good to lay my head down because my neck can relax a little bit. I use my shoulders to cover my ears. My eyes are closed. I'm receiving sensory input at this moment. It would have been a good idea to go home and cocoon there instead of here.

What compelled me to come to the meeting tonight was my fear of falling away from my writer crowd, of being forgotten and having no way to maintain the connections I have forged over the past two years with the talented, engaging writers who attend these two organizations' meetings. And so, I will surely attend the next monthly meeting of WWP, as well as Red Wheelbarrow Writers. These people mean a lot to me, and I will feel my losses more keenly if I cannot interact with my artistic friends.

And yet, I have to ask a question that arrives and will linger until I answer it: *Is the effort worth the resulting pain?*

Medical Leave.
February 12, 2015, 8:00am

My two weeks of short-term medical leave have come to an end. If I were navigating this journey alone, I would undoubtedly try to go back and teach. I would do so as a confused, incapacitated teacher with massive headaches and an inability to get to and from campus.

Fortunately, I married Maureen, who has worked in the nonprofit world for most of her career. She is well-versed in the regulations that apply to the elderly, the injured, and the unemployed, from auto insurance to health insurance, to Medicare and Medicaid. She also knows how the Family and Medical Leave Act (FMLA) works.

Once it became clear that I was going to need a lot of time off work, Maureen contacted our Human Resources people. She set up my leave with them in a matter of minutes. I had some paperwork to sign, and then I was put on full medical leave with full pay for up to six months. While some states may have more generous leave statutes than federal law requires, every state at least matches the federal mandate to require employers (with a certain minimum number of employees) to provide this type of relief for the injured and their caregivers.

Since I am in no shape to return to work, this law is a godsend. Alongside the comfort, however, is the knowledge that I have failed at healing. As I tend to do, I analyze my plight and note how sad it is. I just don't feel the sadness, and I don't shed tears over it. When will tears return?

Ask an Expert.
February 12, 2015, 10:00am

Two years ago, one of my dear friends experienced a TBI of her own. This woman, whom I will call Allison in this story, got whacked in the eye by the hook of a bungee cord when it slipped out of her hand. Apart from a brutal shiner, she learned a couple of days later that she had some sort of fracture around her eye, but her massive headaches stemmed from a concussion.

Allison tried to continue working, but the pain and dizziness brought on by her traumatic brain injury made it impossible for her to work. She took some time off, and she kept us informed of how she was progressing. She found herself unable to write, which was terrifying to her because she is an exquisite and prolific writer of fiction. In a sense, my current circumstances now reflect the arc of the past two years of her recovery. I thought of her as soon as I realized that my concussion was not as simple and easily healed as I had hoped, because her personal journey became her friends' journey with her.

Today I am meeting Allison at the Black Drop. We both frequent this place when we want to think or write. I arrive first. I sit back and admire the blue walls, darker than aqua and lighter than navy. I don't look at the wall that faces the street because the light is too bright. I also find the surrounding conversations a bit challenging to completely ignore.

Over drip coffees at a table along the inner wall, as far from the windows as possible, Allison manages to express very clearly her impressions of, and thoughts on, healing from a TBI. As I listen to her, I gather that I should not expect my symptoms to pass quickly. I should not expect my writing and reading abilities to spring back to normal within a reasonable amount of time. Allison is upbeat about her progress now, but she is two years into her ongoing recovery, and I am just two weeks into mine.

I walk back to my car after we say goodbye, stunned and feeling helpless.

Trauma Therapy.
February 12, 2015, 4:00pm

I've had a therapist before. My previous counselor retired, and she recommended the professional I have approached regarding emotional trauma from my accident.
Her name is Nancy, and I will meet her today.

It turns out that Nancy has suffered from rheumatoid
arthritis since childhood. She is uniquely attuned to the
issues I am having. She has had chronic pain far longer
than I have had neck pain, and she has dealt with her pain
in ways that I can use to manage my own. She also understands the "Why me?" focus that one can feel when it
seems that the cosmos has poured boiling oil on your
plans for your life. These factors are a relief to me.

Today marks two weeks from the date of my accident,
and we are in fact meeting at 4pm, 18 minutes after the
two-week mark of impact. I am still not very coherent, I
am pounding Aleve® in order to calm the headaches, and
nothing I take helps my neck much. Our goal, however,
is to address the psychical effects of this pain, to soften
the after-images of the impact, and to create a future that
I find satisfying regardless of whether I heal completely
or not.

The first step I need to take is to calm my fears that I
will never be able to return to work. If reading makes me
sick to my stomach now, what will happen when I need
to grade a set of exams? If bright lights make my head
pound, how will I be able to create, or even watch, a PowerPoint presentation on a screen? Nancy helps me sort
out my fears and sift them from the realities I will face
down the road. When I make up stories about my future
before I arrive there, she helps me remember that, at
whatever point I find myself in my journey, I am a TBI
Survivor, and my brain will do everything in its power to
become whole again.

She makes two points that I struggle continually to

keep in the forefront of my mind. One is that I cannot allow myself to criticize work my brain is doing. The other is that my brain is doing its very best to perform cognitive tasks while there are detours and roadblocks put up by the collision. The kinder I am to my brain, the more my injured brain will feed off the positive vibes from the part of me that wants to be critical. The end result will be better and faster healing.

Eventually, though not today, we will reach a point where Nancy will ask me if I believe that I have a good life now. When I can say yes, she will tell me, in a Zen-like way, that I have learned to accept whatever deficiencies, or perhaps I should call them features, exist in the cognitive abilities of Seán 2.0. I will then be able to embrace any further improvements in my brain function as a complete bonus prize, an unexpected gift from the same source that allowed my brain to be concussed in the first place.

I see from the start that Nancy's contribution to my healing will be huge. I may be gaining weight from physical inactivity because of my neck and back pain, but I am lightening the emotional load that I carry in my head and on my shoulders. At times, the emotional weight is almost too heavy to bear. Nancy is here to help me offload. We'll see if she's enough to center me. If not, it won't be her fault.

Sophie's Crisis.
February 14, 2015

I've talked about Sophie's importance in my healing. Today could be the day Maureen and I have been dreading; Sophie has had an upset digestive system for several days, and because she has felt nauseated, she has developed taste aversions to the foods she has eaten for several years. When a human decides to go on a fast, a couple of days on a liquid-only diet seems to be good for the system. A cat, especially an eight-pound one, shifts almost immediately into kidney failure after going more than 24 hours without food.

Sophie hasn't touched any food for at least 36 hours. She is drinking a little bit of water, but she is not urinating much. She is listless and shows no interest in any activity other than lying beside Maureen on the couch. Now, Maureen has come to where I am lying on the twin bed I use during the day to talk to me about Sophie. Maureen has tears in her eyes.

I sense that this is an overwhelmingly sad moment, but I'm not really feeling it. I think I am approaching the clinical perspectives of Sherlock Holmes and Mr. Spock when it comes to emotional response. I still have no urge to cry; I hope this lack of reaction comes from brain damage that will heal, rather than some personality change that has resulted from the impact.

Maureen says she plans to take Sophie to the vet for an emergency Saturday-morning appointment. She is hoping they will give Sophie an IV to hydrate her and forestall kidney failure. Such treatment may involve an overnight stay. We will decide what to do next if our kitty does not perk up enough to start eating again.

A problem Sophie faces is that, last October, the vet removed a lump from a mammary gland. The biopsy showed that the lump was adenocarcinoma, but the vet said he got good margins and that Sophie would not have more cancer in that gland. However, Sophie was a breeder at one point in her life, and before she was spayed, she spent considerable time on birth control. Feline birth-control pills frequently cause breast cancer. Removing this tumor does not mean that she can't get cancer in the remaining mammary glands.

We think we have found a new lump. It is the size of a BB, and if it does not grow quickly, it will not present the same problem that her previous tumor did. But that tumor stayed the size of a BB for several months before it suddenly had a growth spurt. We got it removed as quickly as we could after it enlarged. We don't know if this tumor is the result of metastasis or if it developed on its own, but it has to factor into any decision we make about Sophie's future.

My take is that we need to get Sophie's intestinal upset under control, and then we can decide if we should have this tumor removed as well, or just watch it. Yet another complication is that her response to the anesthetic used for her October surgery was terrible to watch.

Should we subject her to that same experience another time? There is so much to think about. I am not cognitively able to help make clear choices about how we should proceed. But I need to be a good, supportive member of this triad and help Maureen make the best decision.

Maureen remembers that she allowed her previous Sphynx cat, Mimosa, to live a little bit too long with cardiomyopathy. Maureen does not want to see Sophie in the level of distress that her previous baby experienced. I understand her point of view completely, but I am not sure that three bad days plus that surgery equate to a terrible quality of life. I can't quite puzzle out the future.

Maureen gets the carrier and puts Sophie in it. I hear the door close, the garage door open, and Maureen's CR-V pulling away. I hope Sophie will come home with her.

I cannot relax. Maureen is suffering at the vet's office, and Sophie surely feels my absence. I can't take the stress. I'm not really ready to hit the streets in my car again, but the vet is not far from home, so I throw on my track pants, grab my keys, and start my trek.

I feel fragile on the surface streets of Bellingham. I have only two miles to drive. I keep that thought in my mind. If I get rear-ended, it will be at 25 miles per hour, not 45 or 50. I drive to the shopping complex and park without incident. I enter the vet's office and ask where Maureen and Sophie are. An office person takes me back.

When Maureen sees me enter the room, her mouth drops open, and tears fill her eyes. Sophie is lying on her favorite blanket on the examination table. She is not struggling to get away from the vet. At this point Maureen and the vet are discussing whether or not to hospitalize Sophie so she can have several days of antibiotic via IV. They both wonder what the stress of being separated from us will do to Sophie.

"The other thing we can do," the vet says, "is teach you how to give her subcutaneous hydration. You can give her 5 mL of saline solution every day for a few days, then back off to three times a week to see how she responds."

I see Maureen start to turn a pale-greenish color. I look at the vet and say, "I can do it."

I see relief in her eyes, and she rewards me with a small smile. "I'll have a tech come in and teach you how to hydrate her."

"Are you sure you want to do that?" Maureen asks. I give her a great, slow nod.

"For Sophie I can do this." The vet tech enters the room. She has a bag of saline solution with her, as well as the needles we will need to perform this task at home. All I need to do is warm the bag of saline, hook it higher than the needle, settle Sophie on her haunches, bunch up the skin between her shoulder blades, and insert the needle firmly, deeply enough that it will not shake out and spray water everywhere.

Rather than perform the hydration herself this time, the vet tech has me go ahead and show her that I will be capable of sticking a needle into my cat. I think the only reason I can do this is because Sophie has spent the last two weeks being my guardian angel. If she's not going to leave my side, I am not going to abandon her to a hospital while I am physically able to save her that trauma. My own psychology will have to suck it up and give me nerves of steel, so I can help my baby.

I take the needle in my right hand. I lean over Sophie and see her gaze calmly back at me. I see deep trust in those eyes. She knows I mean well. I create a bulge of skin parallel to her shoulder blades, and I press the point through the skin halfway up the needle. Sophie doesn't move at all. This little stick does not hurt her. I thank God that we will not be wrestling her to get this hydration taken care of. When I unclip the IV line, the temperature difference of the solution startles Sophie a little bit, but she sits there calmly while a liquid bulge the size of a golf ball forms. We watch the level in the bag drop 5 mL, and I pull out the needle while the vet tech pinches the line.

Maureen has sat down. She is watching in awe as I perform this medical procedure. We take home a bag of solution and a large supply of needles, and, thank God again, our cat.

Once we reach the house I go back to bed, and Maureen feeds Sophie some wet food. Maureen comes into my dark room and thanks me for my efforts to support her and Sophie.

"It was the only thing I could do," I say. "You are both too important to me for me to stand by and let that precious girl stress out."

Maureen lies down beside me and hugs me. I feel her tears trickle onto my neck. I realize we are not done talking about today's trauma.

I gather my thoughts and do my best to lay out our options for Sophie.

"She really suffered after the last surgery," Maureen says. It's true; we did everything we could to make her experience easy. We had a house-call vet perform the surgery at home. His services cost more than taking her to a clinic, but she knew her surroundings and was not frightened by unfamiliar sounds and smells.

"I could barely stand it," I reply. We had to confine Sophie to a small guest bedroom after the biopsy, because the anesthetic made her frantic. Over and over she tried to stand and run, but after making a half-circle, she fell with a thud on her side, often on the side with the stitches. I spent the entire night awake, holding her so she would remain calm.

"We can't do another surgery now anyway," Maureen adds. "We have to get her kidneys working, and by the time we do, it may not be worthwhile to cut out the lump anyway." She starts crying, and I want to join her. But I have no physical urge to do so.

I hug Maureen tightly. There is no easy decision, but we have made one. There will be no going back.

Maureen goes to see Sophie, and I stare at the ceiling, wondering why such a traumatic event has no emotional impact on me. I should be crying with Maureen. I'm not myself.

The "What-Ifs" (I).
February, 2015

In my dream, two young men step into the crosswalk in front of my stopped car. They are both wearing light jackets; one also wears a checked flannel shirt under his unzipped windbreaker. One man nods his thanks to me for stopping. They have walked down a steep stairway from a row of condos that overlooks Bellingham Bay, and they are headed to another set of stairs that will take them down the bluff to Boulevard Park, on the water. They chat, engrossed in their plans.

They pass my passenger-side headlight and have reached the point of no return. My rearview mirror, which had been reflecting the low-hanging January sun, suddenly fills with a black rectangle. A second later, a shattering *bang!* fills my head, and my front tires roll over one man, while my bumper throws the other into the air. I then feel my rear tires run over the first man again, while my front tires crush the second man just as he lands.

I start awake, and my torso jerks upward as I try to sit and catch my breath. The bruised, swollen stalk of my neck is so weak that I can't lift my head off the bed. The pain I feel in that abrupt waking moment will dog me all day. I ease back onto my mountain of pillows and try to relax.

I'm two weeks into this experience, and I have been oversharing about my accident everywhere I go. I hear a common refrain: "At least you didn't hit the pedestrians." I agree that I am fortunate not to have that guilt on my shoulders, and also that I don't need to feel bad for the driver who hit me. He would have pushed me into them if they had not seen him coming. His life would have been damaged more than mine.

I lie in bed in the dark at 4am, manipulating my head with both hands, trying to find a comfortable position, at an angle that will put less stress on the stretched ligaments and sprained muscles in my upper back and neck.

I realize I want to feel some anger. Even though I "didn't hit the pedestrians," I still face the trauma frequently in my dreams, as if I had smashed into them. But I don't feel anger, because I don't feel emotions. When I learn of bad news, I say, "That's really sad." But I am aware that I don't feel the depth of emotional pain I used to experience.

My brain is waking up enough to give me my first dreams, but if dreaming will be like this from now on, I'm not sure I want any part of it.

Part 2: Convalescence.

Sartorial Splendor.
February 16, 2015, 8:00am

I developed a fashion sense in my early 30s, when I took a job where I had to wear a tie every day. Before that, I was willing to go around in jeans and a polo shirt, but once I had to make combinations of dress shirts and ties, I decided that I was going to do a good job of putting my wardrobe together.

Choosing my outfits with care could have been a time suck, so I created a chart where I matched numerous dress shirts with the perfect tie to go with each one. I needed a chart because, when I washed the shirts, I would have to figure out which tie went with which shirt all over again. I hung the ties on the hanger, and the chart told me which shirt to put on the hanger with each tie. I put a few hours into setting up that system, and after that I didn't need to make any changes.

At my current teaching job at Western Washington University, the dress code is more casual. In fact, the only people who seem to wear suits to work regularly are deans, vice presidents, and the president himself. But since I'm used to wearing a tie, I have sometimes decided to wear suits throughout a quarter. I have about 10 suits, plus all those shirts and ties, so I wind up wearing few combinations twice during any course.

In addition to my outlook on dressing professionally for work, there are a few rules I have followed when I leave the house. I wear decent slacks, a matching shirt, and conservative socks. My hair is always washed and combed. On the extremely rare occasion when I oversleep and cannot get into the shower before it's time to leave the house, I put on a baseball cap to hide my bed hair.

But since the accident, I have become far more concerned about comfort than about style. I've also started putting on weight from inaction, as well as eating too much ice cream and chocolate, so my pants are getting tight. Rather than buy dress slacks with a larger waist, I went out and bought track pants that I can wear without a belt.

No matter where I go now, you can find me wearing black or gray track pants, with the occasional foray into a navy-blue pair. Obviously, I am not going to wear dress shoes with track pants, so I have switched to running shoes all the time, even though I can't run. Since the track pants are all neutral colors, I don't feel bad about throwing whatever pullover shirt I have handy on top.

The situation gets worse. When I say whatever shirt I have handy, I mean exactly that. I have worn the same shirt out of the house three days in a row, without any regard for whether or not I will see someone I know who saw me in that shirt yesterday. Now that I know that I have virtually no sense of smell, I cannot discern whether a shirt smells sweaty or not. Since I don't feel like doing laundry at all, I keep my laundry piles small by recycling shirts rather than tossing them in the laundry hamper.

Best of all, or worst of all, I have felt no urge to wash my hair before leaving the house if I have needed to sleep late. I am so tired in the morning, and so groggy when I wake up, for so long after I wake up, that I simply don't get into the shower at times. As my hair gets longer, it looks worse with each passing day if I don't wash it. Part of me wants to rebel against this bohemian approach to style, but 98% of my brain really doesn't care one bit what others think of the way I look. It is hard enough to get out of bed, take medicine, eat some breakfast so I don't faint while I'm out, and shake the grogginess with a cup of coffee. I don't have the time or energy to make myself look good. I have persuaded myself that no one who looks at me cares what I look like anyway.

I suppose that the last time I dressed professionally

was for my ill-fated trip to the Whatcom Writers and Publishers meeting. If I go to the March meeting, I will dress down, just as I have dressed down for everything else since my accident.

I am pondering my lack of interest in hygiene and clothing choices because it clearly stems from some aspect of my brain injury. Maureen very kindly has not judged me for my choice of clothing, and she has not yet told me that I smell bad. I trust her to tell me if I am emitting off-putting odors. I suspect I am not smelly because I am not moving much.

It may not be fair to my brain to say that I pay no attention at all to what I wear. I have been choosing very colorful shirts to wear with my track pants. Red shirts, yellow shirts, neon-green shirts. And then, there are my socks. I went to Target and H & M and bought the most vibrant socks I could find. Some are stripes, some are solids in outrageous colors, and others have unusual designs that I cannot begin to describe.

My TBI Survivor mentor, David A. Grant, talks about how he decided to paint his front door purple. I think bright colors delight the injured brain, much as they stimulate the minds of babies. Novelty helps the brain grow, and I find my new favorite form of novelty in mixing and matching bright colors, often primaries.

I have not yet crossed the line into wearing unpaired socks. For whatever reason, I still think it is important for my socks to match, no matter how crazy the color. Herein lies one of those brain mysteries that I don't expect to see solved within the next century. Why am I suddenly willing to leave the house with my hair dirty and my head uncovered, while I balk at wearing two different color socks? You might see me on the street with my hair looking straggly and me overall looking like a 1960s hippie.

But look at my feet. As long as my socks match, you'll know I have not given up the internal fight completely.

School Visit.
February 16, 2015, 10:00am

I am struggling to accept that my head still doesn't work well after two weeks. I am putting pressure on myself to return to teaching my German classes as soon as possible. There is a small window during which I can return. There would be no point in going back for the last week of classes; I would simply disrupt the rhythm of the class that late in the quarter.

Both of the substitutes for my classes have many responsibilities of their own. It makes me feel bad to think that they are overworking themselves while I sit at home. For perspective, I'll tell you that when I was in graduate school, I missed only one class in nine years. Even on a day when I had food poisoning, I showed up for class. I lasted only 15 minutes, and shortly thereafter I went to the emergency room, but I had no intention of skipping class.

One of my subs has a small child, and the other has a sick family member. How can I make them continue to teach my classes? I can teach with a creaky neck. I can take the bus to school. I might even be able to get rides in a car. All I need to know is that I can handle the cognitive load of being in a classroom. The first step is to visit a class taught by another professor.

A German professor agrees to let me attend her literature class. I sit in the back of the room near the door, in case I have to slip out. My friend lets her students know that I am attending class because I am trying to rehabilitate from an accident. I'm glad she said that, as I am dressed for comfort, wearing wraparound dark sunglasses, and looking overall rather vague.

I can track what she is teaching at the beginning of class. She has an ingenious approach to introducing the biography and works of Thomas Mann. I would like to take notes for the sake of implementing her format on days that I am teaching literature to my students, but I have learned already that when I try to listen and take notes on paper at the same time, I become dizzy and nauseated. I sit back and listen, my eyes closed.

I open my eyes again when she switches to a Power-Point presentation on today's author. The overhead lights were already a challenge for my brain, but with the screen blazing in front of me, my eyes feel as if they are boiling in my skull. Yet I have to look at the PowerPoint, because she is referring to graphics on the slides.

That's the end of it for me. I never should have opened my eyes. Making it through someone else's class with my eyes closed, however, would be an artificial achievement. I can't teach class with my eyes closed, and I don't have the German book memorized. I close my eyes again, but I've waited too long. My head starts to swim, my forehead over my left eye is tingling, and the knife-like pain I get in the top of my skull feels like repeated stabbings.

There's no choice for me but to sneak out of class. In the department chair's office, I let Paqui know that my experiment failed.

Laura Rink, a writer friend who has driven me places before, brought me to campus. Being more intuitive than I am at this point, she told me I could call at any time if I needed to leave early. I call her, relieved that I don't have to sit in my office until my scheduled departure time.

I crawl into bed an hour after I arrived at school. Groggy, my head pounding, I try to analyze the level of victory I achieved by staying in the classroom for 20 minutes. I'm having trouble finding any positive aspect to this experiment. Finally, I settle on believing that my willingness to try attending a class is a victory. In my perspective, though, this experience might serve as the true definition of "hollow victory."

I have a baseline now that tells me just how far I am from being able to return to the classroom. The glass wall that stands between me and gainful employment is still frustratingly thick. One of the frustrating aspects of that wall is that it still allows me to see my old life, the life I enjoyed as Seán 1.0.

Old-Time Radio.
February 20, 2015

My brain is still in triage mode. There is no hum of activity. No background creativity asking me to write down clever ideas for stories, no earworms. The part of my brain that can analyze this phenomenon finds the silence terrifying.

The quietest room in the world is in Minnesota. It has a scientific use, but people are allowed to buy time and sit in it. I have always wanted to go there, because I don't think silence bothers me. They say you can hear your heart beat so loudly that the sound of its pumping, along with other sounds your body makes, creeps people out to the point that many people beg to be let out of the room sooner than they expected.

While I think I could lie back and accept the noises my body makes, I could do so only with the proviso that the background chatter in my brain would serve to distract me from my biological engine sounds. Maybe I could sing into the silence or recite poetry. But if what I am hearing now, or more accurately *not* hearing, is similar to the deafening silence in that quiet room, I could not stand to be there for more than a minute.

I did not volunteer for my current acoustic situation. When it is too quiet in the house, and I cannot relieve the silence with the internal monologue that comes while I read a novel, or watch a TV show, or even listen to whatever music feels like the right music for the moment, I want to tear my hair out; I am frantic to have my brain return to normal.

Yet again, I have started criticizing my brain for being injured. It's not fair to my brain, which is working as quickly as it can to get the power grid back on line. We once had no power at our house for two days because an ice storm tore down so many electrical lines. We had to figure out how to deal with that issue in the cold, but I didn't complain that the power company wasn't doing everything it could to get us back to normal life.

How, then, can I criticize the most vital part of my physical being, the literal nerve center of my machine, the CPU of my system? Maybe it's because Puget Sound Energy posts updates about their progress in restoring power when we suffer an outage, while my brain is not giving me any specific information about a timeline for repairs, or a clue as to what will go back on line first.

Remember, Seán, remember to love your brain. Pay attention to its subtle signals and rejoice in every small step forward.

I've started seeing an injury massage therapist, Cindy. She has offered me a tool that may work to distract me from this silence. If my brain can handle the input, I will be able to count the experience as a step forward. The tool is old-time radio on CD. I enjoy old radio mysteries, but I had not considered the idea of looking for them on YouTube or elsewhere. Cindy's CDs are boxed like audio-books, so I pull out the first disc and put it in my DVD drive. I hit play and lie down.

I steel myself against the potential onslaught of pain and confusion from the noise of the CD, given that the conversations at the writers' meeting presented such a challenge to my ears. But from the moment the dramatic organ music starts the intro to the show, my fear fades, because my brain can now process audio from a single source. Maybe I should have known I could listen to something as simple as one person talking, because I can listen to Maureen and other people individually without becoming confused.

The beauty of these radio shows is that they tamp down the silence. I don't create my own brain noise, but I am distracted by the voice actors and the melodramatic music. At last I have a pain-free pastime.

But thinking hard enough to understand the plot makes me drowsy. It's a comforting drowsiness that takes me out of the story and puts me to sleep. When I wake up, a new episode has begun. I let it run rather than go back, because I will probably listen to these stories several times; the case contains just four CDs.

I'm pretty sure that listening to the dramas will resemble the experience of *50 First Dates*, though I never expected that I would be the person with no short-term memory in that dynamic.

I can understand 10 minutes of a radio drama at one time. I will call this a baby step forward.

Don't Give Up on the Novel.
February 21, 2015

I've mentioned before that I keep trying to do things that I would do habitually before the accident. With all this time off, I am trying to stimulate my mind by visiting with friends in quiet one-on-one conversations. Different places, different people. Today I am going to the Black Drop to visit with Teri, a returning student who used to own the Drop, and who took one of my classes with Stephanie, its current owner.

Teri stands about nose-high to me, with long, dark-brown hair and a perpetual smile on her face. She and Stephanie started referring to me as "Profe," and when Stephanie put me into the Black Drop's computerized loyalty card system, that is the name she used. When I go to the shop and a new person rings me up, I say that my name is Profe, and the barista often says, "Oh! So you're Profe." I love the sense of belonging that the Black Drop has given me.

I scan the room to see if I know anyone at the small tables scattered about the seating area. Nope. Teri is the only one I know, a rare situation. We catch up first on daily life. She is well-aware of my physical and mental state, because I have kept her in the loop. Things are going well for her at Maniac Roasting, the coffee-roasting business she co-owns. I've been getting regular caffeine doses at home, so I will probably need to buy more of my favorite beans from them soon. That thought distracts me from the reason we are here: to create more realism in one section of the novel I hope to finish soon.

The protagonists of my almost-ready novel have driven from Indiana to Cardiff-by-the-Sea, California, so that the woman can visit a friend and help her run a new hospice she has opened. I learned just before my accident that Teri grew up in Encinitas, the city that swallowed up Cardiff as Encinitas expanded southward. Teri has a treasure trove of information for me about Cardiff and everything the locals know about that town.

She tells me about landmarks like VG Donuts, Swami's Beach, and the Self-Realization Fellowship. She describes local practices, including surfers who park and undress in public, so they can put on whatever they are going to wear while they surf. I have not had contact with anyone who could tell me anything about day-to-day life in Cardiff until now. I have never been there. I used Google Street View to find the shopping center where my protagonist buys groceries, and also a large building to house the hospice. Now I can add a decent dollop of local color to my story. I really do need to go to Cardiff and tweak my descriptions of the town before I ship off the final manuscript to a publisher, but I'm a lot closer now to making it look as if I know what I am talking about.

When I have finished my mocha, we say goodbye, and I walk back to the bus terminal to catch my ride home. Teri has promised to send me as much information as she can find about Cardiff through Facebook. I won't be able to do anything with the material for an undetermined amount of time, but I feel as if I have done something a writer would do, for the first time since my accident.

Matt Checks In.
February 23, 2015

I sort of forgot that I had gone to see an attorney about my accident. I'm sitting on the couch, listening to my radio shows, and the phone rings. I do not recognize the number. I'm not in the mood to take a call from a telemarketer. I reject the call and let it go to voicemail.

When I listen to the voicemail, I realize that I should have picked up. It turns out to be Matt, the attorney assigned to my civil suit. He will be working with Paula to keep the insurance companies from keeping all the money.

I call him back. He sounds a little bit surprised that I called so quickly. I'm wondering what he needs from me so early in the process.

"I just wanted to check in to see how you're doing. Have you been getting any treatment for your injuries?"

"Yeah. I'm seeing a physical therapist, an acupuncturist, a craniosacral practitioner, a counselor for my emotional trauma, a neuropsychologist, and an injury-massage therapist."

I hear him pause to think. "I'm glad to hear that. Sometimes people don't look for medical treatment right away."

I smile to myself. Daytime television is overrun with commercials for personal-injury attorneys. Much of their captive audience is truly captive, injured and unable to get out of the house. The TV is the only solace of these people. Matt is probably concerned that I would be one of the few who could be doing something about my health but refuse to engage in treatment.

"I'm looking to see what sticks," I reply. "I want to get healthy again as quickly as possible, so I can return to work. I'm not there yet. I'm kind of worried that it's going to take longer than I thought."

Matt tells me that I shouldn't get impatient. As hard

as I got hit, I should expect to need some time for healing. I know he's right. Everyone says the same thing. I think it's obvious to him that I am looking at every option to improve my physical and brain health. He seems satisfied with my effort. He tells me he'll call or write when he has information for me, and I settle back to listen to my radio drama again.

Artistic License.
February 28, 2015

Valentine's Day, two weeks ago, didn't work out so well for us. We contemplated hospitalization for Sophie in the morning, and we were still so devastated by her health crisis that dinner at India Grill, complete with belly dancers, did not cheer up either of us at all. Maureen and I needed a reboot. We have thought for a long time about taking a painting class together. We decided in January, before the accident, to take a lesson at Uptown Art. Today's lesson, an autumn scene with trees, is the one we chose to create. So, ready or not, off we go.

I have not taken a painting class before. I have always thought I would enjoy this art form, and I have done a few sketches with pencil that somewhat resembled the subject. I even bought some acrylic paints and canvases, because one main character in my novel is an artist, and I wanted to see what it would feel like to brush paint onto a blank surface. I never did get around to painting anything, but I did try once to create a small landscape. The results fell far short of my hopes for the project.

We walk into the painting room. There are three long tables with a dozen easels on each one. The painting we are going to copy is set up. It involves a yellow evening sky, a tree, and a big bushy thing that will be painted with fall colors. Uptown Art serves wine and beer, but the last thing I need right now is to impede the regeneration of my brain. And then there's that whole thing about drug interactions and the possibility of getting a stomach ulcer from mixing Aleve® and alcohol.

Maureen and I sit across from each other, as close as possible to the teacher. It's better if she doesn't watch me work, I guess. My painting will probably look like something a first-grader would produce. Or maybe a second-grader, because that is when my artistic skills peaked. Maureen, by contrast, has painted some excellent work before.

We start by painting the top three-quarters of the canvas pale yellow. I'm using a brush about half an inch wide. Smoothing the yellow acrylic onto the textured fabric is a carnal sensation that reminds me of sitting at a keyboard and painting a landscape with words. Involving textiles in that creative process adds a new facet to my creativity. I am suddenly entranced as I watch my brush swish back and forth, first streaking the canvas yellow, then filling in tiny squares of white that did not capture paint on the first stroke.

I feel less like Bob Ross than Salvador Dalí. We are painting trees today, but I feel something much less formed, much more a product of my inner turmoil, wanting to escape from my brush after I learn how to do what I'm doing now. The background is finished, and we are using the brush to dab green paint onto the left side of the tableau. On the right side I sweep brown paint upward to form a tree.

We switch to small brushes for the detailed work. I love getting into sharper focus and creating small branches and other items that, from a distance, will bring out the story the canvas wants to tell anyone who takes the time to inspect it.

The woman sitting next to me is a regular. The artist knows her by name. The student does an excellent job of fading one color into another. It might have been good for me to watch how she did that so I could use her technique in future work or even this time around. But I needed to listen to what the artist was saying about the technical basics of the landscape, so my work at least resembled hers in some small way.

After an hour, we finish up. At last I see Maureen's painting. She did a better job than I did, which does not surprise me. What does surprise me is that my painting resembles both Maureen's and the one the artist painted as our example. Not terrible for a first attempt.

I take a moment to meditate on the idea that painting

could be a good therapy for my brain. Reading and writing make my head hurt, and my ears are too sensitive for me to enjoy playing the guitar. As soon as I feel comfortable sitting up long enough to do a meaningful amount of painting, I will bring home an easel and a greater variety of colors and brushes. I'll find a place to set up my materials and start the path toward being a proficient painter. If I can't write, I now know that I can paint.

The artist asks me if I enjoyed myself.

"I did! This is the first creative work I've done in a month. I was in a car accident at the end of January. That's why I'm wearing sunglasses. It hurts to look at light, and I can't write. Normally I'm a writer. I write better than I paint." I reach into my pocket for my phone. I pull up the photo of my car after the crash. The artist gasps.

Then I glance at Maureen, and I see her wince because I am once again sharing this picture and my story with a stranger who doesn't really need to know what's going on. I can't explain to Maureen that I believe I am making a terrible impression on people, with my slow brain and my sunglasses. I try to remember that everyone says I am not embarrassing to be around, that I am recovering well. I close my eyes and promise myself that I will resist the compulsion to explain my plight the next time this scenario arises.

The next time.

We take our canvases home, now that they have had a chance to dry. It's after 7pm, definitely my bedtime. As I fall asleep, I remind myself that I did something creative today. Part of Seán 1.0 has not vaporized completely.

Phobias.
March 1, 2015

I have a phobia. It is not uncommon. Just annoying. Somewhat delicate to discuss, too, so be warned.

When I was in high school, on days that the boys who smoked could not go to the smoking area, usually because of rain, they took over a restroom and smoked there. On the few occasions when I had no time to walk to another restroom, I would enter their domain and use a urinal. Several of the smokers doubled as bullies, and they began to walk up behind me and push on my back while I urinated. Over a few such bathroom visits, I became apprehensive of their actions, and it became harder for me to relax enough to do anything at the urinal. I tried sitting in a stall, but the same guys started kicking the door.

I found other bathrooms to use, but the psychological damage was done. I became incapable of using a urinal if any other person was in a bathroom. Sometimes a public restroom would be blessedly empty, and I could relax enough to go to the bathroom. But if someone walked in before I finished, I often locked up. If someone was already in the restroom, even in a stall, I could not use a urinal, no matter how much I tried to distract myself and relax.

Today, I've entered the men's room at Target. No one is here, so I head to a urinal. Just as I begin to go, a man walks in and steps up to the urinal next to mine.

My flow does not stop. I finish without a hitch. *How can this be?* I ask myself. I don't know. Freak accident?

I have another common phobia, a fear of choking. It makes it difficult for me to swallow any pill larger than an Advil®. I often resort to chewing the Aleve®, which burns my mouth. I need to get past my swallowing phobia.

And maybe I just did! If I can pee in a public restroom because of my TBI, maybe I can do a Jedi mind trick and rewire my brain to end the choking phobia while there is construction going on.

I race home, because it's time for my second dose of Aleve® for the day. I take my afternoon pills. The struggle to get it down is just as harsh as it has ever been.

You can't win them all.

On the Road Again.
March 2, 2015

Maybe I should have chosen yesterday morning, bright and early, to take on today's project, which will make feel a little bit more normal. Yesterday didn't fit into my plans, for whatever reason. I think I simply didn't want to leave the house yesterday. I'm sure my neck hurt too much, and my head always hurts, and I probably felt too sleepy to do this task by the time I realized it was the first of March.

Because March 1 was the date I arbitrarily chose to be the day I start driving.

I have an acupuncture appointment at 10:30am, so I go through my morning ritual early. I have an egg scrambled with smoked salmon, about 50 blueberries in yogurt, and a glass of green Naked juice, so I get lots of vitamins. Then I shuffle into the shower, dry off carefully, and throw on my track pants and a long-sleeved shirt that I can wear under my jacket. Even though it's sunny, the temperature hangs in the low 40s, and a steady breeze brings the wind chill much lower.

Today I need my sunglasses more than any day up to now. I'm driving west, so at least the glare won't be in my eyes. I stopped wearing the cervical collar out of the house about a week ago, but I wouldn't wear it this morning anyway, because I need to be able to turn my head as easily as pain will allow.

My new black Civic has been waiting a month for this moment. The car did not frost up last night, which is good, because I would have to put most of the pressure on my left arm if I needed to scrape the windows. I did drive the car to Sophie's vet on Valentine's Day, but I barely remember that trip. Now I get to see what the car can do.

I climb into the front seat. When my left arm bumps the ridge of my bucket seat, I realize my injury came from the impact of my arm on the seat, either when I originally banged into it or when the back seat catapulted me sky-ward. The Charger I rented had a seat with a different shape, so I didn't feel contact with my left arm. There's one mystery solved.

Maureen and I live on a quiet street. There are four houses on the north side of our street, and three on the south side. Our next-door neighbors on both sides have several towering cedars in their yards. I back out of the driveway, enjoying the view in my first backup camera. I glide away from the curb and ease forward to the corner. I turn left onto a longer, busier street and coast downhill to the traffic signal.

Cross traffic has been busy, so the light does not change for two minutes. I turn slowly onto the four-lane avenue and begin the main segment of my trip. After I slalom through a few curves, I reach a portion of my route where the lights guarantee that I will be in stop-and-go traffic. The back of my neck starts to tingle.

I'm waiting at a red light at a busy cross street. I'm watching my mirror. I've had no one behind me, but this round of approaching traffic includes several cars in a string in my lane. The lead car is an SUV. Thank goodness it's not a Toyota. I tense up. Does this driver see me? Is he singing along to his radio, gazing at the pedestrians on the sidewalk? I wince and close my eyes. I don't hear the screech of tires. When I open my eyes and start breathing again, I see that the SUV has stopped half a car-length behind me. The driver is a middle-aged woman who looks very trustworthy behind the wheel.

I promise myself I will not spend my time at every single red light fearing that the car behind me is not going to stop. But I break my promise. I feel as if I am driving an egg carton, and I am the egg. I feel as fragile as the January day when I drove my newborn son home from the hospital in a car seat in the back seat. The day I took him home was January 29, the same date I was reborn as Seán 2.0. I believe it is far too soon for me to have another serious accident, but I cannot help but realize that the people driving behind me are not aware of how fragile I am, and that they will not take extraordinary measures to keep themselves from rear-ending me.

I drive through downtown without mishap, and once I get out of the city core, I am on the final stretch of my trip to the acupuncturist's office.

This is my third acupuncture visit. I had trouble finding the office the first time, and I had no recollection of how to find it for the second visit. I do better this time. I remember that the office is on the third floor. I remember the number of her suite rather than the name of her practice. No matter. I make it into the lobby on time.

Michele is a kind woman. She is tall, with blonde hair and an overall aura of peacefulness and good health. Her work with needles calms my neck spasms and makes it less necessary for me to use Flexeril® every night. At this point, I get only two nights without medicine after a treatment, but I hope that acupuncture will accelerate my neck's healing process.

Michele is thrilled for me that I was able to drive here on my own. She sees it as a strong sign of progress for my brain. I see it as my choosing to follow the deadline I set for getting back on the road, but I don't say that out loud. I have no idea if it was a good idea to drive today. I feel fine, but do I have the reflexes and the alertness necessary to drive safely? I think I would have to be hooked up to a machine that was looking at my brain function for me to know the true answer to that question.

However, the sense of achievement I feel from regaining my independence on the road helps me relax into the acupuncture more than I did the first two times. I enjoy lying face-down, something I can't do at home because I don't have a way to support my head off the bed. But those needles. The muscles in my shoulders and neck rebel at first. Then they stop fighting and start actively cooperating with the treatment. At the end of an hour, Michele's expertise has taken the tension in my head, neck, and back down several notches.

The drive home does not cause the terror that I experienced on my way to the appointment. I see this as one area of life where I can feel like Seán 1.0. One tiny area, so rare, so precious.

Haircut One.
March 3, 2015

I was already due for a haircut when I got hit. I tend to let my hair get a little bit long, mostly because I'm too busy to notice that it has started to cover my ears and fall into my eyes. Having hair in my eyes right now is irritating, so I go see my barber. Already today I have seen my doctor, my massage therapist, and Dr. Schmidt, my physical therapist. I always enjoy going to PT, because Cindy, Dr. Schmidt's wife, and Laurie, their office manager, are both adept at cheering me up. We laugh a lot while I pay for my visits. Sneakily clever of them.

I enjoy my haircuts as well. My barber, Diane, always has interesting news to share. She also owns two dogs, big galoots who love the attention I am willing to give them. The shop isn't large, but there is room for me to toss a tennis ball for the dogs to fetch. They take turns going after the toy.

I have a few minutes to wait while Diane finishes up with her previous customer. Then I take my place in her chair, and she asks me how my neck is doing. It is not doing well today, and she says she will be careful about asking me to move my head.

I can't leave my sunglasses on during the haircut. It's yet another sunny day in the middle of our allegedly gloomy Pacific Northwest winter. The day has been pleasant to move around in, 50 degrees, the birds expressing their joy at the seeming return of spring. I close my eyes, even though I prefer to make eye contact in the mirror with Diane while she works. I also like to watch the progress on my haircut. Not today.

It doesn't take long for my neck to get angry at my head for having the audacity to sit atop it. As so often happens, I start to envision my neck as a toothpick and my head as a bowling ball balanced on top. Despite the massage and the PT, sitting upright for half an hour is wreaking havoc on my spinal column. Tendons and muscles and ligaments begin to rebel. It would have been a brilliant idea to schedule the haircut to take place prior to massage and PT. But I do not fault myself for failing to consider that this haircut would set me back so far after all that medical work.

I don't let on that my neck and shoulders are on fire. None of that is Diane's fault. It simply feels good to be in her chair, doing something normal that I do every few months whether I need to or not.

When I get out of my seat, Diane offers to accept the bottom price on her sliding scale. I thank her for her kindness, but I tell her that I am receiving my full salary. I pay her full price plus a well-deserved tip. I say I'll be back as soon as my hair demands it. I say goodbye to her doggie boys and head home.

By the time I pull into the driveway, I have made up my mind that I am going to let my hair grow out. I have absolutely no idea when a haircut will stop being an excruciating experience. Rather than test the waters every three months or so, I'll give it a year. I may not be able to write, but I can assume the look of a Beat Poet for a while.

My Second Reason to Cry.
March 5, 2015

When my sister Cindy calls me, I always catch my breath. She does call for an occasional catch-up, but usually she has bad news to share. This call is one of the bad ones.

We are not a cancer-prone family, but my dad's sister, Louise, has been diagnosed with esophageal cancer, stage three. She is still a sharp, active woman at 86, so the news stops my heart for a couple of beats.

Aunt Louise offered me a place to stay when I took a job in Indianapolis and was sleeping on a friend's couch. When she saw my piece-of-crap car, she and Uncle Bob co-signed for my first dependable wheels. Even before that, they had taken in two of my brothers to get them out of domestic stress. She and Uncle Bob helped turn them into upstanding men.

Aunt Louise is the type of person you want to see pass in her sleep at age 101 with a smile on her face.

Cindy is telling me the cancer has spread to her stomach. She will begin treatment soon. My brain creaks into action. I need to see her before she is too ill for a decent visit. I'm six weeks post-accident, my neck muscles spasm constantly, and I get a couple of headaches a day in different parts of my skull. But I'm going to travel from Bellingham to Shoals, Indiana, to see my Aunt Louise.

A check of my funds indicates that I will be seeking an inexpensive rather than a convenient itinerary. I weigh the advantages of various Southwest destinations. It's bad enough that I can't fly Alaska out of Bellingham because of the cost, but now I see that the cheapest airport by far is Lambert in St. Louis. A four-hour drive will take me directly to Shoals, whereas the drive from Indianapolis would involve a three-hour trek. The savings on the cost of the flight make me take the risk of driving the longer distance.

Is it a good idea to make the drive? I haven't driven more than a couple of miles at a time since I resumed driving this week. But when I was 23, I drove from El Paso to Indianapolis in two 16-hour days, and I assume I can handle a measly four hours. I love to drive, and I still have stamina, I suppose.

Something to consider: I also assumed I could edit Maureen's paper, and I assumed I could return to teaching after two weeks, but those failures don't cross my mind today. I have to see Aunt Louise, and I need money for food along the way. St. Louis it is.

I generally check my plans with Maureen, at least out of courtesy, but there are times when I have to accomplish a goal, and this plan is a no-brainer, which makes me qualified to organize it. Once I have my trip routed, I ask Maureen to check my work on the Southwest website before I buy the tickets. She says I got the flights I intended to choose, but she asks about the drive.

"That drive will be really hard. What if it snows?"

"I'll have my neck collar on the whole way, and I don't really have any choice. If I can't drive that far, I'll go back to St. Louis and take a bus." I click the button that commits me financially to the trip. I go to bed and sleep a couple of hours, losing the late morning to this mental exercise.

Where Are the Tears? (I).
March 6, 2015, 6:00am

Maureen drives me to the airport shuttle. I'm not dressed for success: black track pants, black sweatshirt, and a dingy cervical support with ring around the collar. But the collar holds my chin steady, easing the strain on the muscles that prop me up because my sprained ligaments can't do their job. I feel stoic, standing erect, not looking to the sides, as if I were a military man at attention. My dark glasses and the green Cubs hat complete the picture. I could be a not-so-discreet undercover CIA operative. The glasses would give me away.

After a gentle hug from Maureen, I step aboard the bus. I ball up a spare jacket against the window, recline the seat a couple of inches, and nestle my head into the soft supportive corner I've created to stabilize my neck. Once I settle, I start to think.

I haven't been thinking much. I still suffer from dead silence in my brain. Despite the lack of logic in the few thoughts I do have, I cherish them as a sign of healing. Today, I wonder what weather I will encounter on I-70. Or will I take I-64? Maybe I should drive over to Ferguson, Missouri, and see the town for myself. Oh! I'll take I-70 so I can stop at the Chuckwagon Café in Vandalia, Illinois, where one of the scenes in my novel takes place. So far, all my information about the café has come from its website. Or was it just Google Images? Have I even seen photos of the restaurant's interior? Well, it didn't matter when I wrote the drafts of my novel, because I saw a stereotypical truck-stop restaurant in my mind. But I may as well get this one right, whenever my brain lets me upgrade the scene.

And then, we reach Seattle-Tacoma International Airport. I toddle to my gate and sit. My neck muscles, jolted by mild bumps on the bus ride, are twanging like plucked cello strings. I take a Flexeril® to mitigate the spasms. When they call for passengers who need assistance, I heave myself to my feet and show my boarding pass. I had even paid to move from the C boarding area to the A area. That was dumb, since my neck is getting me on early.

A flight attendant helps me tuck my backpack under my seat, and I drop into my home for the next few hours. After a smooth ride to the Midwest, my neck nevertheless protesting, I shuffle to my rental car and hit the road.

I exit the interstate at Vandalia and drive a block to the Chuck Wagon Café. I choose a lunch I can't get in Washington, a bluegill sandwich. I take numerous photos of the restaurant's interior so I can describe the place accurately when I revise the scene where my characters have lunch there. It would make sense to pull out my Surface and rewrite the scene now, but I have absolutely no sense of story since the accident. I can't shift my imagination from the original truck-stop scenario to this well-lit, smoke-free restaurant with planters hanging over the booths.

I hear a man talking to an employee, and I realize that he is the owner. He is a Russian man, friendly and kind to his workers. I take a chance and ask if I may use the name of his restaurant in my novel. He agrees readily and tells me that he had bought it recently and considered a name change, but the locals were so attached to it that he kept it. One tidbit I do remember without referring to photos is that my server brought my coffee with a spoon sitting upright in it. It strikes me as a sensible tactic when you have more items to deliver than you have hands.

I eat my bluegill, my mouth and stomach enjoying the nostalgia. I tell the server I'll be back in a couple of days, and I roll east.

The highway is blessedly clear of snow and rain. If I maintain good posture and keep my eyes on the road, no sightseeing, my neck behaves itself. Southern Illinois isn't all that exciting anyway. I stay in the slow lane, not trying to pass anyone, because I-70 serves as a major truck route, and I'm content to let them rule the road.

I don't take I-70 the whole way, because it goes to Indianapolis, far from my destination. I happen upon I-69, which didn't exist the last time I was in southern Indiana. The concrete is pristine, the new path through the countryside inviting and modern. I exit and drive a short way on U.S. 50, a curvy two-lane highway, to Shoals.

My dad grew up in Shoals, and I have spent a lot of time there. My grandparents owned a restaurant in town when I was a child. The locals still know me as Jack's boy. Down the hill from U.S. 50 is the house Louise and Bob bought when they retired. Uncle Bob, at nearly ninety, is a town councilman now.

There is snow on the ground, but it's sunny and fairly warm. The glare of the sun on the snow burns my eyes even with my dark glasses on. I scurry up the short sidewalk and step onto the porch of the white Craftsman. I don't have to knock. My sister Cindy opens the door for me.

I didn't know she was going to be there. I haven't seen Cindy for at least a year, so that's another bonus to the visit. Aunt Louise comes to hug me. She has not lost weight, and she steps firmly across the room. There's nary a gray root to be seen in her dark-brown hair.

Uncle Bob is watching college basketball on a really large TV, in color. I can't let his TV wreck my brain, so even though I sit facing the screen, I ignore the visuals. Aunt Louise sits on the couch, near the recliner where I'm sitting at her suggestion, where she was probably sitting before I arrived. At last, I remove my neck brace. I can't help sighing with relief.

She tells me about the spots on her esophagus, her stomach, and a shadow on her liver. She has a clinical tone as she discusses the clinical issues. I don't know if she has accepted the situation, is resigned to it without embracing it, or if she simply has blocked off her emotional reaction. I do know I would have a hard time maintaining my composure if we swapped roles.

I want to be strong for her. It's an easy role for me right now. I identify the situation as sad, traumatic, but there are no tears for me to hold back. I think, "This is one of the saddest conversations I have ever had." But the recognition is purely intellectual. My nervous system is not responding to my thoughts. No tightness in the pit of my stomach, in my chest, my throat.

No tears.

I'm not afraid to cry. When I wrote really sad scenes in my novels, tears would stream down my cheeks as I reported the death of a character. I have cried tears of joy, of pride, of sadness. But often, in cases of grief, the tears might not come immediately, which is why I'm only mildly nervous about my lack of tears today.

I have assumed since I got the news of Aunt Louise's illness that shock has kept me from crying. But as my aunt talks matter-of-factly about her prognosis, I realize I am objectively, but not emotionally, heartbroken. The wiring from my brain to my heart seems to be broken as well, and there is no response south of my frontal lobe.

I stop fretting about my lack of emotion when my cousin Larry arrives with his mom, Aunt Louise's sister, Aunt Jenny. I'm thrilled at this coincidence. Aunt Jenny and Uncle Eddie took me in for part of the summer of 1970, when my widowed dad had to find care for his kids. I got to enjoy the experience of spending time on the farm Eddie and Jenny owned. Larry became like an older brother, and I developed a set of memories that helped me forget why I was on the farm and not at home.

Cindy makes tea, and we all sit around, enjoying being family. After a couple of hours, I decide I should leave, because I know Aunt Louise will stay in hostess mode as long as I'm there. I sense that she is tired, and I never know when my own fatigue will crash down on me. I give Larry and Aunt Jenny a hug, take a couple of photos with Cindy and Aunt Louise, say goodbye to Uncle Bob, and walk toward the door.

Just before I open it, I turn to Aunt Louise.

"I want to thank you again for letting me stay at your house when I worked in Indianapolis. And for helping me buy my Chevette."

"Well, thank *you* for paying for the car."

I cock my head. "Of course."

"Well, not everyone we helped paid their loans."

"I couldn't let you down."

"And then you came all this way to see me. Thank you." As I hug her, Aunt Louise begins to cry. Diamonds fall from her eyes, and I push myself to reciprocate. I focus on the tragedy: I might not see her again. I came from Washington for this visit so I could thank her for her contribution to my life.

Despite pain and frustration since the accident, I haven't cried. This would be the perfect time for a little catharsis. But nothing happens. Where are the tears? I hold her close and sigh, my face hidden so she doesn't know I'm numb inside.

I kiss her cheek and step out of the house.

Where Are the Tears? (II).
March 6, 2015, 3:00pm

When I reach my car, I look back and wave. The sun is so bright that I can't tell if anyone waves back. But I still feel the love connecting me to my aunt. I drive into town and have an early dinner at Velma's Diner, which used to be the Dwyer Café.

On the half-mile drive across the White River, where I used to fish with my grandfather, I can't shake my concern about the tears I did not cry today. I've noticed before that I can't cry, but today I experience crystal clarity that I may have a problem.

Like most people, I have varying reactions to tragedy. For example, when I was nine, my dad took me to my Saturday-morning basketball game. When we came home, he went to check on my mom, and then he ran to the phone. He took me and my three siblings to a babysitter, and we spent the night there. I told her I hoped my mom was doing well, and she said Mom was in critical condition. I was used to that, somewhat jaded from prior health crises.

When Dad picked us up the next morning, he got us into the house and stripped off our winter gear. He sat on the couch and called us to him. We looked at him, and he put each arm around two kids.

"I have some really bad news," he said.

I thought, *Yeah, Mrs. D. told us Mom's in critical condition.*

He swallowed hard. "Mommy went to heaven yesterday." He started sobbing. The other three kids started sobbing. "Cry, cry," he said.

I didn't cry. I was stunned at my callous response to my mom's condition when I thought she was still alive. Now, she wasn't. I could never apologize for being mad at her for being sick, for not being available to hear about my basketball game. I stared at the wall, willing myself to bawl like everyone else.

My tears came two weeks later, late at night, and I soaked my pillow in the dark. Either Dad slept through my sobs, or he decided to let me get it out of my system.

In contrast to this delayed reaction, I remember the night in 2004 when one of my best childhood friends died from a fall. When I read the email sharing the news, I began to cry instantly. I don't know what psychological nuances bring on one reaction or the other.

I do know that my reaction at Aunt Louise's house is not normal for me. I will be taking this issue to my doctor.

Where Are the Tears? (III).
March 10, 2015, noon

As I write this scene, thirty months after my accident, I cannot remember what happened after my visit to Shoals. Logic tells me that I went to Indianapolis to visit my dad for a couple of days, but I have no recollection of the next steps in my trip.

I do remember driving back to St. Louis. It's a gray day, and I wish it would snow, as I haven't seen snow fall in more than a year. I spend part of the drive pondering my lack of tears, and what people will think of me when I can't react properly to sad situations.

I stop once more at the Chuck Wagon Café. I sit again at the table near the door where I sat the first time. In the far corner of the dining room, a Red Hat Society chapter is meeting. Several of the women are wearing St. Louis Cardinals baseball caps, which I consider cheating. That's a go-with-the-flow hat, not a sign of rebellion and individualism suited to the intent of the Red Hat poem. But I can add them to my novel, when I am up to depicting the restaurant scene. I am, at least, able to recognize important scene points for my fiction.

At a round table near me, a family of six has settled in. Five of them are adults, four mature women and a mature man. And there is a boy in a motorized wheelchair who is probably nearing ten. The boy is ecstatic to be here. He tells his waitress that this is his first time in a restaurant. The huge grin on his face brings me joy. He is bubbly, chatty, gracious, and clearly not defeated by his inability to walk.

I suspect that he lives away from town, that getting his heavy chair into a vehicle is a challenge, that his family had to figure out how to acquire a van to render him more mobile. Or I may have misheard him, and this is his first visit to *this* restaurant.

Regardless of the circumstances, seeing his joy gives

me the sensation of real happiness for the first time since my accident. The breakthrough excites me, but it gives me even more concern about my inability to cry. Maybe happiness will lead to an ability to express sorrow as well. But what if it doesn't?

It took the image of this little boy to make me *feel* happiness. I want to pay it back. And so, when my waitress comes to the table, I ask her to give me that family's bill and not tell them until I'm gone. I pay her, and I go to the restroom, so I won't have to stop before I reach the airport.

When I return to my table to grab my coat, I realize that the waitress thought I had left, and she has told them I covered their check. The man of the family comes over. He shakes my hand, but he says, "You didn't have to do that."

"I wanted to. Your little boy made me really happy, and I wanted to give you folks a gift for being here." He sits down, and we chat for a few minutes.

I can't remember if I went to see my dad prior to this meal. And yet, I remember the name of the man, though I won't divulge it. Such is the spotty function of a brain after a TBI.

On my way out, I go over to the table and meet the boy. I tell him that his happiness has added to mine, and I hope to see him at the café again sometime. I don't tell him how much he has inspired me to push through my own obstacles.

A Quest for Tears.
March 10, 2015, 7:30pm

My return flight takes me through Denver. On my layover, I grab some dinner at a little restaurant near my gate. I'm wearing my cervical collar, and the server asks what happened to me. I show her the photo of my demolished car, and she tells me how lucky I am not to be dead.

That response always sends a chill through me. I would think I'd be able to reply to myself, *But I survived!* Nevertheless, I always wince inwardly.

While I eat, I want to avoid overthinking my lack of tears in Indiana, so I pull out my book of crossword puzzles to distract my brain. I haven't opened it on the trip, because there's a risk it might bother my head. And sure enough, after I look over a few clues, my head starts to spin. I barely get a couple of Aleve® into me before the pain in my forehead and the back of my skull shows up. Then the knife-like stabbing in the top right of my head starts. I become dizzy and sit back, my dark glasses on in the fluorescent lighting, and wait for the episode to pass.

No tears, no crossword puzzles. Now I have even more to think about.

I am able to catch my flight and grab the shuttle bus home. I seek the bright side of the experience. With this visit to my aunt under my belt, I have conquered one fear, which is that I would not be able to travel home to Indiana for an emergency. I can make the trip, even if I can't cry as needed.

I've conquered that fear, but I now seek the ability to react to sadness as Seán 1.0 did.

Unlike my previous self, I will seek sadness. I need to try to force my emotions into outward expressions.

I am now on a quest for tears.

They're Back ...
March 11, 2015

Michele plays soft music during my acupuncture sessions. Sometimes she plays Anonymous Four, other times her iPod segues into classical works. Today's music is an album of cover songs on acoustic guitar. I know the first twelve songs, but I have never heard these versions. The thirteenth song is a melody that is new to me. It is more up-tempo than the rest of the songs, with drums and bass, a change from the guitar-only songs that comprise most of the album. The iPod moves to another album after this song, but I like it enough to ask Michele to tell me the name of the song after she removes the needles from my back.

It turns out that the song is called "Taylor Willobee," by Rodney Crowell. I like Rodney, though I don't own many of his albums. I could not recognize this song as his, because it's an instrumental. It's not quite what I would have expected while I'm lying on the table. It manages to be soothing, even though it is structured and arranged like a pop song.

Before I go to my next appointment, a craniosacral treatment with Karen in the next room, I have 10 minutes to research this song. I learn that it's on a special album designed to show off the sonic qualities of Taylor guitars. I want to download the song I liked best, but the songs are all available only on the complete album. I bought plenty of albums for one hit song when I was a kid. That move didn't always work out, but I often got a pleasant surprise when I listened to the rest of the album. This time, I have at least heard all the songs.

Scheduling me back-to-back is an experiment that Michele and Karen are trying out. We're going to schedule me both ways. Michele went first today; Karen will go first next time. Now, Karen settles me in and asks me to visualize what the back of my head looks like. I contemplate her request for a minute, then I make my report.

"I see the aftermath of a forest fire. The ground is charred; there are stubby black bushes and tall, leafless blackened trees. Smoke still rises from the underbrush."

"Wow. Now, try turning some of the underbrush green while I work."

I sense my legs lying raised on a pillow. I feel the rest my body lying flat on her table. I feel her hands manipulating my skull. I concentrate on the devastated landscape that my brain has given me as an image of its current state.

I perceive that any green growth will be neurons developing new pathways. I push low-growing plants, ferns, nettles, to spring up from the ashes and speckle the landscape with their new, vigorous life. The image begins to look like a graphic of terraforming Mars. Here and there I see a fern anchoring itself in the rich post-conflagration soil. Tendrils of smoke weave through the fronds of these intrepid plants.

The landscape is not regenerating entirely on its own. I see people wearing white overalls who are turning over scorched soil with spades. They seem to be loosening the earth to facilitate growth. I have had dreams about these people who are working to repair my brain. I take the dreams as a message from one part of my brain to my conscious self that reconstruction is proceeding as quickly as possible.

And, accompanying this work, I hear the people playing "Taylor Willobee" on a loop—one usually considered annoying—that constitutes an earworm. It's the first music to play in my head since the accident. I celebrate it.

I describe to Karen the bit of growth I see in the forest that symbolizes my brain. I don't tell her about my earworm, because it might be too hard to explain. I want to cherish hearing my brain produce music out of nothing for the first time in six weeks. I think I have Karen and her visualization of my brain's healing process to thank for the advent of this lovely earworm, this step forward in my brain's self-repair.

I have nothing to do but rest when I arrive home about 12:30. I go to the computer, download the songs on the album I just bought, and burn a CD. I also put the album on my phone. I put "Taylor Willobee" on single repeat and lie down for a three-hour nap.

Sacred Healing.
March 12, 2015

See what sticks. That has been my motto since I started trying to repair my body and my brain. Today I have scheduled an attempt at a shortcut to complete recovery.

When I lived in Minnesota, I once accompanied somebody who had a cancer scare to see the local Catholic priest. He anointed this person with oil and prayed. The sacrament of healing seems to have worked, because the precancerous condition was eradicated much more easily than expected.

I have attended Sacred Heart Catholic Church in Fairhaven about twice a month since I moved to an apartment a few blocks away. Now that I live farther away in a different neighborhood, I am less likely to make it to Mass here. That won't stop me from seeking the sacrament of healing from the priest. I made an appointment to see him today.

I sit down in his office, my sunglasses on as well as my cervical collar. It's not a good day for my neck. Father Joseph is a young redheaded man. I enjoy his straightforward style during his homilies, and I am encouraged that someone his age wanted to serve his church in this profession.

He asks me about my background as a Catholic. I will admit that, after my mother died, I attended a variety of Protestant churches and became skeptical of some Catholic doctrine. I don't bring that up with Father Joseph. I divulge that I made my First Communion when I was seven, that I have not been confirmed, and that I was married in the Church. He asks if I am still married, and I tell him that I divorced the mother of my children many years ago.

Father Joseph asks if I have been taking Communion. I say that I have, and he says that, as a divorced man, I am not allowed to take Communion. The revelation stuns me. For whatever reason, that ritual has been the main comfort I derive from attending Mass. Perhaps because I chose to have my First Communion take place at my mother's birthday as a present to her, I feel a link to her whenever I go up to the priest and receive the Host.

He says I will be able to resume taking Communion if I have my first marriage annulled. All I need to do is to admit that our marriage was not the perfect marriage for me or my ex-wife, and we will both be cleared to be complete members of the Catholic Church again.

I tell him I will consider that option, but I know that my ex-wife would find annulment papers devastating. I see no reason why I should offend her in that way. I would also create pain for our sons, and there is no good reason to hurt them.

I will not take Communion at Sacred Heart any longer. It will feel strange to sit while everyone files past me, but it would feel even stranger to step up to Father Joseph and have him give me the stink-eye for placing him in the awkward position of having to refuse me.

We get these preliminaries out of the way, and the priest goes into healing mode. He anoints my forehead with oil and prays for healing for me. I find the process comforting, but it is hard to overcome the shock I still feel at being banned from Communion because of an event that took place 25 years ago.

When I get home, Maureen asks how the sacrament went. I tell her what happened, and she gives me a big hug. She understands that I feel as if I have lost a part of my childhood this morning.

If I gain a part of my brain in trade, I will call it even. My adult brain is more important to me right now than anything else, including the good spiritual moments of my childhood.

Neurology, Neurosis.
March 13, 2015

There is nothing like the second Friday the 13th in a row to keep you on your toes if you've had a spell of dodgy luck lately. I have two medical appointments today. The second one will be my first visit with my real primary care provider, who has been out since mid-January with a health issue. The first one is with an honest-to-goodness neurologist.

Dr. John Jefferson is in great demand. I scheduled this appointment about a month ago, so I'm glad I'm not too headachy or too nauseated to drive to see him. It might have been wise to make backup plans for a ride if something went wrong with my head this morning, because his office is pretty far from our house. But I'm not good enough at organizing my thoughts, much less a complex agenda, to have thought of this potential issue.

Dr. Jefferson is probably young enough to be my son. That would make him the youngest doctor I have ever seen. He is extremely intelligent, personable, and efficient. I sit on the examination table. He checks how well my eyes track; he hammers my reflexes; he tests my grip strength. He asks me for such cognitive data as my name and where we are. I give him the complete address, and he jokes that he's not sure he knows the full address of his office himself. Then we talk about the particulars of my neurological impairments.

When I tell him about my different types of headaches, especially the knife stabs in the top of my head, he explains that gabapentin, an epilepsy drug, works wonders for TBI headaches. He says that using Aleve® too often can lead to rebound headaches on days that I don't take it. I use Aleve® as rarely as possible, so I don't believe I have yet had any rebounds. But if he has a medication that will prevent these headaches rather than simply push them away after they start, I'm in.

Just to make sure there is no physical issue causing

the headaches, Dr. Jefferson orders an MRI. Dr. Patterson was not a fan of high-end testing, as he did not like the radiation load it would put on my brain. But since I am still suffering pain six weeks later, an MRI now seems appropriate.

I ask him about my trouble reading. He says that I should try to read a little bit each day, not quite to the point where I begin to have headaches. I should then try to add a little bit of time each day to my reading quota until I get to where I can read for a normal amount of time. I also accept this advice as wise.

Then I ask the big question. "When will I be able to get rid of the sunglasses?"

He keeps writing and answers without looking up. "I would hope that you will not have photophobia within a year."

"A *year?*" Six weeks in sunglasses seems like an eternity to me. I can't imagine going a whole year this way.

He senses my dismay. "Much less than a year, probably. I say a year because conventional wisdom dictates that whatever improvement you experience in the year after your injury is all the improvement you will get."

"That doesn't sound so bad. So, maybe six months, maybe nine?"

"Keep working at it."

I don't ask about crying, though I should have. My quest for tears is my personal battle.

Ophthalmologist.
March 17, 2015

I developed an eye condition called nystagmus when I was about six weeks old. When someone's eyes don't develop properly, they sometimes move excessively in search of a crisp image on the retina. My case of nystagmus seems to have developed after I became ill with an intestinal infection and spent a couple of weeks in the hospital.

People who develop nystagmus as babies normally develop filters that the brain creates to steady the image entering the brain from the optic nerves. Essentially this system works like a Steadicam. It doesn't matter if a camera operator moves around, because a system of pulleys and gyroscopes holds the image steady. My brain works hard to give me a visual image free of jitter and has done so since I was just weeks old.

Another way to develop nystagmus is to have a brain trauma. Many times, people who are injured in car accidents and acquire a TBI also acquire nystagmus. Unlike early-onset nystagmus, acquired nystagmus does not give the brain time to develop a compensatory routine. Many people who have adult-onset nystagmus from traumatic brain injury have accompanying vertigo for the rest of their lives. As a part of the nystagmus community, I have known people injured in bicycle accidents who acquire nystagmus and are never able to ride a bicycle again.

Imagine my dismay, then, when I realized that the accident damaged my ability to compensate for my nystagmus. For several weeks now, I have experienced a condition called oscillopsia, where I actually detect the eye movement, and my field of vision jitters. My Steadicam is on the fritz.

The first order of business is to find out if I have actual damage to my eyes from the impact. I have chosen to visit an ophthalmologist, Dr. Carlson, for a state-of-the-art investigation of the health of my eyeballs.

When I sit down in Dr. Carlson's chair, we quickly re-alize that we both attended Indiana University. This fact is important, because the Indiana University optometry school gives its students exceptional, thorough training in the latest advances in dealing with nystagmus. Even though Dr. Carlson studied well beyond optometry, she received the same training, perhaps even more, in nys-tagmus issues. The training becomes evident as she works on my eyes.

She apologizes for shining her bright light at my ret-ina, and with good reason. She might as well be using a light saber, thrusting it through my eyeball into my brain. I have never felt such excruciating pain in my head as what she perpetrates with her little flashlight. She notes that my retinas are not detached, and then she makes a sound that indicates interest in whatever she is seeing in my eyeball.

"You have the foveae of a three-month-old child. When we are born, our foveal cells are scattered on the retina. Around age 3 months, they clump up and give your vision a solid spot to focus on. Your cells never joined up."

I tell her about my hospitalizations for intestinal is-sues when I was an infant. She agrees that, like any med-ical trauma at that age, my severe illness could affect whatever developmental processes were going on in my body.

I'm fascinated to have more information about the source of my nystagmus, and I'm relieved that I do not have issues with my retinas. I was hoping to go to a yoga class today, but I feel a gigantic headache coming on from those bright lights. I drive home as the headache settles in. I sleep it off, and I also sleep through a lunch meeting I scheduled with my colleague Joan at Taco Lobo.

My new medicine, gabapentin, has curtailed the stab-bing headaches in the top of my head. Now I know the limit of its ability to prevent my light-induced headaches.

Capitulation.
March 18, 2015

Fresh from my MRI, I take a seat at a tall table in the Book Fare Café inside Village Books. My department chair, Paqui, suggested it as a convenient place to meet to talk about my plans for next quarter. Paqui has helped me navigate the departmental aspects of my leave. Over the five years I have known her, she has always been a steadfast colleague. Now she is the key to my future.

The Book Fare boasts one of the choice locations in Fairhaven. It nestles in a corner on the top floor of Village Books. Two walls of the seating area are all glass from table height to the 15-foot-tall ceiling. The view is Bellingham Bay. If you take a break from reading, writing, or drinking coffee, you can see how Fairhaven follows the curve of the Bay. You can see the train tracks, the path of long freight trains and Amtrak passenger trains that run from Vancouver to San Diego. You have a view of the boardwalk that crosses the water from Fairhaven to Boulevard Park.

Everyone who sits in the Book Fare seems to be a reader or a writer. Four laptops sit open here. I see several people absorbed in their reading, holding the book in one hand and lifting a fork or a mug with the other. I would love to be writing. I would love to be reading. I am facing outward at the Bay, because it would be strange for me to sit facing the wall when I am alone at this tall table. I didn't think about the intense overhead lighting, shooting into my eyes like lasers, or the daylight streaming through the glass. I am squinting at the table top, unable to look up. I keep hoping I can find sunglasses that are nearly opaque for this type of situation.

I planned to return to work after a couple of weeks. I wasn't ready. *Give it a full month*, I told myself. I wasn't ready. With just three weeks left in the Winter quarter, I finally gave up on finishing the courses I had started.

It's Finals Week now, so I have this week and next to

wrap my head around the material and the routine involved in teaching my Spring Quarter Spanish classes. So far, thinking about standing in front of thirty students makes me dizzy and gives me a headache.

Paqui will arrive soon to ponder my progress and my short-term future. I am going to fail her and the whole Spanish faculty. The idea that I am still infirm embarrasses me.

All around me I hear writers typing on their laptops. I have enjoyed writing in the café, surrounded by examples of persistence from other writers whose typing turned into books. But these books are paperweights that mock me, with their painful, unreadable prose and the dead promise that I will see my name on the cover of a novel if I just keep on writing.

I am growing dizzy, and I feel my few words fleeing me. I need to express my symptoms to Paqui, and it will cost me a headache and hours of fatigue to do so.

Paqui finds me. She is Galician, with the dark hair of that region of Spain, which she wears long. She is slim, not tall, and she has on fashionable eyeglasses that have no tint. I can barely remember not hiding from the light. She hugs me, an unusual action, and joins me at the table, where we sit on barstools.

"How are you, don Seán?" Her nickname for me has always made me feel important, as if I have some stature in society.

"I've been doing a lot of PT, and I hope I can start brain therapy at the Western clinic soon. My neck still gives me a lot of trouble."

I tell her that I can't watch moving pictures yet, and if I try, all I can handle is a few minutes of *The Munsters*, thanks to the lack of color. I can't look at color TV any longer than I can look at the sun. I tell her I can't read, and I depend on uncomplicated audiobooks to keep my mind from spinning on the same simplistic thought loop that, I suppose, must resemble the mental activity of a goldfish in an aquarium.

I stumble as I express my plight: "I can't write a syllabus, but I have an old one that will work if I change the dates. I can't stand for eighty minutes, but I can teach sitting. I can't handle the light of the classroom, and I can't look at a screen for more than a few minutes, even if I use brain-friendly colors. I just won't use PowerPoint. When I come back, I'll need to have someone available to take over if I can't handle the work."

I know she thinks highly of my teaching. I always have good evaluations, and I pitch in wherever I can to help the department. I worked out a plan to implement a placement exam for Spanish, something our department did not have until I arrived. I'm depending on my past to ensure my future.

I see concern in her eyes, and to my relief, I also see sympathy for me. "You are welcome to try, don Seán," she says. "I have a backup plan, though. I need you to do what will help you heal as well as possible."

Gratitude washes over me. I hold my fate in my hands, with no pressure to push beyond my limitations. I know what I want to do, but I also know what I need to do. My desires and reality are like an estuary, with hope and despair pushing against each other, intermingling along a thin border.

As we sit there, deciding my near future, my instinct to curl up and rest overwhelms the go-getter in me. I admit defeat; I capitulate. I will take Spring Quarter off. It's for the best, and Paqui accepts that plan as the safest way to handle my injuries. The part of me that seeks normalcy wants to rebel, but the idea of trying to stand before thirty bright, healthy young minds while I still deal with dizzy spells and light-induced headaches makes me want to vomit.

Taking this huge decision to rest longer calms my nerves. I can stop fighting myself. I understand that my biggest concern was that I *would* have to return to the classroom in March. No matter how willing I am to gut it out, going back now would lead to disaster.

Along with the relief, though, comes the darkest thought I could have: If I do not heal considerably by mid-summer, I will be left with no income when my leave ends. Even worse, I will not be able to teach ever again if my brain does not respond to convalescence and therapy well enough to put me back in the classroom at some point.

Paqui seems to understand my mixed emotions. She can't see my eyes through the sunglasses, but if she could, she would see no tears. That would not mean I am happy. I just have no means to cry, even though this is a perfect moment to do so.

Jacket for Sale.
March 22, 2015

Maureen has planned a round of errands, and I feel well enough to tag along. It's warm out, but we're getting some drizzle with a few windy gusts. Spring has arrived. I prefer this gray weather to our breezy and bone-chilling sunny winter days. In past years I have enjoyed the odor of awakening earth on the breeze. There's a word for that odor, and after a few seconds of fishing in my brain, I find it: *petrichor*. I wish I could pull up the words for common household items when I need them. I still point a lot or use the wrong words.

I don't smell petrichor today, though I'm sure others do. My sense of smell is still failing me.

I feel the barest tingle of excitement to be going somewhere, anywhere, with Maureen. My few car trips have mostly involved doctor visits. Sitting in her big Honda CR-V will be both a hint of normalcy and a comfort because I am not driving.

I head for the closet to grab the perfect coat for this weather. I reach in and pull out a black jacket, thin leather, not lined. It's a recent purchase that fits me perfectly. I walk to the door that leads to the garage, where Maureen is wrestling with her purple parka. I help her find her left sleeve, then she turns and thanks me.

I put my right hand in the sleeve of my jacket, then I freeze. I look at Maureen and see her eyes go wide.

"Did you hurt yourself?" she asks.

I shake my head. "I can't wear this jacket," I admit.

She frowns. "What—oh." She gets it. "That's what you were wearing when you got hit."

"Exactly."

"It's creepy," she agrees. "I feel bad energy around it now."

That's what's wrong. This is the jacket I walked around in while we waited for the investigation to end and my car to be hauled away. I could think of this as the jacket that helped keep me alive, but I don't. I can't.

I'm not superstitious, but for me this jacket has acquired a negative energy. I'll never again be able to slide my arms into the sleeves, zip it up, put my phone in its pocket. This jacket is my enemy.

I would say the feeling it gives me is a product of the short-circuits in my brain, or my imagination running away with me, as the Temptations put it. But since the accident, I have not yet displayed *any* imagination, and I've helped Maureen feel the same vibe from this innocent-looking, stylish, malefic jacket.

I fold it and lay it on the dryer, so I can remember to take it to Goodwill. I go back to the closet and pull out a lined windbreaker. I slide my hands into the sleeves, look at Maureen, and she nods. Crisis averted.

Amid the stops for groceries and prescriptions, I receive a glimmer of a story idea about the jacket. I have not tried to write any fiction since my accident, and this is the first notion I've had that could produce a story. I figure that I'll take a nap when we get home, and when I am rested, I will tackle this other step toward my old normal: writing fiction.

I clear the cobwebs from my head after my nap. I sit down at the computer and open Microsoft Word to start writing my first story since January. I want to talk about how this jacket goes from owner to owner, creating mischief in the lives of each of them, the damage increasing with each change in ownership. Either someone will learn of the jacket's evil properties and burn it, or it will kill the last person who wears it.

I'm having trouble getting started on the story. I write a couple of introductory sentences:

The Blackest of Jackets

Sure, you can tell from the title of some stories

what emotion you're expected to experience when you read them. "Black" doesn't usually connote sweetness and light, but a black jacket tends to attract positive attention.

But then nothing else comes to me. I don't know who the characters are, other than the man who is first wearing the jacket when he is injured. As I try to conjure up an image of the man, my head starts to swim, and I become sick to my stomach. I save the two sentences I have written and go to bed. It's not time to write yet.

Sophie jumps onto the bed to snuggle. "Baby girl, do you know Daddy's sad because he can't write?" She stares into my eyes, then leans forward and begins to groom my neck. Her tongue feels like a rasp on my still-puffy throat, but I accept her desire to comfort me. Soon, we sleep.

Maureen's Journey.
March 23, 2015

Most of the time, my thoughts center inward. Since some areas of my brain are redeveloping from a toddler state, I should not be surprised at my egotism. But I don't like it. I care about my wife, my family, and my friends. There is just so much going on in my head, compounded by the physical pain in my neck and back, as well as the overwhelming sudden-onset fatigue I experience each day, that I have very little time to think about anything at all.

It is time to give a shout-out to Maureen.

Maureen has held positions in the nonprofit sector for most of her career; with children who face physical, mental, and emotional challenges; with elderly adults who need help taking care of their insurance, housing, and caregiving needs; and with able-bodied Americans who are struggling to find affordable health insurance.

And now, five months after our wedding, she has a TBI Survivor in the house.

She doesn't grumble about helping me navigate the paperwork. She does an admirable job of being patient when I forget to do a task I promised to do. She bites her tongue when I show the photo of my car to people. I cannot explain to her why I use the picture as a buffer between my perceptions of my intellect and my projection of how others judge it.

I am fortunate that Maureen does not have to bathe me, help me walk, help me eat, or interpret my slurred speech for people. When I was in graduate school, I worked with students with disabilities, taking notes in classes for students who were blind or deaf. I helped students who used wheelchairs or had cerebral palsy get to class and eat lunch. I know how taxing caregiving can be. If I needed that much assistance from Maureen, I probably would tell her to put me in a nursing home.

But I don't think she would balk at the responsibilities of caring for me. She would seek help for us, and she would never abandon me.

The comfort I get from my faith in her contributes much to my healing. I do not have to wait for the other shoe to drop, the moment when she says she can't take it any more, that I have exhausted her physically and mentally. I am a very lucky man to have such a steadfast ally.

Speaking more generally about caregivers, I have seen many parents and partners who deal with their TBI Survivor's needs with courage and seemingly boundless energy. These are people who did not go to school to learn how to be a caregiver for people with disabilities. The accident occurs, the Survivor spends time in the hospital and then comes home, and the caregiver has to take a crash course in home nursing at the same time that he or she is grieving, losing sleep from worry and the demands of the new responsibilities, and trying to maintain a normal life that includes self-care, social connections, and a job.

I admire everyone who undertakes, voluntarily or not, these responsibilities. Almost all of them have the option of walking away or institutionalizing the Survivor. In my case, I understand very clearly that I was given exactly the right partner to help me navigate this journey. I cannot express my gratitude as well as Maureen deserves to hear it.

Teaching Mockumentary.
March 25, 2015

Thinking is so hard. My head reels when I try to read or write. I can't sort out the plot of an audiobook unless it's a reading of a book I know well, like a Father Brown or an Agatha Christie mystery.

And yet, the day looms when I will have to interact with my brightly colored Spanish textbook, with the classroom computer, with the projector screen on which I will show PowerPoint grammar presentations, and with 20 sharp minds that crave the knowledge I have stored in my head.

I feel more intimidated now than I did the first day I stood in front of a class, when I was 23 years old.

Today, I am going to teach a mock class. I will be in the classroom I will use in four months for Summer quarter. I have been dragging my feet when it comes to this step in preparing for my return to the classroom, because I know it will hurt my head. It will hurt my neck.

And I may fail completely and learn that I am unable to teach ever again.

Maureen has been the catalyst for this therapy exercise. She is understandably concerned that I will struggle during the real teaching if I don't give my brain a workout ahead of time. The truth is that six months off will not really be enough for my brain to be ready to teach anyway. But my paid medical leave ends after six months, and I am ambulatory. Thus, I will teach to keep food on my table.

The point of practicing in the exact classroom I will use is to gauge how I react to the light, and so I can get a few volunteers to be mock students. I could pretend at home that I am teaching, but talking to an empty room won't give me the stimuli I need. When my mock students ask me questions, I can see how well my brain responds to their queries. So, here we go.

I walk into the room. It's cloudy and rainy, but the

room still seems as bright as a greenhouse to me. In the back of the room there is a three-sided nook comprised of 20-foot-tall windows, and until late afternoon, daylight intrudes into the room. The shades are designed to let in some light even when they are pulled down.

I walk past three rows of tables and chairs and place my book on the workstation desk. I log into the computer, and the first thing it tells me is that I need to change my password, because I am supposed to do so every six months. I see a small triumph in my ability to remember the password that has overstayed its welcome, and I take a moment to think of a solid new one.

Then I look up and see that several friends have come to support me. Karen, my craniosacral therapist, sits in the second row, center. Maureen is here, as is Tosia, a steadfast former student and a TBI Survivor in her own right. Tosia's boyfriend, Andy, who met Tosia in my class, is here to help out. Two grad students from the Speech and Hearing Clinic have walked up from their building to lend a hand. I have six mock students to teach today. Only Tosia and Andy have studied much Spanish.

Already my stomach is rebelling. It's pure nerves, nothing to do with overuse of my brain. I am nevertheless relieved that Maureen drove me here, because I don't see myself being able to drive home. I am going to teach until my brain locks up. Doing so will give me a baseline from which to judge future efforts.

I'm going to start easy. I'm presenting the verb system in the present tense. I uncap a marker and turn to the white board. The marker feels natural in my hand, a talisman of normalcy after two chaotic months. I graph out the stem and the endings on the white board:

habl	o	habl	amos
habl	as	habl	áis
habl	a	habl	an

and then I explain how the endings indicate who is doing the action of the verb. My non-Spanish speakers recite the verbs at my behest, and they are able to transfer the concept from *hablar*, my example verb, to *tomar*. I can still teach, even if all I am providing is information from the first week of Spanish 101.

I start to show how these common verbs work in sentences. I leave the verb grid up on the board to the left of the Smart Board screen and move to the board at its right. I start composing example sentences, reaching up to use the entire board. I am writing my third sentence when I begin to stumble over my words. I wobble, and I grab the marker tray to avoid falling. All I can say is, "That's it."

I lasted 22 minutes. That's not the three hours I will have to handle when class starts in August. I don't know if I should be scared for my future or pleased that the first indications show that I can recall Spanish grammar.

I sit down in my chair and take a couple deep breaths. The room stops spinning, but I feel the tingling in my frontal lobe that tells me I've pushed too hard. It was my goal to use up my brain, to lead my cognition to the precipice and dangle it over the edge. I've met that goal, and now I surrender to the ministrations of my caregiver, Maureen, who will walk me to her car and put me to bed for the afternoon.

As we all pack up to go, one of the grad students mentions that I presented the verbs more clearly than she had ever seen them. In 20 minutes, I gave her a greater understanding of the verb system than her teachers had done in a full year.

That's my first glimmer of hope in a transitional stage full of fear for me, one where I feel as if I am on a tightrope, with teaching success on one side, cushiony and inviting, and early retirement on the other side, a sharp, rocky menace threatening to tear into my body if my fate takes me that way.

To some degree, which way I tip off the tightrope depends on my resilience, my determination to succeed at any cost. But if I believe I can overcome absolutely every aspect of this injury on sheer willpower, I am deluding myself. If my healing stops at any point, my desire to return to the classroom won't matter.

I have no choice now but to resume my teaching. I hope I can reconnect enough neurons to make the plan work in time for my debut in four months.

Handing Over the Reins.
March 26, 2015

The Rustic Café is a cozy spot in Fairhaven where I meet a lot of my friends for coffee. I have written many pages in this venue. I have read the works of other authors here and shared mine back. Today I will be sharing some of my other intellectual property, the syllabi for the two Spanish courses I am giving up for the Spring quarter.

Paqui has called in our most dependable part-time instructor, Sarah, to teach these classes. She will be teaching some people I taught in the Fall quarter. I was looking forward to seeing them, and to see their progress after a quarter away. I can't even get up the energy to go to the classes on the first day to say hello and goodbye.

Sarah has lived in Spanish-speaking countries for a number of years. Her Spanish is impeccable, and her teaching skills earn her admirable reviews. I know the students I was looking forward to teaching will be in good hands. I wanted them to be in my hands. Getting paid to teach them, while not teaching them, is no comfort.

I am sitting with my back to the window. To my left is a small gas fireplace. I am wearing my sunglasses, even facing into the café, where the predominant color is dark brown, and the overhead lighting is not overwhelming for most people. The gloomiest part of this experience is not looking at the brown walls through sunglasses, but rather watching as my hopes of teaching this quarter dim and flicker out like a candle that has run out of wax.

I must be exuding melancholy. After we talk for half an hour, Sarah thanks me for the materials and wishes me quick healing, her tone serious and heartwarming. She is probably feeling excited about teaching these classes, but she has cued into my somber demeanor and matched it. I thank her for taking over for me and make myself smile so she knows my mood has nothing to do with her.

We finish our meeting at nearly 6 o'clock. It's still light out, but when I get home, I collapse into bed.

Near-Death Experience.
April 8, 2015

My friend Marla Bronstein invited me to have coffee. I see her sitting at Boulevard Park, and I buy a coffee, welcome heat on a cool, sunny morning. My dark glasses guard against the glorious sunshine that glints off the choppy waters in the Bay. A steady breeze ruffles my windbreaker. This is one morning where, even with my emotions slowed by my TBI, I feel glad to be alive.

Marla knows everyone. She is probably the most gregarious person I know. We have one major link in common. Marla had brain surgery five years ago for an acoustic neuroma. It is a non-cancerous tumor caused by abnormal growth of certain cells around the main nerve that leads from the inner ear to the brain. While pressure from this growth can be life-threatening, surgery usually takes care of the issue.

Marla has written a book about her acoustic neuroma, *A Whole New Normal: An Acoustic Neuroma Journey*. She named her neuroma Norman. Norman caused balance issues before he was detected. She suffered some hearing loss as well. She is now as healthy as she could possibly be, and she is a warrior for the cause of acoustic neuroma. She keeps us up to date on her many endeavors via her blog, "A Whole New Normal."

She waited two months for me to get to a point where I could comfortably have a conversation about my accident. Marla is intuitive about timing. We decide to walk the boardwalk that extends above Bellingham Bay in Fairhaven, and we walk all the way to the Alaska ferry terminal. We catch up on the day-to-day activities and happenings in our lives, and eventually the talk turns to my accident.

She hasn't gotten the details before now. The photos come out, and so does the story in word form. She listens patiently while I piece together orally what I can see in my mind. I mention at one point that I intend to be an advocate for TBI Survivors and TBI prevention, almost as if I had had an epiphany after a near-death experience.

"You did have a near-death experience," she replies.

"My heart didn't stop on an operating table or anything," I counter.

"How close did you come to dying from the impact?"

I stop walking to think about her question. "When my head snapped forward on my neck, it knocked me out for a few seconds. I guess I could have awakened paralyzed."

"If you woke up at all."

I ponder her words for another few seconds, then we resume walking.

After we part ways, I pick apart Marla's perspective on my accident. Some of my behaviors since then–wanting to advocate, deciding to improve my diet, waiting impatiently to be able to do more exercise, everything I want to do to ensure that the extra years I have been given will be quality time–these are the behaviors of someone who, like Ebenezer Scrooge, receives insight into what matters in life after a traumatic experience.

She's right. I've escaped death. Now, to make use of this new perspective.

Can I Write? (No Fiction).
April 18, 2015

I've been feeling isolated at home, and I haven't been able to write. But I won't let this stop me from helping other writers be productive. At the April meeting of the Red Wheelbarrow Writers two weeks ago, I suggested a Write Out at the Calico Cupboard in Mount Vernon. Several writers agreed to come, and I also contacted people who did not attend the meeting but often come to Write Outs.

I will try to tap a few lines at this Write Out, using a dream I had in late March that I can turn into a story. My first attempt at writing fiction was a disaster, so I'm keeping that experience in mind and promising myself that I won't be as disappointed this time as I was that day. I know what I'm facing now.

I carpool with one of the other writers, because I'm never sure I'll be able to drive after I spend time using my brain. The restaurant has a small room in the back of its upper level. I've reserved it, so we start to settle in at the long table. One by one, the writers arrive, and we get down to business.

A Write Out involves working quietly, maintaining focus on the creative thoughts trying to escape our brains. Background noise becomes a comforting hum, and we're always just far enough out of town that no one is tempted to run home and drop some clothes into the washer. We write, and then we share our day's work. That's all we do, apart from buying enough food that the restaurant is glad we came.

I turn on my Surface for the first time since the accident. I have sat at my desktop computer frequently, but I have not left the house with the intention to read or write. I might not be able to drive home if I do.

My food is ordered, I have coffee, and my screen is on. Even with my dark glasses, I turn down the screen brightness. Now, the moment of truth. I open a blank Word document and rest my fingers on the keyboard.

I try to recall my dream. It had something to do with medieval knights, not my standard writing topic, and how a swordmaker got revenge on a king who disparaged his perfectly forged weapons. I could guess that there is some subconscious reference to *The Princess Bride*, where Íñigo Montoya seeks the man who killed his father. I am happy right now to have any story idea at all in my head, which is just barely beginning to give me background thoughts.

I wrote a couple of paragraphs on April 12 to get the tale started. I don't know where to go from there. A bit of background about this kingdom? About the king himself? About the weapons supplier? Start with battlefield action? A scene at the king's court? It's bewildering, unlike prior to my TBI. Sure, there have been times in the past that picking the right starting point, like deciding where to apply the first brush stroke to a canvas, is a challenge. I normally just pick a scene and start writing it. But this array of options already hurts my head.

I almost decide to flip a coin. My frontal lobe has started to tingle above my left eye. The right side of my head is beginning to ache. I brought Aleve® for that contingency, so I take two. Swallowing the pills distracts me just long enough to be able to settle on an opening scene. And I write.

I finish the seven-page story in five hours. I write in short spurts, a paragraph here, one there. I take short walks when I feel a fog settling over me. My typical writing pace before the accident would be five pages per hour if I had a scene firmly in mind. I don't have anything concrete in my head this time, but even so, I should have settled into a groove and whipped out this piece in a couple of hours.

At least I finished the story, yeah? Well, the first attempt to write was brutally bad, and this one is just...bad. The fun of writing fiction is that I sit myself down in the midst of the characters and the setting and record what unfolds: what the people say, what they do, what the scenery looks like.

In this post-accident experience, my interaction with the characters resembles that of a television viewer who is watching a show on a flat screen. I don't find myself amid the characters; I'm a reporter, not a creator of a world. I don't get insight into the characters' psyches, their pasts, their futures. My description, and my descriptors, are neither vivid nor compelling. The story line is basic and not much to read.

I do know now that it's far too early for me to write more of the scenes I am supposed to add to my finished novel. I don't dare mess it up with the sort of grade-school prose I've concocted today.

My writing friends listen to my story and congratulate me for getting over the first hurdle. I have written my first post-accident story, and it's no worse than what I was writing in the eighth grade, when I really started to pick up steam and learn how to make words sing. What I need to do now is write little bits on as many days per week as I can, to stretch the damaged areas just beyond their limits for just a few minutes, to create new pathways as I create new words.

Brain Camp (I).
April 20, 2015

The paperwork was horrendous. The Western Washington University Speech and Hearing Clinic reports to so many entities that I had to fill out seven pages of paperwork to complete the application for services. I should say rather that I looked at how many pages I had to fill out and handed the sheaf over to Maureen. She filled out everything she could, and then she asked me questions about such things as my Social Security number.

Repeating the data over and over made me dizzy and gave me a headache. Just dredging up the information they wanted and saying it out loud to Maureen forced me to take a three-hour nap. We got the paperwork turned in, though. That happened a month ago. Today I have my initial assessment, done by graduate students in the program.

I submit to testing unlike any other I have ever taken. One task requires me to look at a map and find all the icons for restaurants. Another gives me instructions about how to schedule the workday of an office worker who has to complete every task between nine and five. The graduate students also interview me to interpret my attitude toward healing.

One thing I learn is that I cannot do the agenda-building exercise by thinking inside my head. I can't calculate the agenda merely by looking at the paper. I start saying out loud the tasks the office worker faces so I can shuffle them around and make her day as efficient and productive as possible. Somehow, hearing the words makes it feasible to reach my objective. I will remember that talking through tasks out loud may be a good workaround for complex textual work.

When the testing ends, my assessors tell me I am extremely accurate at the tasks. They tell me I also rank at the 30th percentile in speed. I time out on some of the exercises, probably ones that have more test questions than anyone could reasonably be expected to complete. But I have always been a fast test-taker, and I am disappointed to learn how much I have slowed down.

I'm not sure what I will be able to do about Seán 2.0's slowness. When I try to work on strengthening my visual cortex by reading paper books, the nausea and pain and fatigue shut me down 10 to 15 minutes after I start reading. I then need a two-hour nap to recover. Even while I'm not working, I don't have the luxury of spending most of my day sleeping, in an attempt to repair my visual cortex well enough that I can read up to pre-accident standards. If someone wants to pay me to stay home and read from 9am to 9:15am, then nap until noon, have lunch, read from 1pm to 1:15pm, then nap until 3pm, let me know. If that person will also take out the garbage, clean the cat's litter box, and do my laundry, we might have a deal. Otherwise, reality will continue to strike, and it will continue to bite.

I face a conundrum: my assessors have noted on my chart that one of my characteristics that will prevent me from healing at the maximum possible rate is my strong desire to get back to work as quickly as possible. It seems I am already pushing myself too hard. I want to be able to read novels if I am going to be sitting around healing. I can't do that. If I can't sit around reading novels, I may as well be teaching classes. I can't do that, either.

I am three months into my convalescence, and in many ways, I still feel like a complete invalid who has made absolutely no progress in healing. If I look back three months, I see considerable improvement in the health and function of my brain. But if I look back two weeks, I see no real change. The indication to me is that I am healing and repairing my brain at a glacial pace.

I once cracked a bone in my right forearm. I wore a cast for a month. When I saw the doctor at the two-week mark, I was hoping she would have me remove the cast. My arm didn't hurt any more. But she said it was a good idea to leave the cast on for a full month to make sure my bones were healed. I had already spent two weeks learning to write on the white board at school with my left hand, so my functionality at work was not impaired by keeping the cast on.

Right now, I have no functionality at work. I cannot see my brain to know if it is healing. The clock is ticking on my medical leave, and thus on my paycheck. It distresses me to face an unknown time span for this recovery process. I do not believe I would prefer to be permanently disabled, but I truly wish technology were farther along and better at sorting out subtle improvements in brain function. Not knowing where I stand in the healing process is for me the definition of frustration.

A Bright Idea.
April 25, 2015

Maureen thought it would be a good idea to get away from the house for a weekend. She knows I like the unique atmosphere of Point Roberts, Washington, and she surprised me by renting a cabin there for a three-day weekend. All I knew when we left the house was that I should make sure to have my NEXUS card with me. I always carry the card anyway, because you never know when you're going to be 100 yards from the border and in the mood to head for Vancouver.

Point Roberts is a geographical anomaly in the United States. When the border with Canada was set, it became clear that a piece of land jutting south from British Columbia fell below the 49th parallel. The United States offered that spit of land to Canada, but Canada didn't take it. Point Roberts is part of Whatcom County, which also includes Bellingham. School-age children who live on Point Roberts get on the bus in the morning, cross the border into Canada, cross the border into the United States, and go to a school near the border. They reverse the process in the afternoon. Gasoline is expensive on Point Roberts, and it's sold by the liter. Most of the people who buy gas there are Canadians who still find it a bargain.

Maureen and I had visited Point Roberts on day trips before. We have hiked around most of the coast there. Now, we are going to spend two nights in a log cabin at the end of a road, a short hike away from the water. It's a two-story cabin. The sleeping area is upstairs, and it's not walled in. I feel very close to nature. The wood is all light-colored pine, giving the small space a sense of being larger than it is.

The only heat in this cabin is a wood-burning stove. Maureen is far better than I am at making fires and keeping them burning. We have brought food with us, and we cook simple meals in the kitchen. Maureen packed a book, and she is reading short essays to me while I lie on the couch. Being away from our house and staying in such a peaceful environment is providing delicious novelty to my brain. I am not suddenly, miraculously healed, but my surroundings are not overwhelming me, either.

There is a collection of DVDs in the cabin. Saturday after lunch, Maureen tells me to choose a movie to watch. The TV we'll watch it on is an old-school set with a small screen. I choose a horror movie, I don't remember which one, and I wear my sunglasses while mostly avoiding looking at the screen. The story is intriguing, not dependent on gore to be interesting. When the movie is over, we start cooking dinner.

I'm chopping onions when something clicks in my head.

"I just got an idea for a story," I say.

"This isn't the first idea since the accident, is it?"

"No. I had the idea I got in a dream that I wrote last weekend. I got this new idea from watching the movie."

My idea is nothing like the movie plot, but there is a hint of similarity in that the character in my idea has accidentally killed someone, and no one realizes it, including my character. He doesn't know anything is wrong until the person he killed haunts him.

This cabin seems like the perfect place to get the first good idea for a story since my TBI. On Sunday, I write 500 words to start this story. I think they are keepers. When I finish this novel, I will know I have found Seán 2.0's way to creativity.

Teaching for Real, Sort Of.
May 9, 2015

My friend Michael Fraas is a specialist in sports concussions, but he has taught a wide variety of subjects at our university. This year he will be leading his second summer group on a service-learning trip to Guatemala. The students sometimes build housing for residents of a village near Antigua, and in other years they work in the clinic with children who are awaiting treatment for cleft palate.

In 2014 Michael asked me if I could give his students a quick lesson in survival Spanish. I created a little booklet for them that included dialogues they might encounter, as well as lists of vocabulary words related to their coming experience. It was easy for me to teach that lesson a year ago. Today, the lesson will be my first live teaching experience since the accident.

The first time I taught a mock class, I lasted 20 minutes. The second time, I lasted thirty. I expect today's lesson to require about 45 minutes. I'm a bit nervous about overdoing it, since my track record so far doesn't show that I am prepared to teach that long.

The students are spending the weekend together at a retreat center east of Bellingham. Like the cabin where Maureen and I stayed two weeks ago, this place is designed to let in a lot of daylight. I will wear my sunglasses while I teach this lesson.

I warm up the group by asking them their names. I ease into the first dialogue, which has to do with meeting and greeting their homestay families in Guatemala. We move on to vocabulary about construction materials and tools. We talk about food, especially tropical fruits. I have a drawing of the human body, and I tell them the obvious body parts while supplementing detailed anatomy of the mouth that they have been learning in school.

The energy of the group provides me with an unexpected boost to my own stamina. For one thing, in my mock classes I do almost all the talking. Here, there is enough back and forth that I talk perhaps half of the time. I have not taken into account that my job in the classroom typically is to impart a little bit of grammatical wisdom and then step back and let the students practice with each other.

This is a good perspective to gain. I will need to be able to talk to my students for at least 45 of the 80 minutes we are together, but I will almost never need to deliver an 80-minute lecture.

Maureen drove me here, and she will definitely drive me home, because I am beat at the end of this lesson. The students put together lunch after I teach, so I get fed in gratitude for my efforts. The food restores me somewhat, but there is still no way I would be able to drive after this experience.

I can say, at least, that I have faced a live audience of students who are learning the material I am teaching for true academic reasons. Reacquiring my sense of purpose marks another milestone on the journey back to the classroom.

It crosses my mind that I should be shedding tears of relief after discovering that I can teach a full class, even an informal one with no stakes. But all I can do is contemplate dispassionately the step forward. "This is good news," I tell Maureen. As for tears, the quest continues on a path with no visible endpoint.

Crosswords and Lumosity.
May 19, 2015

I fill out crossword puzzles in ink. I don't do that because I know every answer to every clue. I do it because I don't like smearing graphite across the puzzle. Ink will dry, but pencil marks are always vulnerable to smudges. But I let people think I work crossword puzzles in ink because I know all the answers. It's part of my mystique.

Crossword puzzles are considered to be good therapy for aging people, because the puzzles keep the mind active. Sudoku has the same effect, I'm sure, but I'll admit right now that I have never been able to figure out a sudoku puzzle, not even quote-unquote easy ones. Words are my bag, man.

Not so much since the accident, though. My attempts to work crossword puzzles have met with brain pain, sudden-onset fatigue, and irritation when I give up after four clues. The first crossword puzzle I finished after the accident took me two weeks to work. I am used to finishing a relatively challenging puzzle in half an hour or less, perhaps over two sittings. I think now that, while I do have trouble figuring out some answers, my primary problem is that writing what I am thinking is a nearly impossible task.

My lack of neurological progress leads me back to see Dr. Tedd Judd on May 19. I have a baseline with him from February, and I am looking forward to seeing if there is any progress now. I perform the same tasks I performed in February. Among them is a process where I look at words printed in red, green, or blue ink and say either the word or its color, depending on the task. I also move some discs from one wooden pole to another, with the goal of getting the largest disc on the bottom and the smallest on the top.

When we finish the exercises, Dr. Judd informs me that I have improved my scores from the 33rd percentile to the 50th percentile. Then, I bring up the fact that I just turned 55 today. I asked what my percentiles would have been yesterday, when I was still 54.

It turns out that yesterday I was still in the 30s percentile-wise, whereas I entered a new age bracket today and climbed above a whole bunch of my 64-year-old peers. I find small comfort in this alleged improvement.

Dr. Judd does suggest that I might ask my doctor to prescribe Ritalin. He says it wouldn't hurt to see if part of my issue is damage to the areas that help me focus. I am the guy who is willing to try anything that will improve my cognition, so I make a note to request Ritalin from the doctor when I next see him.

In the "see what sticks" department, I also have a tip from the brain clinic at Western to try Lumosity, an online brain-therapy program that uses games and problem-solving to keep the brain strong. I buy a family package for a year, in case Maureen or her mom wants to give it a shot. I start doing my exercises daily. I do arithmetic problems that show up in bubbles that pop when they hit the bottom of the screen. I do tasks where I have to recall the names of customers and what their preferred orders are when I serve meals to them. The exercises are enjoyable and, I believe, useful for the creation of those precious neural pathways that are under reconstruction.

I find encouragement in the fact that, unlike my frustration with crossword puzzles—which I *know* I should be able to complete easily—I have no prior experience with Lumosity. Therefore, I can relate my current scores only to the previous scores on this program. Whether my scores started out being pitiful or not, any improvement is exactly that: improvement.

A crossword puzzle I cannot finish in less than a week is not an improvement on what Seán 1.0 could do. For now, crossword puzzles are one of my demons, a reminder over breakfast, while I fill out a few clues, that I am not whole. Slogging through the mire of healing my brain is not much fun, but Lumosity is a beacon of hope, a program that allows me to see progress in real time.

The "What-Ifs" (II).
June, 2015

I have known about the Brain Injury Alliance of Washington, Bellingham Chapter, for a couple of months. My wife, Maureen, also knew about it, thanks to her work in the nonprofit sector. She had suggested I wait a few months before attending a gathering, so I did. But now it's time for me to start going.

The session takes place in the dank basement of a PeaceHealth building on Chestnut Street. Mary, a nurse nearing retirement, runs the meeting. We, the TBI Survivors, fill both sides of three eight-foot tables. The westering sun blasts through the windows, and no one in this group has the physical capacity to close the decrepit blinds. There are several men here, but I am the steadiest on my feet, and I can't handle the strain of pulling on the cords. Between the sun and the fluorescent overhead lights, my dark glasses are nearly useless, and I bow my head. I have to wonder if the decaying building foreshadows revelations about the lack of attention paid to the needs of TBI Survivors.

Mary calls the meeting to order. She has us introduce ourselves. I learn quickly that I am not the only Survivor who notes the date and time of my accident. For all of us, the moment our brain became something different is the moment our old selves died. Many cannot talk well. Many cannot walk well. Many start a sentence and can't remember how to finish it. One or two can't stop talking.

One of the Survivors interrupts people's bios to compare her experiences to theirs. Mary clearly knows how this woman interacts with people and feels the need to makes frequent, general stern reminders that we need to raise our hands before we speak. Conversations derail easily here.

Some TBI Survivors say they can't sleep. Some can't stay awake. After the introductions, we have a contest to win Independence Day swag. Mary gives us basic multiplication problems to do in our heads. For many, this exercise is the toughest cognitive challenge they can handle and still succeed. I win a flag-themed hard-plastic drinking glass that comes with its own permanent hard-plastic straw. Some others would find more need for this glass, as I learn over time.

After the meeting, I'm sad. And scared of what the future holds. I see why Maureen wanted me to wait until I saw personal progress before I joined forces with these Survivors. Many of them have been in recovery for years.

As I do several times a day, I review the accident in my mind. This time, for some reason, I get stuck on thinking about the "what-ifs." What if I had turned my head the wrong way during the crash, and I suffered injuries that prevented me from talking properly or moving freely? Or what if I cannot regain enough brain function to return to work when my six-month leave ends? As it stands, I'm teaching several mock classes to get myself into shape for teaching a summer course. What if I have to retire after that? What if I am never able to write well again?

As I carefully drive home (I will always be more than reasonably careful when driving now), I decide to throw myself into being supportive of my TBI peers, because I feel gratitude that I am not facing the struggles some of them endure. I also feel guilt that, for reasons I cannot take credit for, I have fared better than they have so far. My mind whirls with possible ways to improve the lives of others: providing respite care for caregivers, giving talks to heighten TBI awareness, simply being a friend to the injured. What else can Seán 2.0 do?

Part 3: Seán 2.0 Is Partially Operational.

Start the Story.
June 3, 2015

Back to the Book Fare Café. The mood is much lighter today than it was in March when I gave up on teaching for Spring quarter. There is no sense of defeat, of inadequacy. I am here to attempt to write.

One of the members of Red Wheelbarrow Writers, Jes Stone, has made my return to writing a project of hers. Who am I to turn down an offer of collegial support for the activity I most love?

Jes is a perky, grounded, talented writer with a PhD in Marketing. She has published several books, including *Doggy on Deck: Life at Sea with a Salty Dog—Absolutely Everything You Need to Know Before Cruising with Fido*. Jes has been the captain of her own boat, sailing up and down the West Coast of the Americas and across the South Pacific. For several years she sailed with Kip McSnip, a captain's canine best friend. Now that she has given up the boating life, she has settled into writing mysteries and the story of some outrageous women who escape a nursing home. Jes is prolific, and she likes the premise of my novel. She wants to help me get my writing back on track.

I have my Microsoft Surface with me. I bought it prior to my accident because I wanted a light tablet I could always carry with me for whenever a writing opportunity arose. I also wanted a tablet that would let me save my work to a flash drive, rather than depending on cloud storage, because some of the places where I like to write have no Wi-Fi.

Jes and I spend a few minutes catching up, and then we get down to work. She asks if I am going to continue incorporating the novel edits I received from my editor, Laurel Leigh, and I say no. Dr. Judd and I discussed whether it would be a good idea for me to try to write fiction. We decided that I could always segregate my new work and look at it later to see if it belonged in the book. When I tried, after some time resting my brain, to do some of the rewrites Laurel had suggested, I found that I could not visualize in my head the story I knew so well and previously could see in great detail, as if it were part of the real world.

With that disappointment firmly in my mind, I decide now that I am going to start a new project. That project is a memoir about my accident and my struggle to return to normal: reading, writing, crying.

Jes is working on her fiction while I stare at the screen of my Surface. I have no idea what title I will want, but often I have no clue about titles until I am well into a project. Where do I start? At the beginning, I reply to myself. I begin typing.

Jes's strawberry-blond hair is all I see of her behind her screen, but when she hears the clicking of my keyboard, she looks up and smiles. I am guessing that she feels good that she has achieved her goal of getting me to put some words on paper. If what I write works out, I will eventually have a manuscript I can try to sell to a publisher, a book that will in my best dreams be a resource for TBI Survivors, their caregivers, and the medical community.

I write for as long as I can. What am I accomplishing? I am describing what I was doing before I got in my car to drive from Fairhaven to downtown Bellingham. At the same time, I am reliving the accident, a scary thing to do in public. I go over and over the scene when I am at home, but I try not to think about it when I am out. Remembering makes me jittery. I don't want strangers to worry about my well-being if they see me getting twitchy.

I do have Jes here to help me calm down if the memory impacts me too much. I am trusting that I will know when to stop working so I don't become too foggy or fatigued to drive home. There is always the option of having Jes drive me home and coming back later for my car. With this backup plan in mind, I urge myself onward in the telling of my tale.

I Always Wanted to Be a Mascot.
June 19, 2015

The year was 1989. Domino's Pizza had a TV campaign involving a fictional character called the Noid. This character destroyed your pizza if you had it delivered by anyone other than Domino's Pizza. The Noid was a bright-red creature with big rabbit-like ears that stood straight up. I worked for Domino's Pizza in 1989, and when there was a 24-hour sports event on the Indiana University campus, our store was given a Noid costume for a personal appearance at the gym. The only person willing to wear the Noid getup and appear was yours truly.

I enjoyed the experience. The only problem was that my wife brought my small children to see me in the costume. I approached my sons, forgetting that they would not recognize me. I scared the bejeebers out of one of them when I went to give him a hug. I won't say which one, out of respect for him as an adult.

In early June of 2015, Maureen noticed on Craigslist that the Bellingham Bells summer-league baseball team was looking for a mascot. She joked that, since I couldn't do any real job that involved thinking, I could do a job that only involved walking around and giving high-fives to children. She might have been kidding, but I took the opportunity seriously. I applied for the position. And by golly, I got the job.

It really does feel good to do something out of the ordinary. No cognition involved, frankly. All I do is follow the schedule, show up to run the bases with the kids after the fifth inning, supervise a few between-inning games, and glad-hand anyone who wants to interact with a six-foot-tall hamster in a baseball uniform. Dinger is the mascot's name, so when people start yelling "Dinger," I have to remember they are talking to me.

The staff I deal with are nice people, running a strong baseball organization. Based on a short chat with the other guy who plays Dinger, I have a good idea of what

I'm supposed to do today. I go to the equipment room, which is a large closet at the back of the beer stand. In here are reminders of most promotions that the Bells have done over the years, as well as the paraphernalia for the between-inning games. The Dinger suit hangs on the wall. I slide on the pants, then I jam my feet into the enormous hamster shoes. I wiggle into the shirt, which has an umbrella-like frame to give Dinger a big belly. I put on the head, which has eyeholes that are the only source of ventilation. Finally, the gloves. I am now Dinger.

The sky is overcast, so it's not particularly warm. Even so, I heat up quickly. I have brought a water bottle, which I leave in the equipment room. Over the first three innings I guzzle my water. I go in search of a refill, and I contemplate buying a beer and pouring it into my water bottle.

There are two problems with that idea: the first is that for a long time I was allergic to hops, which made drinking beer a life-threatening activity. I recently learned that my allergy is in remission because I went without drinking beer for so long. Since my allergy could come back, the only time I drink beer is on St. Patrick's Day, and then I make sure there are people around to get me to the ER if I have an allergy attack.

The second problem is that the staff might be concerned if they have a mascot who cannot work through a full baseball game without drinking alcohol. And maybe there's a third problem, which is that I can't drink alcohol anyway, because of drug interactions with my brain meds.

We reach the fifth inning, and the clouds are getting lower, heavier, and darker. There is a sense of impending baseball doom. The Walla Walla Sweets, named for the onions grown in the area, bat in the top of the fifth. Then come some scattered raindrops, followed by more raindrops, followed by a solid downpour. The umpire halts the game. The fans in the grandstand don't get wet, but the fans who bought cheaper tickets to sit on the left-field hillside have to figure out where to go to stay dry.

Dinger faces a conundrum. What does a mascot do when there is no game to cheer on? Well, I look around and see that all the people in the grandstand are glued to their phones. The PA announcer has turned on some music, but no one is reacting to it. I decide to try a social experiment.

I read an article a while ago that dealt with a person who was sitting in a crowd of people on a grassy field. Music was playing, and this person stood up and started dancing. Sociologically, that person was an outlier. But then, a second person stood up to dance. This second person was the key to starting a social shift. With two people dancing, the concept of dancing while nearly everyone else was sitting became less threatening. More people on that grassy field stood up and danced, and pretty soon, there were more people dancing than sitting.

I start dancing in the grandstand. I'm down at the bottom where everyone can see me. In a sense, I'm dancing as if no one is watching, because truly, almost no one is watching, and also because they aren't seeing Seán. They are seeing Dinger dance. In the same way that people who put on a Halloween costume might act in unusual ways, Dinger can do a lot of things I would not do at a baseball stadium.

I dance through nearly a whole song before my Number Two shows up. It's a boy, maybe 10 years old, and he comes down and joins me in dancing to the tunes. We face the grandstand and dance for the people up higher. Then comes person number three, another tween. Finally, an adult joins us, a woman who knows how to dance. She dances with me, and she dances with the boys.

And then something truly magical occurs. One of the Walla Walla Sweets steps out of his dugout and starts busting a move. Now, the people in the grandstand start cheering. He dances through most of a song, then he goes back to the dugout. The PA announcer picks up on what is happening, and the next thing you know, a Bells player steps out to the next tune the announcer spins.

First a Sweet, then a Bell. Back and forth they go, showing some serious dance moves. The announcer, now acting a full-blown DJ, keeps the momentum going. It seems that all these baseball players can use their athletic skills on the dance floor. By the time the umpires give up and call the game off, nearly every player on both teams has stepped out to show the fans a good time.

I go and high-five all the Bells players after the game, and one asks me why I didn't go over to the dugout and take my turn with the players. In my mind, I think the moment was so special for the fans, seeing the players from a different perspective, that I didn't want to step on the magic. What I say is, "I didn't want to get the costume too wet."

Then comes my second outing as Dinger. I read that the day will be sunny and hot, in the mid-80s. I go to REI and buy a shirt that allegedly has cooling properties. I also buy a CamelBak device I can wear on my back that holds a liter of water and has a straw that comes all the way around, with a big mouthpiece so I don't have to reach under my head to reinsert the straw.

It turns out that today, the Western Washington University mascot will be here as well. The staff gave this guy a list of all the activities we are supposed to do. They never gave me that list. Everything goes well until we run the bases with the kids. The Viking mascot is probably 21 years old, and I'm 55, with a neck injury. My strategy in the first game, out of compassion for the kids even more than because of my physical health, was to run with the slower kids. I figured that the little ones and the slow-moving ones would get a bigger thrill from having Dinger in their midst than the fast-moving tweens would.

But the Viking takes off like a track star, and I don't want to look like a loser, so I make a push to catch up to him. Running kills my neck. Even worse, about 20 feet from the left-field fence where we exit the field, the heat overwhelms me. My heart starts racing, and as soon as I get off the field and through the fence, all I can do is stand there and hope I don't either vomit in my suit, as the vomit would come out the eyes, or flat-out keel over, which would both traumatize the tykes and prompt my second EMT response of the year. I stagger away from the fence, six-year-old boys swarming me, giving me hugs and requesting high-fives. I hold my paws up and let the kids slap them while I try to catch my breath and get the black spots to dissipate. There is one kid, there is *always* one kid, who has to be a jerk and try to bully Dinger. He chooses this moment to try out his technique on an innocent victim. It crosses my mind to take off the head and tell him that if he hits me again, I will call the police and have him charged with assault. But I stay in character and wave a finger at him to say no.

It turns out that, on the directions that the Viking mascot got and I didn't, after the seventh inning, we were supposed to dance on the Bells' dugout. I was pouring water on my head when the eighth inning started, and one of the staffers came over to chide me, no, let's be honest, berate me, for not being on top of the dugout. In the first game, I was getting my direction inning by inning. We never made it to the seventh inning, so I was never told to dance on top of the dugout.

When I finally could take off Dinger, I realized I would probably drop dead the next time the temperature was higher than 70 at game time. I wrote an email to the guy in charge of me, apologizing for not being able to continue as mascot. And that is the end of my attempts to diversify my skills in case I can't return to the classroom.

Powers of Observation.
July 15, 2015

Time is really winding down now to the day when I start teaching. Summer language courses at Western Washington University run from mid-June to mid-August. If students decide to take the entire 200-level series during the summer, they go to school for three hours a day, five days a week, for 40 days. Right now, we are in the second course, Spanish 202. I will teach the third course, beginning August 3. I am observing the group today, because most of these students will take Spanish 203 as well.

I come early and take a seat in the back of the classroom. The instructor, Amy, shows up and nods in my direction. We have decided that it's probably good for me to make a low-key appearance and not be introduced to the students.

I really would like to sit through the entire class as an affirmation that I can stick out a three-hour classroom experience. It would be very helpful to me psychologically to know I'm not going to halt the class after an hour or two once I take over in August.

Amy is an exceptional teacher, sure of her approach and extremely proficient in Spanish. She interacts with the students in such a way that they pick up the material with greater ease than they would with a lot of other instructors. I follow along with her instruction method, intuiting where she is going with the grammar explanation that she is weaving into examples of the topic. It all sounds clear to me. I think I would be able to teach this particular lesson well.

As the end of the first hour approaches, fatigue sets in. I have started describing the sudden-onset fatigue as walking into a glass wall. I don't know where the glass walls are, and I don't know when I'm going to bump into them. They get in my way every single day, and on a good day the only remedy I need to apply is a nap. On a bad day, I take Aleve® to calm a headache before a nap will do me any good.

Amy gives the students a break at 10 o'clock. I debate with myself: should I try to stick around for all three hours, or should I just go home while I can still drive? It feels important to tough out the entire class, since I'll have to do the same soon as their professor, but I do have to get home safely.

As the break comes to an end, I realize that my fogginess is increasing. Sitting through another hour of class will make me sick. I give up, give Amy a wave, and walk to my car. I drive home and, as I so often do, I crawl right into bed.

What am I going to do when I start teaching on August 3rd? Where are my tears of frustration?

Back in the Saddle.
August 3, 2015

Paqui, my department chair, showed a lot of faith in me when she slotted me to teach the third part of the Spanish second-year series this summer. With three mock classes under my belt, ranging from 20 to 45 minutes before my brain gave out, I suddenly have to teach three hours per day for thirteen days. I need to have faith that I can remember the grammar and answer questions quickly and efficiently, and that I won't pass out halfway through a lesson.

The first task today is to get myself out of bed in time to teach at 9. I have not forced myself out of bed at any particular hour, except to get to early medical appointments, since the accident. I need to prepare my brain to be alert, not just awake, at nine. My past efforts to get up this early have delivered mixed results. I have driven in a brain fog to medical appointments, and I have met people to take walks at this hour, but there has been no need for me to think at my best level this early in the day.

I set my alarm for seven, because I move so much more slowly in the morning than I used to. Maureen helps me out by cooking breakfast for me. Sophie contributes by licking my face with her rough tongue until I wake completely. I get my shower. I put on the lightweight clothes I picked out last night, based on the weather forecast. We're in the midst of a string of sunny days. The sunshine in the classroom will add stress to my brain. I can't let that specter control my approach to the class.

I'm going into this course hyper-prepared for the first week. I made absolutely sure that every little thing I want to say is on paper. Spanish 203 is essentially a mop-up course that combines all the grammar taught in 201 and 202 and teaches students how to synthesize everything they have learned, so they can write and speak like educated professionals. Six months ago, I wasn't even speaking *English* like an educated professional. Here I am, though, back in the saddle, as Steven Tyler said in a somewhat different context. I have a manageable number of students, about half that of a class during the school year.

I drive to a parking lot near campus and walk to Miller Hall. I don't have a parking sticker for campus, and I won't risk a neck sprain by taking the bus from the Park and Ride lot. In my office, I prep my materials for the first class, take a deep breath, and walk down to the classroom.

I introduce myself and have the students tell me a bit about themselves. I do this with every new class, usually to make sure everyone knows how to say, "My name is." It always surprises me how many students say that phrase incorrectly, even this far up the ladder in Spanish courses. This group nails it. Some of the students in this class took 202 in the Spring quarter, and some of the students who took 202 in Amy's summer session did not continue into this 203 class. I do remember the skills I saw in the students who are continuing from the 202 class that just ended. I'm confident that this group will be able to succeed at 203 even if I don't deliver my best work.

Will I even do acceptable work? I make myself remember the perspective my friends offered at the birthday gathering Maureen put together for me in May. She reserved a shelter at Lake Padden, and a heartening number of my friends came out to share in a potluck and show their support for me. At that gathering I mentioned that I would be teaching in August. I brought up my concern that I would not be as good a teacher now as I was prior to my accident. One of my friends mentioned that she knew my work, and that I, at even 80% of my previous abilities, would provide better teaching than what most of my students would receive with someone else.

I appreciated that sentiment. I still do, as I stand before these students, trying to affirm to myself that it's as acceptable now to flub a thing or two as it was prior to my accident. But am I capable of knowing in my heart that I am teaching at 80% of my former skill level and still feel comfortable standing in front of a crowd of people who have paid a lot of money to learn from me?

Maureen and I have talked about this topic several times. She thinks I can teach without letting on that I have been injured. I go back and forth between thinking she's right and thinking I should fend off any doubts my students have about my abilities by coming clean. Now is when I have to decide what to do.

The deciding factor is my sunglasses. The light in the room is dazzling. I am in full hide-from-the-sun mode. I picture a scenario where my students go home and tell their friends that their new Spanish prof is buying into some 1960s retro hip cool shtick that is not at all cool. I can't push that image out of my head, so I do triage.

"I need to tell you all something before we get started. This is my first class back after six months off because I was in a car accident. I had a brain injury, and that's why I'm wearing these sunglasses. The part of my brain that knows Spanish grammar and how to teach it is intact. Otherwise, I would not put you through a course where you were getting less than a complete education."

Instantly the group coheres into a support team for me. I tell them I will do my best to give them three hours of class each day, and they tell me not to overdo it.

The kindness in their eyes gives me courage. It looks like every little thing is gonna be all right. This first step back into the classroom is going to be something I did not expect, a healing experience.

50th State.
September 16, 2015

The "life goes on" aspect of my before-and-after life has involved the completion of activities we planned prior to my accident. In many cases, I slog through those events, which pose an extreme challenge to my cognition. One of my long-term projects is so epic, yet easy at the same time, that it makes up for all the accomplishments that are so tough to complete. Today marks the day that I set foot in my 50th state, Alaska.

Yes, I know Hawaii is the 50th state. But Hawaii is *my* 49th state, and Alaska completes the set for me. When we were in our teens, my best friend, Tom Gruber, and I talked about planning a bicycle trip that would take us to 48 states. That discussion morphed into the goal of visiting all 50 states. Montana was my 48th state, in 2006. I spent a lot of time dreaming about moving to Alaska, and I even applied for a teaching job in Fairbanks, but I didn't get serious about traveling to the outlying states until I met Maureen.

Here we are in Anchorage, 40 years after I set the goal of coming here. A Facebook friend, Karen, drives us north from here to a glacier. The glacier we visit is receding rapidly. Viewing its retreat is one of the few somber moments of the trip.

Karen gives us a tip for the next adventure, so Maureen and I drive south on our own to the Alyeska Resort. We park and take their tram up to the restaurant and ski area.

I learn a lot of things on this trip. I see lynx, bear, and porcupine. We get life-saving advice: If a moose crosses the road in front of your car, and you can't stop in time, duck when you hit it. You will knock its spindly legs out from under it, and its body will come crashing through your windshield. If you're out of the way, the moose will fly over your head, and you may survive the crash.

An amusing highlight of the Alyeska trip comes when

Maureen and I are at the ski area at the top end of the tram route. We walk up a gravel road toward the ski area itself, which is closed for the summer. To the right, we see small, narrow glaciers amid the taller mountains. We are nearly to the ski area when my phone rings.

I would normally not take a phone call while I'm climbing a mountain in Alaska, but the caller is Cami Ostman, the second person I called when I was looking for a ride away from my accident scene. I pick up the call.

"Hi, Cami," I say as nonchalantly as I can.

"Hi, Seán. Whatcha doin'?"

"I'm hiking up a mountain in Alaska. What are you doing?" I give Maureen a big grin.

"Oh, come on. What are you really doing?"

"Just what I said. Maureen and I decided to go to Alaska. I'll have her take a picture of me for proof after we get off the phone. What's up?"

We chat a moment about something related to writing and to Red Wheelbarrow Writers. She tells me to get back to my hike, and we hang up. I have Maureen take the photo. I text it to Cami, so she knows I'm not messing with her the way I so often do.

Another good thing that came out of this trip is that I forgot my dark glasses, and at Walgreens in Anchorage we find the perfect pair of wraparound dark glasses, far better for shutting out light than the glasses I have been using since February.

This trip is the perfect end to the first summer for Seán 2.0.

Fall Quarter.
September 23, 2015

The day is here. I know I thought at some points in March and April that this day would not arrive. I go to my office in Miller Hall, then I go upstairs to the main office of the department. One of the first people I bump into is Shannon, who took over one of my German classes in the winter. He is pleased to see me back on campus, as are the support staff in the office. Paqui is on the phone, and I give her a little wave.

It's 8:25, and I recall that I teach Spanish 101 at nine. Later in the day I will teach two sections of 104, accelerated first-year Spanish. All I need to do at this moment is print a copy of the syllabi for my classes, print out the lesson plan I have typed up, and wait for the moment when I make an entrance into the classroom. In the class I took about teaching college Spanish when I started graduate school, my professor, Diana Frantzen, told us all to show up exactly on time for the first class. Showing up early leaves one being stared at by the students, while showing up late is simply bad form.

In my tiny office, I open the syllabus document for Spanish 101. I happen to glance at the heading on the first page, and I get my first shock of the new school year. I don't teach Spanish 101 at 9 o'clock. I teach 101 at 1 o'clock. So what the heck do I teach at nine? I open the syllabus for a Spanish 104, and I teach that class at 10 o'clock. I'm really confused now. I open the third syllabus, and my stomach drops. I teach Spanish 104 at 8:30. It's 8:29. I heave a sigh of dismay and send the two syllabi and the lesson plan for Spanish 104 to the printer upstairs in the main office.

I run to the main office and grab my printouts. I run downstairs to the hallway where I teach, then I walk casually the rest of the way to the classroom. I walk past the rows of tables to my desk, log in to the computer, and say, "¡Buenos días!" I hear a few mumbled replies. I say that they need to wake up and repeat my greeting. I get a more robust response this time.

I apologize for showing up three minutes late. I tell them I was having a conversation with my department chair. I tell them we were talking about strategies for Fall quarter because I was returning from a medical leave for a brain injury. I fudge on the reason I was late. I don't think it will inspire a lot of confidence in these new students to know I forgot when class starts, and which course I'm teaching.

I do make sure I explain clearly that I am a teacher with "features." One is my sunglasses. Sometimes I hate so much that I depend on them day and night. Lately, there has been social commentary about guys who think they are too cool to walk around without sunglasses. While I realize that my wraparound sunglasses could not possibly be construed as an attempt at coolness, it would be even worse if someone saw me wearing them in the grocery store at night and thought *I* thought the glasses were cool. Boy, do I feel like a dork sometimes.

But just like my summer students, my new groups rally around me. All I can say about the student body at Western Washington University is that those young adults do an amazing job of being kind to the vulnerable.

I set aside my insecurities and get down to the business of teaching. All three 80-minute classes go well. I survive them without dizzy spells. I've gained a lot of stamina since I sat in Amy's summer class for a single hour. Even though I have to be on campus longer than in my summer course, interacting with people and battling the fluorescent lights, my brain holds up.

I typically learn the names of my students on the first day, and I recite them back before I dismiss class. Today, none of the names stick. I spent considerable time in the past few days looking at the photo roster of my classes, so I could get a head start on learning at least a few names. It didn't help. There's another skill lost, at least for now.

I check in with Paqui before I go home. I tell her about the snafu with the time. She points out that, prior to this year, I taught five days a week, and classes started on the hour. Now that I am the guinea pig for experimenting with longer, three-day classes, it's not surprising that I would forget that class starts on the half hour.

Her reasoning brings me some solace, but I wonder if I would have made such a rookie mistake if I weren't fighting my way back from my TBI.

Maureen and I debrief the day, and she agrees with Paqui's assessment of my error. I am so relieved that the first day is over that I wish I could cry. But there is still no catharsis for me.

Cindy.
October 9, 2015

It's Friday afternoon, and I have finished teaching my three classes for the day. I'm organizing my thoughts for Monday-morning classes when my phone rings. It's my sister Cindy, she of the calls about family triumphs and crises.

Which type of call will this one be? There is just one way to know.

I can tell from her voice that this call will not be pleasant. She starts out by asking how I'm doing, and I ask the same of her.

"Well, I was just diagnosed with breast cancer."

The news is a bare fist that slugs me in the gut. I react as I would if I were really struck. Anger floods through me.

"No, you do not have cancer!" I scream. "That cannot happen. No."

I wonder why my brain chose to unleash anger rather than letting me feel sadness. What a mixed-up brain. I suppose I should be glad I am emoting at all. This is my baby sister, the youngest of eight. The situation is surreal.

Cindy tells me she noticed a lump and went to have it checked. A biopsy showed cancer, and a scan showed that the first lymph node was enlarged. She has had genetic testing, and she is negative for the BRCA1 and BRCA2 genes. She tells me that is good news for me as well as for her, because BRCA1 and BRCA2 are also related to prostate cancer.

Her tumor turns out to be what is called a triple negative. That means it has no receptors for the three leading chemotherapy drugs. The tumor therefore may be resistant to treatment. If it does not respond, she will have a mastectomy, and possibly two. If she is going to go through chemotherapy for one breast, she believes there's no point in undergoing that hell again in a few years and perhaps not catching the second tumor as early as the first.

As we head toward the end of this conversation, I hear Cindy sniffle. I want to reach through the airwaves and hug her. I want to get on a flight to Indiana and take her to her medical appointments. She has a good support system at home, so she doesn't need me there as much as I need to be there for my own comfort.

Of course, while she is sniffling and probably dabbing her eyes, I am not crying. Since the accident, my Aunt Jenny hasdeveloped congestive heart failure, my Aunt Louise is sick but recovering, I have a cousin who is fighting a devastating bout with cancer, and now my sister has it. My inability to respond emotionally in a cathartic way to all this trauma is really getting old.

Fall Down.
October 21, 2015

I've reached the halfway point of the quarter. I have a pattern now. I teach from 8:30 to 2:20, with one 80-minute break, on Mondays, Wednesdays, and Fridays. I gave in and bought a parking pass for nearly $400, so I drive home at 2:30 and nap until 5 on teaching days.

I have dinner with Maureen, and I listen to the TV while she watches a show for half an hour. Then, at 7pm, I go to bed for the night.

The days after I teach, Tuesdays, Thursdays, and Saturdays, I sleep in until 9am. After breakfast, I sit and listen to some music. After lunch, I take another nap. When I wake up, I prep my classes for the following day. I go to bed at 7pm, so I am rested for teaching.

Sundays are my day to enjoy being alive. Maureen and I go for a walk, and sometimes she drives us to a park on the Bay, where we enjoy the autumn breezes that will soon turn bitter.

I have given two exams in each course, to a total of 90 students. I can't grade the exams without pain and nausea, so I have started dishing out $10 per hour of work to advanced students. I check their work and decide how many points to deduct for each error they find. Paqui and I talk about the situation. She tells me that she senses my struggle and already called Human Resources to see if I had any FMLA time left. At this point I would gladly take it. But I had to use some of the leave time when I wasn't teaching, because I couldn't pause the leave and restart it later for the same incident. I've used up my medical leave.

She asked also if I could receive funds to pay a grader. HR says that grading exams is part of my job description, and thus we can't pay someone to do what I am being paid to do. My eventual cost for having my exams vetted before I grade them works out to $300. But I can't shoulder the task all on my own.

Therefore, I do what I have always done in tough situations. I persist.

Saturday Night at the Movies.
November 5, 2015

My seemingly endless push against my visual problems takes another step forward tonight. We used to host movie nights and have friends over. The first time it happened, we had been discussing *The Princess Bride* with a friend. I own the DVD, so Maureen suggested we put together a potluck and have people over to watch the movie. Movie Night became a fairly regular happening, sometimes with themed food.

I can't handle movies visually, and while it would be fine if Maureen had people over to watch a movie while I listen to it, we just haven't arranged a gathering. I've watched enough episodes of *The Munsters* without pain now that I think I can handle a black-and-white movie. I think first of Hitchcock, because I have a number of his older films on DVD. But then I get a better idea: *Young Frankenstein* is not in color. We send out the call for guests, and now we're going to watch the movie.

It feels good to have eight people in our living room, enjoying a movie the way we used to do it. I watch the entire movie with my sunglasses on, but my stamina is good, and I don't get a headache from the brightness of the screen.

I do notice that I don't laugh much at the movie. I have not laughed much in general since my TBI. I'm sure laughter and tears are linked in my emotional wiring. Am I going to be an emotional zombie for the rest of my days? The idea disturbs me to the point that I can't concentrate on the last third of *Young Frankenstein*.

I have to test myself. After everyone goes home, I decide to check my ability to laugh by watching what I find to be the funniest moment I can think of in a movie. This scene used to make me laugh when I even thought about it.

I pull out my DVD of *Rat Race* and find the segment of the movie I want to watch. I sit down and press play.

The scene plays, and I chuckle.

"That was funny," I say to Maureen. But just like my rational reaction to sadness, I am not showing the capability to respond the way I used to to funny moments on video.

When I can watch color movies, I will have people over to watch *Rat Race*. Maybe their laughter will be infectious. Maybe then I'll have them over for a sad movie, and their tears will lead me to the end of my quest for tears of my own.

Sophie Speaks.
November 20, 2015

Maureen and I agonized in February over a decision not to treat Sophie's second tumor. The lump has grown, though not much so far. What if we are not doing what Sophie would want by standing by and ignoring it? We made an appointment to speak with Joanna Schmidt, an animal communicator who has talked with us on Sophie's behalf before.

Joanna calls at 6pm on the dot. Maureen, Sophie, and I have settled in on the couch, fleece blankets covering us. Sophie sits between us, her special beige blanket covering her up to her neck. She is pensive, not interacting with us, as if her mind were somewhere else.

We have a list of questions for Joanna to ask Sophie.

"Is the tumor causing her any pain?" Maureen asks.

"She is barely aware that there is a tiny bit of weight on her chest. It doesn't hurt at all, and she almost never thinks about it," Joanna replies.

It's my turn. "Does she wish we had intervened so she could be here longer?"

"No. She has had a good life with you two, and going through surgery and chemotherapy would have damaged the dynamic she loves so much."

I sigh with relief. "Do we need to do anything now to make her comfortable?"

"Sophie says she wants things to continue as they are. She is more concerned about how you will handle the loss than she is about going. She knows she can stay aware of you when she's gone, and she will be off on her next adventure. You have no reason to worry about her."

"How will we know when it's time to help her move on?" Maureen asks this one, because she has a painful remembrance of hanging onto her previous cat, Mimosa, somewhat too long.

"Sophie will let you know in no uncertain terms

when she's ready to go. She won't let you face an ambiguous situation. She knows you will know how to help her when it's time. And then she'll be stardust, headed off to another place where she will be as much of a queen as she has been here."

I smile at Maureen as I ponder this image. Maureen smiles back, her eyes watering, unlike mine.

"One more thing," Joanna says. "Sophie will make sure you have a new baby Sphynx within a month of her departure. She thinks you need a baby to love when she goes away."

When we end the call, Maureen looks at Sophie. "I don't know how you'll keep your promise, little girl," she says. "Kittens are hard to come by. Don't worry if you can't manage it."

Sophie stretches, toes spread, and then she climbs onto my chest and tucks her head under my chin.

The Clocks Are Ticking.
January 19, 2016

Resilience. Determination. My efforts to recover from my TBI have been described as involving these two qualities. I don't know that I have applied every bit of effort possible to recovering some of the skills I had prior to the accident. My teaching/resting routine leaves Sunday as the only day that I can possibly spend time repairing my brain function. But after a week of teaching, I don't feel like applying a cognitive load to my brain on Sundays, either.

However, this is Martin Luther King Jr. weekend. I rested Friday night, and after I ate breakfast on Saturday, I implemented a plan to read a novel over my four days off.

I need a short book. I should probably reread a plot I know, to keep me from having to think hard about the story line. I settle on one of Agatha Christie's shorter mysteries, *The Clocks*.

I read 20 pages at a sitting. I drink coffee while I read. When I hit the 20-page allotment, I put down the book and either take a nap or go for a walk, whichever my body demands. I read 80 pages on Saturday, and I split the rest of the book between Sunday, Monday, and Tuesday.

My copy of this mystery is an old, very cheap paperback edition. The pulp pages have gone from yellow to tan. It's possible that the sepia color of the paper has made it easier for me to read the book. There's no question that my knowledge of the plot allows me to read without having to guess what is going to happen next, and I have less trouble remembering what happened 20 pages before.

I read the last page. I close the book. I take a deep breath and drop the paperback beside me on the bed. I have read the whole book, lying down to keep my neck supported. I read it all with my sunglasses on so glare would not undermine my efforts. I seem to have found a formula for pushing through a book.

I assume I have reached an exciting tipping point in my battle to return to normal from my TBI. I own many books I have not been able to read. I bought a bunch from fellow writers after the accident, as well as new novels in multiple series by my favorite novelists. They await me on my bookshelves. However, Presidents Day is several weeks away. I will have to teach for a while before I can sit down to read another short mystery.

In the meantime, I keep wondering about the greatest mystery of all: why do I have so much trouble with reading in the first place? Why is it so slow, so laborious, so demanding? Two steps forward, one step back.

Smashiversary.
January 29, 2016

I have tried to maintain a positive attitude about my recovery. My brain will do better if I allow it to think cheery thoughts and believe that it is doing an amazing job of repairing itself. I have a sense of humor that sometimes turns depressing situations into tales that amuse people. When I tell a story about my recovery in such a way that I make people laugh, they often clap their hand over their mouth and apologize for laughing. I reply that I was trying to look at the amusing side of this train wreck.

Thus it is with what I call my Smashiversary. It is the one-year anniversary of my accident. Three weeks ago, I decided I wanted to acknowledge this anniversary. I remember many dates, both good and sorrowful, and I knew I would be mindful today of how my life changed one year ago. I'm gathering my friends for my Smashiversary, because this would be a very lonely day otherwise.

I found a Mexican restaurant on the north end of Bellingham that could host 40 people at a reasonable cost for dinner. The responses to my invitation have rolled in. I'm thrilled that 40 people are willing to spend their Friday evening with me.

The day starts with my teaching two classes. I mention to both groups that today will be a hard day for me, and they should forgive me if I get emotional. But what am I thinking? That was Seán 1.0 talking. I am painfully aware that I can't express cathartic emotion, and most especially I can't cry. There is never any concern that I will make a fool of myself in the classroom by weeping in front of my students.

I grab my phone after my classes and call my eldest son, John. Today is his birthday, and I didn't call him last year because of the accident. I catch him at work and give him a brief greeting.

Jes Stone wants to do some writing today; we decide to meet at Mi México at 2:30 and knock out a few pages before the Smashiversary party begins at 5:30. I hoped fervently not to drive through the scene of my accident today, but I find myself on the Boulevard shortly after two, driving in drizzle that would make it hard for someone behind me to stop if a pedestrian steps into the crosswalk. I do my best to keep the "what-ifs" at bay.

I make it through the danger area without any issues, and I navigate the roundabout as well. My stress level drops when I leave that area. I meander through Bellingham without feeling nervous about other drivers. I stop on my way at a Mexican grocery and buy a piñata of a car. I get to destroy this effigy of the vehicle that smashed into me. Then, on to the restaurant, where I settle in to work on some short story I hope will be worth reading.

I'm not particularly fast at writing these days, but even if I scrape out just one or two pages, sitting one-on-one with someone like Jes makes me feel that I am a member of my tribe, even if I am sidelined by injury. It's one reason why Major League Baseball players who are on the disabled list sit in the dugout with the team during games.

Five o'clock approaches. The most prolific novelist I know, Jennifer Mueller, shows up for the Smashiversary, as does Maureen. Jennifer and Maureen chat while I shut down my Surface, and we migrate to the room where we will have the party.

Friends from all my worlds congregate here. Black Drop people show up, university people show up, but the primary constituency is writers. Above all, as I sit in one corner of the large room, I see before me a broad range of lovely human beings, people I want to interact with because of who they are. I realize that I genuinely don't care what they own or who they know. And I would like to think my choice of friends speaks well of me, and also of them.

I of course stand to address the crowd, as the guest of honor and the "most likely to stand up and speak at a party." Then, I display the piñata, and everyone laughs. I do find some catharsis in pounding the crap out of this papier-mâché representation of my nemesis.

But then, to my surprise, my normally reserved wife, Maureen, says she has something to say. I give her the floor. And wow, she makes an absolutely beautiful, touching speech about me and to me:

> *The earliest writer in history whose name is known was Princess Enheduanna of Akkad in Sumeria. She tells the story of a goddess who descends to the underworld as a path to claiming her blessings. In the journey she is stripped of all her resources and killed. Unlike the male archetypal stories of the lone warrior conquering his enemy, this goddess is freed through the assistance of friends. The friends come to the underworld and show great compassion and empathy for its queen, who is giving birth. The queen, who has never experienced such support, agrees in her gratitude to free the goddess. Then, like all great archetypal "dark night of the soul" stories, the goddess is restored, claims her gifts of knowledge and power, and gets to exact revenge on her enemies.*
>
> *I tell you this story because we have all been its players 4,300 years later. Seán, I have watched you suffer, work hard at recovery, and experience the ups and downs of healing. I have watched you reach out to your community who together has joined you in the walk out of the underworld. We were not lost in the dark night, because all of*

*you helped to light the way. I hope you
know how important you are to me and
Seán and how thankful I am.*

*Seán, I am proud of you and your re-
covery. I know with certainty that recovery will continue, and I am grateful
for your tribe.*

More than one eye has to be dabbed before she finishes talking. My eyes stay dry, to my ongoing frustration. Because if ever I could do someone the honor of
weeping at their words, I would conjure up tears in response to Maureen's speech.

She finishes talking, and she pulls from a small bag a
plaque. Glued onto the plaque is a metal print of the
photo she so hates to watch me show to strangers at restaurants and coffee shops. On the plaque is engraved the
date of the Smashiversary, as well as an encouraging
statement about me: "Stronger Than Steel."

My response to this overwhelming gift is to stare at it
and gasp for air. My chest has tightened, not from a heart
attack but from emotion. My body has begun to cry, even
if my eyes have not. It's the first deep sensation of emotion I have felt in a year. Maureen has touched me pro-
foundly with this thoughtful gesture, as she has so often
since the accident. The crowd gazes at us, savoring the
magic of the moment.

I go home feeling loved, knowing there are people
who are glad I'm still around a year after the accident.
Whatever glitches still occur in my daily life, my people
understand, love me, and roll with the punches.

Rashani.
February 2, 2016

One of the most valuable contributions to my life that Maureen brought along with her is that she introduced me to a wise soul named Rashani Réa. Rashani lives in a 16-acre sanctuary on the Big Island of Hawaii. People come to stay in one of the cottages on her land to clear their minds and learn perspective from her.

Rashani comes to Bellingham from time to time to do workshops. I have participated in one two-day weekend retreat with Maureen. This past Saturday I started my second Rashani retreat, but I woke up Sunday morning with a terrible headache from all the thinking I did Saturday. Rashani's workshops are both peaceful and thought-intense. My brain could not handle the cognitive load.

I could not attend the Sunday session. Normally, Saturday lays the groundwork for Sunday breakthroughs, for the group as a whole and for each individual attendee. I am frustrated at my fragility, at my inability to hold together my system long enough to derive full benefit from this opportunity. It's especially demoralizing because I was eager to hear Rashani's insights into my quest for tears. I rage against myself for missing out.

But Maureen, ever considerate of my needs, arranged for me to be able to meet Rashani for an hour today, the Tuesday after the weekend retreat. I arrive at the house where Rashani is staying. I find her, a short, slender woman with long, graying black hair, in the living room. Her skin is weathered by sun and wind, and her dark-brown eyes pierce me with their gaze.

Rashani and I sit on throw pillows in the middle of the living-room floor. We talk first about my symptoms and the headache that kept me from coming to Sunday's session. Eventually we get to the topic that preoccupies me most about my cognitive state: my inability to cry. I have read one book since my accident, and while I don't know when I will be able to read another, I do have one under my belt. When the stars align again as they did in January, I should be able to read another short, simple book.

But I have not yet cried.

When I finish describing my circumstances, Rashani sits back on her heels and looks deeply into my eyes. What she tells me seems simplistic, but it resonates with me as a deep truth, a comforting truth.

"You aren't able to cry now because you are not supposed to cry now." She looks at me with compassion as she shares these words. In her eyes I see excitement for me as well, because there must to be a strong reason, a deeper mystery that I will uncover as I continue my healing journey.

I gaze into her eyes, but I am pondering the message her words send me. If I am not supposed to cry now, it could be because I don't yet need the catharsis that crying brings. It could be because right now I need to appear strong, in society's view of what defines strength. Finally, it may be that I am not supposed to cry yet because the bridge from my brain to my tear ducts is not yet completed, and there is no way of knowing where the emotions would go if they hurtled toward the gap in the middle of the bridge.

I understand instinctively that, in some ways, she is offering me the peace of not knowing the future, not worrying about it. Her perspective is a huge gift. I have kept track of so many details of my response to stimuli, had so many hard days, slept so many hours, eaten so many blueberries, needed Sophie so much, depended so much on Maureen. I feel bad for needing this support, and not at all entitled to it.

Being given the option to believe, and trust, that it's best for me to achieve the peace that patience brings is critical in this moment. I am not the only TBI Survivor who feels impatience, feels despair; I hope I can convey to my community that, whatever is now missing from their lives in comparison to what they had prior to their brain injury, the peace of knowing that, sometimes, it's just not yet time to know, and that this challenge is perfectly appropriate to growth as a person, is perhaps the most important perspective I can share. Our monthly meeting of the Brain Injury Alliance happens in two days. I should take this message to my friends there.

I come away from this meeting focused on demanding less of my brain. If something about my journey indicates that I should not seek to cry right now, I will wait patiently for this aspect of my return to normalcy to manifest itself whenever the time is right.

Wild Ride.
March 20, 2016

For a somewhat delayed honeymoon trip in December, 2014, Maureen worked out a trip to Hawaii for me. A high-school classmate who lives on Molokai introduced us to a friend of hers, Steve, and he let us stay for a week at his house. His backyard is a beach that faces Lanai. We fell in love with Molokai and decided to return for spring break this year.

Molokai never disappoints us. Kaunakakai Town has two grocery stores, two gas stations, no traffic signals, and a number of little shops that cater to the few tourists who visit. We spent a lot of our first trip exploring areas away from the house, including the white-sand beach on the west side of the island and an ancient temple to the east. Steve told us he had kayaks, but we never got around to trying them out.

This trip is different. We have gone kayaking nearly every morning, before the breeze springs up and makes the water choppy. Steve's beach lies within a fish farm, which was built by indigenous Hawaiians out of lava rocks to a height just below the water at low tide. At high tide, fish would swim over the fence and become trapped. They had plenty of room to swim and lots of food, but when the local people wanted to go fishing, they had a plentiful supply within easy reach.

Parts of the wall have broken down, and I take the kayak through one of the breaches and out into more open water. I am wearing a life jacket and my sunglasses, so I feel that I have all I need to be comfortable in this area. I don't stray too far, because I have not consulted with the expert kayakers to see what would be in store for me if I paddled toward the open sea.

One result of this kayaking is that I am getting exercise that does not hurt my neck. I am working my upper body as well as my legs. In fact, I have been coming off the water with stiffness in my psoas muscles, which lie in the lower abdomen just inside the pelvic girdle. Maureen has felt the same strain, and today she tells me that she, too, feels abdominal pain.

We rinse off the kayaks and move to the second activity of our day. We are going to the north end of the island, up to a cliff that overlooks an inlet that used to house a leper colony. We could take a mule ride down to that area, but Maureen doesn't relish the idea of sitting on the back of a pack animal for two hours or more, as sore as she is. It is also possible to walk down, but we don't have a four-hour round-trip in us. We opt for a picnic atop the overlook.

Maureen and I eat sandwiches while we gaze out over the ocean. We then walk into a magical copse of oddly bent trees. Maureen suddenly feels unwell, so we return to town. We are both tired, and we lie down. I start to doze, but she begins to writhe in pain. She calls her friend, who is a medical professional, and her friend suggests that we go to the ER.

The staff is small at the hospital, but we don't have to wait to get treatment. They give Maureen something for nausea and pain. The doctor says there is an extremely small chance that her problem is appendicitis. She doesn't have a fever. He wants to do a CT scan to rule it out.

Nurses slide Maureen onto a gurney and cart her away. She comes back quickly, and we wait for the results. Maureen is resting comfortably now, thanks to the meds. The doctor returns, a sheepish look on his face.

He says, "The scan says your appendix is inflamed. We need to send you to Honolulu for surgery."

We are supposed to fly to Honolulu tomorrow morning and catch our flight to Seattle. Maureen's appendicitis seems to be giving us a few extra days of vacation. I'm not sure, though, that she will consider these days to be very much of a treat.

The medevac plane will come for us shortly. I have half an hour to gather one bag's worth of belongings to take with us. Everything else will be shipped. But I forget that this is Molokai. One of Steve's friends is flying to Honolulu in three days. She has privileges that allow her to bring extra luggage on the small plane for free. We do pay for one bag, but it's far cheaper than having our goods shipped eventually to Bellingham.

After an ambulance ride on Molokai, the flight to Honolulu takes off. Maureen lies on a gurney, two medics at her side. I sit in a cramped corner at the front of the passenger compartment. The takeoff and landing are blessedly smooth, which helps Maureen's comfort level. After an ambulance ride to Queen's West Hospital, we meet Maureen's surgeon. She says Maureen should stay in the area a couple of days post-op before flying home. I call and extend our stay at the Ramada in Waikiki. In the meantime, Maureen has her appendix removed.

There is no place for me to sleep at the hospital. A nurse brings me a chair, and I try laying my head on the end of Maureen's bed. I can't find a comfortable position for my neck. I go out to a waiting room and lie across a couch. The lights have a motion sensor, so even in the middle of the night, when someone walks through, an explosion of light startles me. I stay awake all night.

By two the next afternoon, Steve is there to pick us up and take us to our hotel. I settle Maureen in the room and set about trying to find soft foods she can tolerate.

We spend three days at the Ramada. One of my jobs is to take her on short walks in the hallway, starting at 50 steps. I also need to find a grocery store where I can get her a greater variety of foods. The closest pharmacy is in a mall about a mile from the hotel. I walk back and forth to the mall a lot over those three days. Each night, I crash as hard as if I were the one who had surgery.

On the last full day in Honolulu, I take Maureen out in the hotel's wheelchair so she can get some sun. We roll over the sidewalk and go to the mall, each uneven spot in the sidewalk making her yelp.

I take her to the Prada store, just so we can say we

went in it. I eat abalone in the food court and bring the shell back to the hotel so I can take it home as a souvenir.

Our flight home doesn't stress her system too badly. It's a great relief to get her into our own bed after several days of hotel living. Once she recovers from the flight, she tells me something I would not have considered:

"I know you have a lot of trouble organizing your schedule, but you did a wonderful job of keeping track of my medication and taking care of me."

I'm thrilled that I accomplished everything she needed. I also feel good that I was able to muster up enough executive function, a phenomenon sadly lacking in my day-to-day life, to make everything work. I wondered why I was so fatigued every night. It was my brain trying to do what it now finds to be superhuman tasks of organization.

Thank you, brain. Thank you, life, for letting me return to Maureen some of the care I have received over the past 14 months.

TBI Conference.
April 18, 2016

I learned in 2015 that there is a Washington State conference for TBI Survivors. The Traumatic Brain Injury Advisory Council, under the auspices of the Washington State Department of Social and Health Services, runs this conference every year. Thanks to the Tommy Manning Act, this council exists, because two dollars from every moving violation, speeding and such, ticketed in the state goes into its funding.

I learned about the 2015 conference too late to apply for a scholarship to attend. I didn't even ask how much the conference cost; I simply decided not to go. It turns out that the conference would have cost about $150. It would have been money well spent.

I have a scholarship for the 2016 conference. It covers the cost of attending, as well as two nights in a Seattle hotel near SeaTac airport. A bunch of us from the BIAWA Bellingham chapter are going to the conference. I won't feel lonely here.

The conference organizers provide a wide variety of services for TBI Survivors. There is a yoga class that runs several times each day, and several massage therapists are providing 15-minute massages for free. Snacks are plentiful. So is the chocolate at the tables in the information room.

On both days there are speakers during lunch and dinner. At other times there are breakout sessions that deal with many different aspects of the TBI experience. Until this conference, my only source of information from other TBI Survivors was Brainline.org. Brainline.org is a vast website that includes information for everyone who has even a peripheral connection to a TBI Survivor. My own engagement with Brainline.org comes from reading the blog of one of the site's frequent contributors, David A. Grant.

David's story parallels mine in many ways. He was

unable to read for three years. He became fond of bright colors after his TBI. He set up a fountain in his yard to provide a bit of sound that masks his tinnitus, which is a goal I have set for myself.

The article that drew my attention to him was one in which he discusses how much transparency is too much. Oversharing about our injuries is one symptom of TBI, and it certainly is one I experience. Reading David's post comforted me with the knowledge that I am not the only person who experiences these issues. His words also have lessened my sense of guilt when I see Maureen wince while I show that terrible photo of my crushed car yet once more. Doing so is part of the TBI experience.

I am now surrounded by TBI Survivors who have stories to tell and experiences to compare. One of the speakers is a woman who fought her way back to normalcy from her TBI, only to be involved in another accident that gave her a second TBI. A Double Survivor—I can hardly imagine the challenges involved in having a second severe injury after working so hard to overcome the first one.

An unexpected bonus of this conference is meeting a Survivor in her 20s, Amy, who lives in Bellingham. She has been getting all her treatment in Seattle. She has not been aware of our local TBI support group. I introduce her to Mary Hughes, our facilitator, and to several people who attend the group each month. Amy will begin to attend our meetings in May.

In the information room I find organizations that have items available to help TBI Survivors live easier lives. One company sells plastic overlay filters, and it has an assessment that shows you what color filter would help you be able to process visuals more effectively. I take the assessment and learn that a peach-colored filter makes the text on a page slightly easier for me to look at without the pain that white paper causes. I buy the filter for when I read text on paper, but I learn also that I can make the background on Microsoft Word documents the same color as my filter.

The University of Washington is conducting a study on people who take gabapentin for head pain from TBI. I take the information, but I do not know if I will remember to follow through. My executive function may have worked well when my wife was in crisis, but when it comes to organizing something that benefits me, I don't seem to feel the proper amount of urgency at this point.

Talking to other Survivors reveals a lot about my own injury. As I noted earlier, Survivors who discuss their accidents frequently note the date and time of the trauma. We are all so different from our former selves after we experience TBI. The way I sense it is that my brain looks at the way its older version worked and tries to bring order from the chaos that has occurred. The trauma leads to an enormous amount of brain activity, and my brain, at least, seems to see its previous version as an artifact from a different time and place.

I have lived with this new brain for nearly 15 months, and I am still horrified by how much it cannot do. The Survivors I meet at the conference are either suffering ongoing frustration or are resigned to their new fate. Many asked me how long it has been since my injury. When I tell them it has been 15 months, they say, "It's early still."

My neurologist would say I have stepped through the window of healing for my brain, and it has closed behind me. Other Survivors know better, and their words are meant to be comforting. But I discover that I am a newbie in this world. They, the pros, are much more aware of how time drags on, of plateaus in healing, of losing hope for a complete recovery. I can only wonder if I will be facing years of agonizing cognitive struggles like theirs, until the day comes when I realize I will never be whole. It's early still, but my inability to predict my future makes the possibility of incomplete recovery a depressing specter.

But everyone at the conference has experienced improvement since their accidents. Absolutely everyone.

The degree of return to the cognitive function they once knew varies among Survivors, but no one I meet would prefer to be in a coma or dead. Everyone has a positive outlook, even when walking well is a distant goal or returning to school seems impossible.

The lunch speaker for Day 2 is a person who has recovered rather well. He was hit by a car while he was riding his bicycle. His helmet did not help him much, given the force and the angle of impact. He did not realize he had been knocked unconscious. A friend of his helped him reconstruct what he remembered. He realized that, if you get hit and then find yourself in an ambulance as your next memory, you spent some time unconscious.

I have an epiphany, thanks to his comment. I remember that my seat collapsed from the original impact, then I was flung into the air. I thought I rolled a very short distance, which turned out to be 136 feet. I could never understand how I misperceived the length of the roll. Suddenly, I understand. I was knocked out, even though I have stated that I never lost consciousness. This realization makes attending the conference worth every second of it.

The speaker has been talking for about 10 minutes when his story starts to sound extremely familiar to me. I finally look at the program and realize that the man talking is David A. Grant, the blogger from Brainline.org. I don't know how I missed this fact during the introduction, but perhaps it's a good thing. David is my rock-star TBI Survivor, and had I seen his name on the program, I might have squealed with excitement.

One thing that affects me and gives me even more reason to emulate David is that, as he tells his story, he has trouble holding back tears. He apologizes frequently for crying, and he tells us that his control over his emotions has been compromised by his TBI. At another point I notice that David refers to his previous self as David 1.0. Since I call myself Seán 2.0 now, I gasp when I hear someone else use the same terminology, even if we focus on different versions of our software.

After lunch I go to the vendor room and get in line to talk to David and his wife. They sell out of books before I reach them. I get ordering information, so I can buy a copy by mail later. I mention that I'm jealous of him because he can cry. He tells me of a Survivor friend in his home state of New Hampshire who did not cry for four years and then suddenly became able to cry.

That is one breakthrough I would love to experience. Nothing will make me feel more normal than crying at appropriate times. I would love to experience this same healing shift.

Knowing now what I know about the conference, I intend to budget for it during any year that I do not receive a scholarship. The new information I receive, the old information I forgot and hear again, and the networking make this conference an essential part of my healing strategy.

Sophie Stands Down.
May 10, 2016

I can't thank enough the friends who have stepped up to support me since the accident. But, as I noted earlier, one particular friend has gone to great lengths to be a source of comfort for me. That friend is Sophie, the Sphynx cat who adopted me in 2013 and nurtured me through the early months of my convalescence. Sophie snuggled with me, kissed me, groomed me, purred sweet somethings in my ear. She has been my steadfast shadow, my selfless caregiver.

She took care of me while she was experiencing health issues of her own. We dodged a bullet fifteen months ago, when her kidneys nearly failed. But the little bump we noticed at that time turned out to be another malignancy. We let the tumor grow. It grew slowly, but now it is the size of a golf ball. She showed no awareness of it until a couple of weeks ago, when she started to lick it. Even then, she showed no obvious distress.

No, that's not completely true. We had to prepare for the moment when the tumor would split her skin. We bought a onesie for her, because we needed to be able to bandage the wound and keep her from attacking the dressing. We tried the onesie on her, and she hated it. That was her only distress. After that, the trauma was ours, because we kept waiting for the skin to split and create a mess for her.

But Sophie, in her typical dignified way, worked to make things as easy on us as she could. Yesterday morning, before I went to teach my Monday classes, she stumbled and nearly fell as she walked from the living room to her food bowl. Maureen and I looked up, and we saw in each other's eyes the knowledge that the dreaded moment had arrived. Tears welled in Maureen's eyes, and my tear ducts gave me a grinding sensation, as if a dry well were trying to eke out a drop of water.

"I'll call the vets," Maureen said. I blinked my agreement and swallowed hard. At our feet, Sophie nibbled at her wet food, unaware that we had just decided her fate.

I have today off, so I've cleared my schedule, and I am going to spend the day with Sophie. She sits, lithe and dignified, gazing out the window of our guest room. She likes to curl up in the sunshine that streams through the window, and she has a turquoise fleece blanket she can burrow under if she gets chilly. Even though it's not particularly warm in the house, it is blessedly sunny, and she stretches out in the golden rays.

She will get my full attention today, and we will both benefit from the us-time. Lying on the twin bed we're sharing, I might have turned on an audiobook on any other day, but I choose soothing music, Rashani's album of music for the dying. Sophie settles into a half circle, curled up against me on her left side. Her skin is a light pinkish-white, and as I by happenstance am wearing black today, we form the yin and yang of the taijitu.

She purrs, even in her sleep.

When her eyes open, she stretches, her toes spread wide, extending claws that will never again be trimmed. She stands and moves to the window to peer outside again. A robin pecks at the grass, and Sophie makes the little Huntress murmur she always utters when she wishes she could get at the birdies. She's so alert and full of joie de vivre that I wonder if we should postpone her vet visit.

And then, out of nowhere, she loses her balance for no reason. She lists far to the right, and she barely catches herself by clutching the bedclothes. She shakes her head, and I hear her ears and cheeks make little flapping sounds like butterfly wings. She is truly ready to fly away to her next adventure.

As noon approaches, I feel a need to use the bathroom. When I stand, she looks at me as if I have betrayed her. She utters an offended "meow."

"I'll be right back," I say in my soft voice. She settles on her haunches. She doesn't follow me, as she always did before today. A minute later, I resume my position in our circle, and she sighs with relief. She starts to lie on her right side. She remembers she has a big lump there and switches to the left side. She presses her back against my belly and smiles.

My mind wanders back over our decisions regarding her health. Should we have put her under the knife again? We could have cut out this tumor when it was tiny and then waited for a third tumor to be the one we ignored. Since we knew which anesthetic caused her distress, we might have been able to find an alternate that would have allowed her to withstand surgery better. I take a breath into my tight lungs, deciding there is no point in rehashing our choices now.

Instead, I focus on the conversation we had about Sophie last November with Joanna Schmidt, our animal communicator. Sophie knows we have done our best, and she agrees with our moves.

After that conversation, Maureen and I discussed the idea that Sophie would get us a kitten right away. We didn't think it could happen, because Sphynx kittens are not easy to come by. We were introduced in April to a breeder in the southern part of the state, and yesterday Maureen asked her to put us on her list for a litter to be born in September.

Now Sophie is facing her final hours, and it seems that we are looking at being without a cat until October. Sophie's end is so sudden that we were not planning to get in the queue for a kitten so soon. As Joanna said she would, Sophie has given us emphatic evidence that she is ready to move on.

Maureen arrives home at 4:30. She comes to the room where Sophie and I are still snuggling. Maureen looks miserable. She has tears in her eyes and a catch in her voice. Sophie murmurs to her but doesn't get up. Maureen sits down and kisses this cat with whom she has shared her life for nine years.

The doorbell rings at 5 o'clock. Our house-call vets, Jill and Juli, step inside. We take them back to the master bedroom, and I carry Sophie in. Jill and Juli are keeping an open mind about Sophie's prognosis. We point out her balance issues, and we mention that she jumped off the bed yesterday and yelped with pain. Jill checks her hind-quarters, and Sophie makes a peep of discomfort. Both Jill and Juli frown.

Sophie helps the vets make their decision by stum-bling again. When they see that she is having trouble walking, they look at each other, then at us.

"It's time," Jill says. Juli nods in agreement. So do we.

All three women begin crying. I'm the outlier. Not be-cause I'm a man; if I could cry, I would join them. All four of us give Sophie kisses and strokes on her head and un-der her chin. I put my cheek next to hers, so she can rub her face on my stubble one last time.

The vets give her a strong sedative. She stands stock-still for a moment, feeling the strange sensation, then she tips over on her side with a thump. She's in dreamland. Maureen strokes her flank nevertheless. I'm sitting too far away to touch her, or I would gather her into my arms. I rub Maureen's back instead, and we both murmur soothing goodbyes, the last sounds Sophie will hear on Earth.

The vets hook her up for the final IV and administer it to her. Jill pulls out her stethoscope and listens to her heart. It doesn't take long for her to tell us that Sophie is gone.

After we kiss our baby, the vets gather Sophie in a blanket and walk with her out of the room to the front door. The four humans exchange hugs, and the vets take Sophie to their minivan. She will come back to us soon as ashes.

Right now, our hearts seem to consist of ashes. I hold Maureen while she cries. I do not cry. My chest is tight, and I have a small lump in my throat. I had hoped to honor Sophie by having today be the day I cried. But I cannot give her a proper sendoff with tears.

As I hold Maureen while she cries, I whisper to Sophie's soul: "Enjoy your new adventure, baby girl."

New Moon.
May 21 and 28, 2016

On May 9, the day before Sophie left us, Maureen called
a Sphynx breeder, Patricia, to tell her that Sophie was
fading quickly, and we would be in the market for a kitten
sooner than we thought. We came well-recommended by
another breeder, and Patricia put us down for an October
kitten. We asked for a black girl, so she would not resemble Sophie too much.

And then, an extremely strange thing happened. On
May 11, the day after Sophie died, Patricia called
Maureen back and told her that someone who had requested a kitten from her current litter had reneged on
the purchase. She had a black kitten available if we
wanted her.

I said, "Sophie told us in November that she would
get us a kitten before she was gone a month."

"I know, but I was wanting to hold her in my thoughts
for a while." We both had welcomed the breather until
October to let Sophie's passing make its way through our
system.

"We'll have at least two weeks," I replied.

Maureen told Patricia we would take the kitten, who
would be available on May 28, after she healed from being spayed. I drove down to the Olympia area on the 21st
to meet the kitten. When we were talking to Joanna
Schmidt in November, the name "Luna" popped into my
head as the proper name for our next cat. We let Patricia
know to start calling her Luna.

Patricia has an amazing array of kittens. One little
pink girl attaches herself to me instantly, climbing on my
shoulder and nuzzling my neck. It crosses my mind for
just a second that the easiest thing might be to take the
kitten that likes me already. But I can't get out of my
mind the notion that the kitten I came to see is the one
Sophie intends for me to take home.

That one is a feisty Alpha girl with a tiny smudge of

black fur on her nose, enormous bat ears, and inquisitive green eyes. On the 21st I took a lot of video of Luna to show to Maureen, and we spent the week falling in love with her. My favorite video shows Luna sitting atop an armchair, batting away the other kittens when they try to join her, even the ones a month older than she is. I like her assertive personality. She will be an only cat, so I don't worry about feline strife in the household.

On the 28th, she handles the trip home with reasonable grace. She doesn't get carsick, but she's bored, and she lets me know at times that she would like to be set free, please. I tell her she will be set loose soon enough, and she will get to meet her mama, who stayed home.

And here we are, done with the long trip. When I open the door to the carrier, Luna heads right for Maureen. The four-month-old kitten is tiny compared to Sophie, and she's so black she appears blue; she is designated a blue Sphynx. She snuggles up to Maureen and starts purring. I recall that, toward the end of my visit on the 21st, Luna stopped ignoring me and gave me a tiny head bump. Sophie got us a snuggler, an affectionate creature who will make her own way in the family.

There is no crying now for Maureen. We are simply hopeful that this kitten will fill the empty space Sophie left behind.

Mental Fatigue.
June 3, 2016

My first year back at school is coming to a merciful end. I have slogged through three ten-week quarters of teaching with minimal breaks, I have recalibrated seven syllabi to transition from teaching five days a week to three longer classes, and I have graded homework and 33 sets of exams. I have done little apart from teaching, prepping, grading, and sleeping. My life pattern resembles the days when I worked 60-hour weeks in the pizza business and left work so drained that I never did anything in my time off.

It's the last day of classes for the year. I have dragged myself out of bed one last time, earlier than I would like, because I scheduled acupuncture for 9am, before my classes. I feel frowsy, and I'm not sure my shower will help much. All I have to do is make it through until 2:20. Then my school year comes to an abrupt halt.

A good way to start is to get the coffee flowing. I fill the carafe to the 4-cup line, as always. I open my small tub of ground coffee, as always. I grasp the ¼ cup I use to scoop coffee. And I freeze.

I can't remember if I use one quarter-cup of coffee for eight cups of water, or four. I cannot visualize myself preparing the coffee. Muscle memory lets me know I use one scoop, but do I have the right quantity of water? I set my elbows on the counter, lean my chin on my hands, and stare at the coffee tub.

I have prepared coffee for most of my adult life. I made a science of it when I worked in an office in 1997. There, I sorted out exactly how much coffee to use when I brewed a pot for my co-workers and me.

How much was that?

I scrunch my eyes shut. I rub my temples with my fingertips. Nothing. I do not know how to make coffee today.

Time for another workaround. I'll put a quarter-cup

of ground coffee in the filter and brew four cups. If it makes double-strength coffee, I'll add water after I taste it.

I start the machine, and a couple of minutes later, I sip the dark liquid. It is exactly as strong as I expected. Crisis averted.

I'm not going to write down the coffee-to-water ratio for future use. I need to make my brain work to remember the simple tasks I have been doing for 30 years. If they get away from me, I'll have bigger problems than not being able to cry.

Testing...Testing.
June 5, 2016

Haven't I gone through enough testing? An MRI, and three back x-rays. The MRI showed that I have no abnormalities in my brain. A side benefit of that MRI is that I now also know I do not have any tumors or aneurysms lurking in my gray matter.

I also know an MRI does nothing to diagnose what is wrong with my cognition. While knowing what I can do to regain the ability to read is important to me, I still can't shake the notion that I would be fine with having my reading remain poor if I could just cry. But the MRI doesn't tell me anything about tears, either.

My attorney, Matt, has done an amazing job of finding information to support our case. The more I've gotten to know Matt, the more I like him. He is forthright and personable, much more than most lawyers I have met.

Now, he thinks I need one more test. This test is called a Single Photon Emission Computed Tomography scan. Doesn't that sound like fun? Known informally as the SPECT scan, it is part of the next wave of brain imaging that can look at how you think what you are thinking.

A little background: When people think, the brain dilates arteries in the area where the type of cognition should occur. If we read, one area is flooded with oxygen. If we see someone we love, a different area of the brain receives the increased blood flow.

I don't know what happens when we see a book we love.

I liken the scan to an image of what happens when one sprains one's ankle. We experience pain to prevent walking or running on the injured foot. The body's goal is to heal that area more quickly by resting it. I say as a layman that the brain does the same thing when part of it is injured. The SPECT scan demonstrates how certain areas, which are supposed to light up when we think, have the blood supply to them *cut* when we try to use injured portions of the brain. That keeps the injured area safe from overuse, but it also prevents any use at all.

On a SPECT scan, areas with increased blood flow light up as yellow to orange. When the brain sees damage and diverts blood from the injured area, the color shifts to green and blue. The darker the green and any shade of blue indicates a strong shunting away of blood from an area that has suffered brain damage. This coloration is indicative of both TBI and dementia. The fact that the brain treats these two conditions in the same way terrifies me.

In Glen Campbell's music video for "I'm Not Gonna Miss You," at 0:43 there is a similar but different imaging scan (PET) that shows a lot of dark-blue areas in his brain, which has been devastated by a form of dementia.

I am in Denver for this SPECT scan. There are very few places to get it as of now. I don't care about the bells and whistles of this cutting-edge scan. What I want to know is how my brain responds when I apply a cognitive load. The SPECT scan will give us that information. It's good for my healing strategy, and for my legal case.

The scan itself is easy to take. First, I get a shot of radioactive liquid. Then, I do a short cognitive exercise. It is the Stroop Color and Word Test, the one Dr. Judd gave me two weeks after my accident. I do it on a laptop in a small room. When I finish, the test administrator takes away the laptop and turns off the light. I rest for a certain amount of time. Then they scan my brain.

The next day I have another scan that does not involve a cognitive load. After that scan I undergo an interview about my symptoms and how my brain responds to my attempts to think. The doctor who will read my scans will not know any information about me prior to the reading. The goal is to achieve the most accurate understanding of what happens in my brain without any influence caused by knowledge of my history.

A few days after I return home, the clinician sched-ules a video conference with me. Maureen asks to be with me when we receive my results. We set up Maureen's lap-top in her home office, where there's more room for us to sit side by side. I don't know what I hope will come of this meeting: Do I want proof of damage, or do I want to be told I'm a hypochondriac? The latter option has never oc-curred to me, because the symptoms are so strong, but one never knows.

We get our first glimpse of what my brain does when I think. My scans show a lot of dark-green and blue spots, which indicate areas of brain damage. I am diagnosed with traumatic brain injury that affects my frontal, occip-ital, temporal, and parietal lobes. My amygdala is also compromised. All this scrambling occurred because of the one-two punch I got from having two impacts.

The beauty of the SPECT scan is that it is impossible for me to underperform on this test by consciously shifting blood flow away from all four lobes when I think. You can fake a limp, but you can't fake a brain injury when a scan detects it.

The tingle I feel in my frontal lobe above my left eye when I try to read is really my brain turning off the flow of blood. My brain shuts itself down for self-preservation. That same process occurs all over my brain. My visual cortex is clearly compromised.

The clinician has gone over all the important data and has logged off. Maureen asks me now how I feel.

"I'm not happy that there is so much damage in my head. But if that damage is going to be there, I want evi-dence of it. Now people will believe that I really have a problem. And knowing what the problems are will give us a better shot at fixing them."

Mind you, we had these scans done 16 months after my accident, when some healing has already occurred. I can only imagine what the scan would have looked like a year ago. I truly hope that, if I do this scan again in perhaps two years, I will see vast improvement. Time will tell.

Brain Camp (II).
June 9, 2016

Fresh off my trip to gather more brain data, I return to the Western Washington University Speech and Hearing Clinic for more Brain Camp. Over the course of my second summer program, my therapists bring many new assessments to the table. From them, I learn a lot about workarounds for the tasks I cannot do well because of my brain damage. One huge example I learn today is from a task called a "two-back." This type of test involves images or words on a screen. For example, if the first image I see is an elephant, and the second image is a chimpanzee, if the third image is an elephant, I hit the space bar. If the third image is not an elephant, I do nothing. Then I look to see if the fourth image is a chimpanzee. If it is, I again hit the space bar. For image number five, I refer back to image number three to see if they match. And so on.

When I sit and look at the images on the laptop, I get an average of 65% correct. I decide then that I might do better if I use my audio tactic and describe the images out loud. The images are a mix of animals, flowers, and shapes. For complex shapes, I come up with a quick descriptor, such as "square plus triangle." When I describe the images out loud, I get 95% correct. My therapists and I share high fives. Even as the amount of time the images are shown decreases, my accuracy does not drop if I give a verbal description of the image as I view it.

I finally get it! From this discovery I intuit that the problem continues to be an issue with my visual processing. I can understand audiobooks. I cannot read novels. I can listen to radio dramas. I cannot watch color television. I need sunglasses day and night, outdoors and indoors. I wear them when I drive at night. It's all about my eye-brain connection.

I ask myself, of course, if having this much damage after 16 months of repair work means I will never read well again. Will I always need sunglasses? Will grading exams always require a struggle against headaches and nausea?

My response is that I need to calm down and start reading out loud to take some of the cognitive load off my eyes and transfer it to my ears. Today's breakthrough in understanding my new workaround will be valuable only if I make use of it.

I Saw the Light.
October 31, 2016

I open the bedroom drapes when I get up. We're having a gray, rainy day, the type of day for which the Pacific Northwest is famous. If it keeps raining into the evening, I may have a lot of leftover chocolate from my Halloween treat bowl. The local kids would be willing to go out in the rain, but I'm not sure about their parents.

I watch the birds—Towhees and Steller's jays—peck around beneath the feeder. One designated jay comes and sets the feeder spinning. Birdseed flies off it, and then all the ground-feeders hop onto the patio and get their fill. I take a photo of the Steller's jays to share with my cousin, Kristi, who loves these jays. She is ill and will enjoy the birds from her home in Indiana.

I notice suddenly something has changed in my morning routine. I am looking at the birds for far longer than I usually can. It's a gloomy morning, certainly, but usually any light, especially daylight, burns my eyes so much I have to look away within a few seconds. I should be reaching right now for my wraparound dark glasses. But I don't need them.

I walk down the hall to the kitchen. The big test will be the overhead lighting that began to bother me the morning after the accident. I turn on the switch and look at the floor. No burn. I look straight ahead at the stove. No burn. I dare to look up at the light bulbs. *No burn.*

I take in the view of the lit-up kitchen with a sense of wonder, my mouth hanging open. I'm not sure what has happened, but if this sudden ability to tolerate light holds, I will have experienced the most significant moment of healing in this entire journey to date.

I call to Maureen. "I don't need my sunglasses!" I exclaim. She comes running down the hall.

"*Really?*" She sees I'm not joking, and she gives me a big hug.

"I don't know if it's because it's cloudy out, but I have the kitchen lights on, and no sunglasses."

I don't try to tax my brain by shining a flashlight in my eyes or any such nonsense. Yesterday I needed sunglasses, and this morning I don't. I am going to do everything possible to maintain this fragile truce my brain has established with the light of the world.

When I drive to school, I wear my sunglasses just in case the light becomes unbearable. I park and start walking toward my building. I take off the shades, and I look like everyone else, walking on a rainy, cloudy day without sunglasses. Normal.

I have offered my students two points of extra credit if they show up in a Halloween costume. No scamming me by claiming they dressed up as a normal student, for example. My novelty-loving brain will enjoy whatever they come up with. A number of them have taken me up on my offer, and they are dressed in a variety of clever costumes.

I am holding the sunglasses in my hand when I enter the room. I hear murmurs of surprise.

Finally, a student exclaims, "Oh my God, I can see your eyes! They're green!"

"Yeah, I decided to dress for Halloween as a person who doesn't need sunglasses."

My students may be nearly as excited for this sudden advance as I am. The overhead lights are on, the computer screen is lit up, and the projector is going. My sunglasses are still off.

I murmur my thanks that Dr. Jefferson's training was wrong about my brain-healing timeline. He is correct in saying that *conventional wisdom* teaches that the brain stops healing after a year. But I wonder if somebody said that a long time ago without any hard data to back up the statement.

I think of the story about the Viceroy butterfly. I was taught in grade school that the Viceroy resembles the Monarch butterfly because the Monarch tastes bitter, so birds don't eat them. The Viceroy tastes good, so it adopted the same coloration as the Monarch in order to be left alone by birds that are looking for a meal.

The problem with this hypothesis is that eventually, when I was completely grown, someone finally chopped up a Monarch butterfly and fed it to birds. They gobbled it right up. They also enjoyed eating a Viceroy butterfly. It turns out both butterflies are toxic to birds, so the coloration is a warning to predators. But the Viceroy isn't colorful to mimic a Monarch. Whoever said the Viceroy's coloration was a protective mechanism related to the Monarch was just guessing.

And whoever claimed that the brain stops healing after a year was similarly stabbing in the dark. Perhaps I should feel sorry for whoever wrote down that hypothesis, because it's likely no one had done longitudinal studies on brain-injury patients beyond the one-year mark.

Dr. Jefferson never said I would stop improving, stop healing, after my Smashiversary. He merely relayed conventional wisdom from the training he received. Again, I am glad this extremely intelligent doctor was given less-than-perfect data. He is smart enough to see that his patients continue to heal, and thus they change his outlook on what he knows compared to what he was originally taught.

I will have to tell my friends who are recently diagnosed with a TBI that, if they find themselves beyond the one-year anniversary of an injury, they *must* not assume they will not continue to heal. We cannot give up hope!

W.
November 2, 2016

I've been here before, both literally and figuratively. I'm at Anna's house, watching a game that will decide a championship. The last time, it was the Super Bowl, and this time, it's Game 7 of the World Series between the Chicago Cubs and the Cleveland Indians.

I say I've been here figuratively because this is the fifth time I've watched the Chicago Cubs play a deciding, do-or-die rubber match in a playoff series. In the previous four, the Cubs won a couple of early rounds, only to lose before they reached the World Series. This year marks their first World Series since 1945, and the first chance to win it all since 1908.

I began to follow the Cubs in 1968, and I felt the heartbreak their fans know starting with their collapse in September of 1969, after leading the National League all season. This year is a new experience for nearly all fans of the team, as people who were eight years old when the Cubs last reached the World Series are now 79.

For the first few games of the World Series, I've been watching the games at a restaurant called the Real McCoy. I love their small plates, especially oxtail with fried quinoa, and the lighting is dim, the TV a manageable size for my sunglass-covered eyes.

However, Anna asked if I wanted to come over to watch Game 7 with her and Frank, her husband. Remembering how hard their huge TV was on my eyes and brain when I watched the Super Bowl with them three days after my accident, I might have declined the offer a few days ago. But now I have a new reality: brain plasticity and its relentless drive toward healing has made it possible for me to watch TV without sunglasses.

I do have my shades with me, because I don't expect my brain to handle nine full innings of color on an 80 inch screen. But I am determined to go as far as I can into the game without them, just to establish a baseline for what my brain has done for me.

The Cubs get off to a good start, but about the time I decide it's prudent to don my sunglasses, for the eighth inning, the Indians tie the score. No one scores in the ninth, sending the game into a tenth inning. And then it rains.

I have been texting another superfan, my cousin Kristi, throughout the game. We were worried after the eighth inning, and now we are really nervous.

At first, the rain delay between the ninth and the tenth innings strikes me as a sign of doom for the Cubs. They started to look frazzled in the eighth, reminiscent of Game 6 of the 2003 series against Florida. But the delay gives respite to both the Cubs and to me.

I watch the tenth inning without my dark glasses. The Cubs score twice. They give up a run in the bottom of the tenth, but they win their first championship since 1908. Kristi and I exchange jubilant texts. In her case, the victory is all the more important because the horrid cancer she has been battling for a year might well have taken her life before she could witness this spectacle. She held on to see her team win, and they came through.

The extra-sweet fact that Kristi is still around to enjoy this game hurts my heart. I feel the typical buildup to tears, but unlike the Cubs, I do not win my long battle over futility tonight.

Cardiff.
December 14, 2016

How long have I been trying to visit Cardiff-by-the-Sea, California? I started writing *Chocolates on My Pillow*, the novel in which the town figures, in 2007. I wanted my Indiana-based protagonist to travel to the coast to visit a friend. I was thinking of a picturesque name for a town. I looked on Mapquest and found Cardiff. Google Street View helped me find some landmarks I could mention in passing. I wrote the first draft of the novel.

I made plans several times to travel to Cardiff, but they all fell through. I finally have worked out a trip to visit my children and spend some time at Cardiff-by-the-Sea Lodge. It is a landmark in a town full of them. Each room in the Lodge is decorated differently from the others. There is a Hawaiian-themed room, for example, as well as the obligatory Sweetheart Room, complete with a heart-shaped Jacuzzi.

Thanks to my friend Teri, a native of the area, I know I need to visit VG Donuts, as well as the Self-Realization Fellowship's meditation gardens. Swami Paramahansa Yogananda constructed the gardens on a bluff overlooking the Pacific Ocean around 1920. Since then, his name has been linked to a major surfing spot, Swami's Beach, as well as several local businesses. I also need to visit the obvious places I included in my novel prior to coming to town, as well as seek out new local color to enhance the book.

After I reach town early in the morning, my first foray is to the Starbucks on San Elijo Avenue, in the same shopping center as the grocery store and several other businesses I built into the book. My protagonist goes to this Starbucks the day she arrives in town. I want to experience the scene as she does. I buy a latte and sit outside in the cool dawn. I learn numerous details that I did not know: there are commuter trains that pass between San Elijo Avenue and the beach every twenty minutes or so. There is no sticky saltiness to the breeze that reaches me. This Starbucks has no drive-thru, and the locals, or commuters heading to or from Encinitas, park and walk inside to get their drinks.

The most valuable revelations come later in the day. The Lodge suits me perfectly. It is comprised of two tall, circular buildings, with an open-air walkway between them. The barrel-shaped constructions are covered in brown shingles, probably cedar. The hospice I have invented for my novel would fit nicely in the quirky Cardiff Lodge.

The other inspiration I get comes when I dine at the Besta-Wan Pizza House. The interior walls are painted bright primary colors, there is a veranda with tables, and the televisions show horse races from Santa Anita. The customers at the bar discuss the races. They know this sport.

I pull out my Surface and stare at the screen. I am right in the middle of Cardiff, and I can feel the vibe this section of my novel needs to have. I start to write a new chapter to add to the book.

My brain tells me it's tired after I write two pages. I wish I could push myself farther, but I need to respect my brain's limits if I am going to enjoy my time here rather than spend it in bed with a headache. I can also accept the small amount of fiction I was able to write as a gift from my brain, because it feels like the best fiction I have written since my injury. I can look around and see the area I'm describing, rather than having to picture it in my mind. I hope I don't always have to be where my scenes are set in order to write about them.

I walk the following morning to the Meditation Gardens at the Swami's Self-Realization Fellowship. The gardens are terraced, leading up to a cliff. I learn that the swami had a center up here that eventually fell victim to erosion and was declared unsafe. But the gardens remain, with a huge variety of plants and trees, many nooks for meditation, and a burbling pond filled with koi.

I realize that another scene I want to write should be set in one particular nook, atop the garden, overlooking the Pacific. I make notes in my phone.

I'm packing to return home. Just as when I met my friend Teri and got a lesson in Encinitas-Cardiff life, this visit gives me a huge amount of data I can draw on to strengthen the novel.

I'm willing to accept the idea that slowing down and not publishing this novel in early 2015 was a healthy thing for the book. I do wish I had learned that lesson some easier way.

Back to School.
January 3, 2017

One result of the accident is that I took stock of every life goal I have not completed. The biggest one has always been finishing my education. Even though I have been a prolific writer, I never got to complete my doctoral dissertation. The reasons involve money more than they do laziness or disorganization, so I think it's time I set myself up to finish this task.

The University of Washington did not have a PhD program in Spanish when I moved to the state. When I learned that they were going to restart their PhD program, I considered applying. I was not moving very fast on my application. I intended to start the program in the fall of 2015. I was finally getting around to the paperwork when I got my TBI.

I still have not been accepted into the PhD program for the 2017-18 school year, but I do have provisional admission to the university as a state employee. One of my job benefits is that I can take a course for free each quarter. I have chosen to take a course at UW that I can apply to my PhD program if I am accepted.

I am enrolled in a film course on the history of Spanish cinema. The course happened to fit the time that would be easiest for me to drive down to Seattle weekly, and it has the added benefit of requiring less reading than the literature classes I would have taken instead. I don't know much about film courses. I'm excited both to be back in class as a student and to study a field new to me.

I have worked hard to get my application in order. I made a list of tasks required for the process, and I met my deadlines. The damaged executive function that makes my daily agenda a challenge to fulfill does have its workarounds. I use my Google Calendar constantly, putting in reminders and scheduling time for tasks that most people do without prodding. Even remembering to check to see if I had received information I needed to finish my application was a challenge. Into my calendar went a reminder to look online.

The application is in, after much determined effort on my part. My film professor knows that she is going to have an out-of-town student who is already teaching full-time at a college. She is aware that I will be working with a cognitive deficit. I should probably be more daunted by the circumstances than I am.

The graduate students look like freshmen to me. There are Master's and PhD students in the course, some from the Spanish Department, and others from Film Studies. I am the only outsider, the only older student. I face the challenge of being out of the loop for a long period of time. A lot has gone on in academia of which I am not aware. It's as if I had been on the design team for Windows 95 and decide to go back to work on Windows 10 without knowledge of any intermediate version of Windows. It's a good thing I don't know what I don't know.

Class goes well. I make sure I raise my hand and participate. We do some small-group work, and I contribute as much as possible to the discussion. Over the course of a few sessions, the students realize that I am serious about this course. I don't feel like an outsider any longer.

The time comes to design a paper and write a ten-page final essay. I settle on a topic that involves the role of female characters in movies by Luis García Berlanga and Guillermo Del Toro. My thesis statement is that the female characters subvert the plans of the men who think they are in control of their own lives and destinies, as well as those of the subversive women.

As soon as I get this idea, I look for conferences where I could present the paper. I need to have recent activity on my curriculum vitae. I do find a conference in April that will be held at Gettysburg College. I have missed the entry deadline by a few days, but the organizer of the conference has a presenter drop out, and he accepts my application. I get to go to Gettysburg in April.

Writing the paper presents a greater challenge than I

expected, even though I knew it would be a difficult process. I watch the movies carefully, multiple times. I am fortunate that two of the movies are black-and-white, and I have detailed knowledge of the third one, *Pan's Labyrinth*. The issue lies in the fact that I must read academic articles about the filmmakers and the movies.

I build a decent-sized but not enormous bibliography for my paper. It is certainly sufficient for backing up and broadening my argument. I finish the paper a couple of days prior to the due date and email it to my professor. Then I spend the time from March to April elaborating on aspects of my argument. I'm not limited to ten pages for the conference.

Maureen and I, as well as others who have watched my progress, are astounded that I was able to put together the application for admission, do the work for the course, and write a paper that I turned in *before* the deadline. If the TBI has taught me one thing, it is that time is too precious a commodity to disdain it. My ability to push through this paperwork and do the academic writing are newly regained skills, signs that my brain keeps battling back from the silence it experienced right after the accident.

I am sitting with Maureen in a hotel in Victoria, British Columbia on spring break when I get the news that I was not accepted to the PhD program at the University of Washington. I had set my sights on finishing my PhD because I decided right after my TBI that getting my doctorate was one piece of unfinished business that required more effort than luck. The Spanish Department gives the explanation that the budget has been cut, and it is a year to focus on bringing in more Master's students. Few PhD students are being admitted, and the few who are have far more academic publications than I do.

This email from the graduate director at UW is a real downer, detracting for a moment from the healing powers of this vacation. To cheer me up, Maureen suggests we go across the street to a place we have been thinking about visiting.

Up a flight of stairs, we enter a room paneled in dark wood, complete with a gorgeous bar that matches the tone of the room. This is a Scotch bar. I have never been to a Scotch bar, and Maureen normally would not suggest that I go to a bar and drink alcohol after receiving disappointing news. But this place is different. I look at their menu and ask the bartender questions about several of the Scotches. He gives me enough information that I can choose something that suits my current mood.

While I sip my Scotch, Maureen asks me how I feel about my academic setback. I think for a couple of minutes.

"I'm kind of shocked. I think they don't see much likelihood that I'll produce a lot of academic publications. I explained that we were told not to try to publish too much until we had a tenure-track job. But the new thing now for students at Latin American universities is to get a lot of publications before they even start the PhD program. There's nothing I can do if I'm being compared to those students."

Maureen takes a sip of her water. "I'm proud of how well you organized your application process, and for getting into the class you took. And you're going to read at a conference. All of this, when a year ago you could barely work a crossword puzzle."

I give her a slow nod and take a meditative sip of my Scotch. "I think I have to change my perspective on what Seán 2.0 needs to do. Instead of saying I am going to get my PhD, I need to say t I will do everything in my power to get my PhD. Many things are outside of my control in every aspect of life." Another sip. "All I need to do is my best in every endeavor, and the ones that are meant to work out will come to pass."

I don't drown my sorrows in Scotch. But I do enjoy the new taste experience that sipping a highly regarded, carefully crafted Scotch gives me. I'm in exactly the right place and with exactly the right person to be making this paradigm shift for my goals for Seán 2.0.

Kristi.
January 30, 2017

It's now the day after the second anniversary of the accident, and I still can't cry.

I met the Underwood family via my stepmother in 1970. Bill and Robyn Underwood had five kids. Michael, the oldest, was one of my two best friends throughout our teen years. Kristi was the baby of the family. I met her just after her first birthday.

My sister called me in October, 2015, a week after she told me she had breast cancer. I still see in my mind the artwork in the shop I was browsing when she called. Each time I return to that shop in Edison, Washington, I remember the conversation. She told me Kristi had cancer as well, and her prognosis was dire.

I didn't cry, of course, but I felt my throat tighten, as well as my chest. I stared at a ceramic bowl during the entire call, trying to absorb the idea: the cancer-stricken baby of our family was telling me about the cancer-stricken baby of the Underwood family. All I felt was the wrongness of the scenario. I wanted to scream with rage, cry at the injustice. All I got was a tight chest.

The call took me back to 2004. One night, I got an email from Robyn: "Michael died today. I thought you would want to know." It took me two seconds to start bawling. When I could breathe, I called Robyn, even though it was late at night.

When I hear of someone's cancer diagnosis, the two thoughts that cross my mind are that the person might die, and that treatment is much better than it used to be. I assumed the best for Kristi, and that attitude protected me emotionally through the winter. I kept track of Kristi's progress. She had chemo every Tuesday, as well as radiation. She called the family members who took her for treatments her Chemo-Sabes, a reference to the Lone Ranger. She maintained the most positive warrior attitude possible throughout the battle.

In February, 2016, my mom's last surviving sister, Aunt Eileen, died. I flew home to Indiana for her funeral. She and I had been close, though not as close as I am with Aunt Louise, who is healing miraculously well.

The trip also allowed me to visit Robyn, my "Aunt Robbie." I went to her house, a cabin in a woods in Northwest Indiana, and she told me the truth. Aunt Robbie stared into space as she spoke, her voice weary.

"Kristi's cancer is in her liver, in the back lining of her lungs, in her spine. People with this cancer rarely survive six months. Kristi was at five months since diagnosis." Aunt Robbie sighed. "If you look up this cancer, the data show that the effects of chemo can't be assessed. That's because no one lives long enough for the chemo to do its work."

It was flu season, and Aunt Robbie was hoping Kristi would catch it in her immunosuppressed state and die without pain. And yet, she knew Kristi had upcoming milestones to live for.

Kristi met her first husband when they both worked at Tower Records in Nashville. Shortly after their son was born, the husband died. Kristi came home to her parents, who were then living in Philadelphia. I was there visiting when she arrived, shell-shocked, with an adorable little boy.

Over the years, she did more than get back on her feet. She educated herself further, became an adjunct teacher at Purdue University, and raised her son to be a clear-thinking, kind, talented young man. Now, he was on the verge of graduating from high school, and his impending choice of colleges was upon him.

Kristi, according to statistics, should have died in March of 2016. She was well enough to throw a graduation party for her son in June of 2016, she saw him off to Purdue University in August, and she watched our beloved Chicago Cubs win the World Series in November. For most of the season, and to this day, her Facebook profile picture is a blue W on a white background, the

Win flag that flies after a Cubs victory.

Kristi went into hospice in late January of 2017. Aunt Robbie sent me a message to tell me, and she also told me that before her final decline, Kristi said that I was loved more as a real cousin than as just a friend, and that I was always very kind. The message slammed into my chest. I could not imagine a person in so much pain, only partially masked by morphine, thinking of me at all, and much less in a reflective way.

But that was Kristi. She loved birds, so I shared videos of the Steller's jays that wreaked havoc at our feeder. They were one of her favorite birds, as was the Bald Eagle, which she never saw flying. I invited her to come to Washington and see them, but she was just on the edge of being unable to travel, and she stayed home. I sent her videos of the ones I saw fishing for salmon off the British Columbia coast.

On January 30, 2017, my sister texted me: "Kristi died this morning." It is over. Her pain, her future. She was supposed to get her son off to college and go see the world. It didn't happen for her.

My temples are pounding. Again, I want to scream out my rage at the injustice of the situation. I remember telling Aunt Robbie that, if I ruled the world, there would be two laws above all others: No parent would lose a child, and no child would lose a parent before turning thirty.

She agreed that those would be good laws. She, having lost two children and her husband, and I, having lost my mother when I was nine, would both have benefitted from such an arrangement.

But for now, all I can do is admire Kristi's warrior attitude, her lifelong determination to give her son a good life to the point of frequent self-sacrifice, while living a rich and interesting life as a jewelry maker, a lover of humanity, and a true cousin-friend.

And here I sit, two years after my accident, not crying, my stomach in knots, my nose and tear ducts burning, yet dry. I know Kristi understands why I cannot yet give her the gift of shedding tears for her. She gives me even more incentive to keep Seán 2.0 healthy and make something of himself.

Thank you, Kristi, for the example you have set for me, and for your friendship. I wish you all the best on your new journey.

Haircut Two.
March 14, 2017

Two years have passed since I last sat in a hairdresser's chair. My neck still has ligament issues and is easily sprained. But I've decided it is time to cut off my hair, which now hangs to the middle of my shoulder blades, as a donation to someone who needs a wig because of the effects of chemotherapy.

Maureen takes me to her hairdresser. The young woman is well-versed in the procedure for preparing my hair for donation. I will be driving my hair across the border to Langley, British Columbia, where I will drop it off at a hairdresser who collects donations for Wigs for Kids, a service of the Canadian Cancer Society. That organization is the most flexible one I could find with regard to graying hair. They will use my hair, and the hair of several other people, to make a wig. Then they will dye the hair to a uniform color.

I am used to getting haircuts when my hair is collar-length and having it shortened to where I can feel the breeze on my neck. Today we are cutting off 10 inches. That still leaves me with collar-length hair. I don't want to have hair short enough that I need to schedule frequent haircuts. My plan for now is to donate it every two years. It crosses my mind that I'm lucky to be a hair donor, rather than an organ donor.

The neck pain from my TBI has a silver lining. It has changed my outlook on haircuts, along with so many other aspects of life. From this point forward, I want my efforts to lead to contributions to the well-being of other people. If I don't torture myself by getting frequent haircuts, I can provide a child with part of a wig every two years. I have seen videos of children, usually girls, getting wigs during chemotherapy. When they unbox the wig, they are thrilled to have hair again.

Today I am donating this hair in honor of my sister

Cindy, who is completely cancer-free now. I will donate it the next time in honor of Kristi.

Battle of Gettysburg.
April 6, 2017

The film conference at Gettysburg College is structured
as a seminar. We all turned our papers in beforehand and
then read all submissions, to be prepared to make valuable comments during the discussion of each paper. The
organizer of the Gettysburg College Philosophy and Film
Seminar, Prof. Vernon Cisney, has put together a stellar
collection of scholars who are at the top of their game ac-
ademically. I am in awe of their intellect and their writing
skills.

It took me a long time to get over my case of Imposter
Syndrome related to my creative writing. Now I am faced
with yet another whopping case of self-doubt. I am hoping that someone, anyone, is less experienced with conferences than I am, and that my paper is at least as good
as the worst paper presented. I refuse to think of myself
as the least-qualified member of this crowd, not because
it's unlikely to be true, but because, just as with writing
this memoir, persistence pays off. I will ignore my doubts
and put my best foot forward in both academic and social
interactions with these amazing intellectuals.

I have taken the time to write down some questions
and comments for each of the seminar participants. I get
in the groove pretty well. My paper will be the last one
discussed on day two, which gives me time to show my
interest in the work of the others and thus earn gracious
collegial treatment.

We hold our meetings in a small, yet comfortable
conference room. We sit at a long table made of light-colored solid wood. The overhead lighting leads me to don
my sunglasses, except when a speaker is showing a film
clip. The mood is light, the conversation is cordial and
stimulating, and the material opens intellectual doors to
me. No one asks about my sunglasses. In case they're cu-
rious, I'll make sure I let them know why I wear them.

We have a great dinner Friday night. No one displays

toxic ego. The only thing I would change about the experience so far is that I am having allergy attacks from pollens I don't encounter in Washington. The reaction seems to be settling in pretty quickly.

It's Saturday. D-Day for me. We have moved to a room with lots of windows, which balances the overhead lighting and makes it a little easier for me to tolerate. Random luck like this helps me navigate my life, for sure. I ask them for permission to record the presentation and comments because I can't write notes without getting a headache. Everyone is fine with my doing so. I give a short description of my research to the group, and they respond with very valuable feedback.

I manage to give a coherent presentation despite the coughing and sniffling that have taken over my entire being. After dinner we gather in the bar in the hotel where we're staying. I share in a few conversations, then I realize that my energy is flagging, more from the allergies than from my TBI. I go to bed much earlier than everyone else.

I have a plan to get up Sunday morning and walk over to the Gettysburg battlefield. But about two in the morning, I get up and have a coughing fit so bad that I collapse onto my bed, black spots swirling before my eyes. It's all I can do to eat breakfast and wait for my shuttle back to the Baltimore airport. I have a plan in Baltimore as well. I bought a ticket to an Orioles game. I'm miserable, but I figure I might as well go and add another stadium to the collection of ballparks I have visited. I know I'm not infectious, or I would have stayed away.

There are a couple of things they do in Baltimore that I have not seen before. Maybe it's just because I arrived early, but the staff have hosed down the seats, and the usher who directed me to my seat dried it off with a towel. It seems to me that this level of personal attention involves a lot of work. I appreciate it very much, since it keeps my rear end from getting wet.

Another Baltimore quirk that doesn't occur anywhere else is that, during the singing of the national anthem, the crowd is mostly quiet until they get to "Oh say, does that star-spangled banner yet wave?" Then, because the Orioles are also called the O's, everyone shouts, "Oh!" Then the crowd quiets down again for the rest of the song.

I enjoy the first two innings of the Orioles-Angels game. I don't enjoy the third inning, as I am getting sicker by the moment. Defeated, I leave the game early, after I worked so hard to get to it.

The pressure changes in the cabin of the descending plane create some of the worst head pain I have ever experienced. My ears are so full of gunk that they won't pop to equalize pressure. I hear a creaking sound inside my head, and I wonder if my eardrum is going to split open.

Maureen picks me up. I'm sick enough that I go to the doctor the same day, unlike my lack of attention to my TBI. I have an ear infection so bad that the doctor gasps. But a round of antibiotics fixes me right up.

What I learned from this trip is that I was able to hold my own in an intellectual community. I still struggle with reading, but there are enough workarounds now that I might well be able to go to a conference every year. If I work hard enough writing these papers, I can get some academic publications as well.

Watercolors in the Rain.
July 8, 2017

Mary and Janet from the BIAWA came up with a great summer activity for the TBI Survivors. We are going to the Fairhaven Public Library to learn to paint. We are going to work with watercolors, which will be a new experience for me. I'm excited to add another technique to my art. I haven't painted much since shortly after my accident. Maybe this lesson will jump-start my urge to paint.

The library is housed in a stately old building. It boasts a reading room with a fireplace. It's an excellent venue for a painting lesson. Our instructor has come up from Seattle to teach us first how to draw with perspective, then how to use watercolors.

Our instructor gives us pencils and paper. She shows us how to start a landscape with mountains in the background, foothills closer in, and trees in a meadow in the foreground. Once we have learned this concept, she turns us loose to reproduce those sketches on watercolor paper.

Except I don't want to paint a version of my landscape. A message is pushing through me. It wants out. I sketch Bellingham Bay from the vantage point of the top of the bluff on the Boulevard.

Anyone who needs to use the crosswalk where I stopped on the day of my accident would take these stairs down from the housing atop the bluff. At the top of the paper I draw Lummi Island. I then draw the crescent shape of the Bay from Gooseberry Point all the way around to Boulevard Park.

I sketch the road below the bluff. On that road I put three cars, one headed south and two headed north. The first northbound vehicle is a small, black car. It is sitting at a crosswalk. Right behind it is a large SUV. The SUV's bumper has just made contact with the rear of the small car.

My sketch is done. I dab water on the sky and paint it

blue. I paint Lummi Island a smoky gray. I paint the shoreline all the way around a sandy shade. I paint the southbound car red.

I have my trauma therapist, Nancy, to see about the stress the accident still brings me. But sitting here and creating a physical version of the moment of impact draws a surprising amount of emotion out of my system. The paper feels charged with the peril I depict in the image I painted.

Karen, my craniosacral practitioner, is taking this painting lesson as well. She is part of the Brain Injury Alliance as both a professional and a TBI Survivor. I show her the painting. She gazes at the cars and tells me that my scene is quietly disturbing. That is what I meant it to convey. I suspect that the people who saw my accident happen saw a big SUV crunch the back end of a little Honda Civic. They saw the Civic roll away from the crosswalk. But no one saw me bounce around in the car.

No one but me experienced that trauma.

I hope that a moment frozen in time, showing the first moment of the disaster, will give people something to think about as they drive.

Monday Night Goofballs.
October 2, 2017

Dr. Michael Fraas has played a huge role in my recovery from my TBI. We were friends before I was injured, and he was the one who, a day after my accident, saw me and immediately diagnosed concussion. It was Michael who worked with his graduate students to get me on track with brain therapy in the summer of 2015. He came up with an idea in the spring of 2017 to have a social-skills class during the 2017-2018 school year. He asked me to participate as someone who had recovered enough to be articulate with both the facilitators of the group and the TBI Survivors attending.

This opportunity seemed like an effective way to begin to give back to the TBI community. I fully expected that I would learn ways to improve my own social interactions as well. Now I find myself in a conference room at the Speech and Hearing Clinic at 5 o'clock in the afternoon. Michael has chosen two graduate students to lead the program. There are eight Survivors here, including me. The only persons I know are Adam and Jeff, who also participate in BIAWA. With those two in the room, I expect this to be an enjoyable quarter.

The sources of our injuries are varied. One man was electrocuted. Another suffered accidental asphyxiation. One person fell off a horse. There are, of course, several victims of car accidents. We all take our new lives seriously. We're all happy to be able to attend this program.

The man who fell off a horse has been dealing with the challenges of his accident for 20 years. He was a healthy, tall, strong man in his early 20s at the time. He became an invalid in a matter of seconds. His mother has been his caregiver for two decades. His prognosis was that he would never walk or talk again. He spent considerable time in the hospital, and he still walks with a cane and has speech challenges. And he has a wicked sense of humor.

Another guy got distracted while he was driving his truck, ran off the road at highway speeds, and rolled the truck about four times. He shattered one arm, and he enjoys showing the x-ray of the array of pins still in his arm. When he shows that photo, he reminds me of my own need to show the photo of my car to people.

I don't know if the graduate students running this program knew what they would be getting into. They probably did, because part of their clinical work has involved TBI Survivors. They would be well-aware of how easily we get sidetracked in conversation. Conversational tangents and rabbit holes certainly are not new concepts to them. Even so, I see them exchange looks of despair as they try to figure out how to get a conversation back on track three minutes after we have taken it far from its original purpose.

The facilitators have a thorough curriculum to explore this quarter. We discuss such topics as not derailing conversations, not interrupting other people as they talk, ways to be assertive rather than passive or aggressive, and sensing when we have talked about one topic too long. I have been especially sensitive to this last issue since my accident, because I can feel myself beating a subject to death, and yet I cannot always stop myself from talking or repeating myself. This course helps me with that issue, if with nothing else.

When I call us "goofballs," I am mostly making a pun on "Monday Night Football," but Adam, Jeff, and I certainly talk some smack and tease one another a lot. Jeff has picked up some gutter Spanish along the way, and he harasses me with it most weeks. When he tells me to go screw myself, I tell him to do the same thing. Then I say a few things more to him that he does not understand. I win.

We are not rude in class. We do our teasing outside of the time we should be paying attention to the important work our facilitators are doing. Michael observes part of each session, and he and I also banter occasionally, though our humor with each other tends to be drier than what Adam and Jeff toss out. What matters most of all is not what we say, but the fact that Adam and Jeff are using their speaking skills. Over the course of three school quarters, I see these two men, and Morgan, who spoke haltingly when we first started, become more articulate and refined in their conversations. The same holds true for the women who attend the group, though in some cases most of their issues stem from challenges they face as they interact with people outside of the group.

Michael is taking a sabbatical for the 2018-19 school year, and there is no one to continue this program for a second year. I feel a sense of loss, and I'm not the only one, which led some of us to set up an informal group to continue conversation this fall. The group will be run by TBI Survivors with no facilitator. It will do all of us considerable good to stay banded together for as long as we find it useful. Our topics of conversation range far from the guided discussions we had in the program. In that shift I see how we have progressed in our language skills.

Almost 1,000 Days.
October 19, 2017

I have a massage to calm my neck this morning, so I'm up early, in the kitchen, getting my routine underway before Maureen finishes her shower. It's time to take my antacid capsule and the gabapentin I use to stave off headaches, so I lay the capsules by the stove before I turn on the burner under my cast-iron skillet. I pull out an egg and my bag of frozen hash browns, as well as a small container of chopped onions I keep handy for the days I want hash browns or an omelet.

I drizzle olive oil into the skillet and look at the onions in the container. The bits are not discolored, and when I sprinkle a handful into the skillet, they are not slimy. I judge their integrity this way because I can't smell them, even when they're burning. As firm and dry as they are, I'll be able to use what's left for a couple of days longer.

Once the onions are sautéed to my liking, I remove them from the skillet and spread a thin layer of shredded potatoes on the hot black iron. Another drizzle of oil, and I sprinkle the cooked onions on top. They will cook more when I flip the potatoes. It will take several minutes to brown the bottom of the potatoes, so it's time to take my meds.

I pour a small glass of water and ready myself to take the antacid. I still have some trouble swallowing pills, but I've done enough biofeedback to be able to get these capsules down easily, once I've set my mind properly. I look out the kitchen window at the Japanese maple at the edge of the patio, at the Rainier cherry trees and the Bartlett pear tree that follow the fence line at the back of the property.

I take a deep breath and pop the capsule into my mouth. I take a mouthful of water and prepare to swallow. But I have gulped too much water, and some liquid trickles into my windpipe. My reflexes engage, and I start to choke on the water. It's in my vocal cords, so my wind-pipe spasms. I take a second to assess my condition, then I try to draw a slow, light breath. I get some air past the moisture and into my lungs. That allows me to start coughing up the water, which I then swallow the right way. My body takes full advantage, doubling me over with coughing spasms. Breathe in, cough out water. Over and over.

Maureen, dressed but still toweling her hair, comes running. I tell her what happened, and I sense that the capsule isn't in my mouth. I wonder if I swallowed it or inhaled it. I figure I'll know in a few hours, if I start to feel heartburn. Then I realize that the capsule will dissolve in my lung, and the medicine will still work. So, whichever way it went, I'll get my medicine, and I won't need surgery to remove the blockage.

A few final coughs, and I stand upright. Maureen relaxes a bit. "I think your hash browns are burning," she says.

I lift them with the spatula, and she's right. Some of the bits have gone from brown to black, while others are still where I want them. I flip the starchy mass and take a cleansing breath. She looks at me, and I see surprise in her eyes.

She says, "You have a tear on your cheek!" I raise my hand to my right cheek, and there it is, both a small liquid trail and a droplet of water showing that I have shed a tear. One on the right side, none on the left. I taste it to see if it is salty water or a splash from the glass. I lick the moisture on my finger. Salty. I know anyway that it came from my eye. After I wipe my cheek, I wish I had saved the drop in a vial.

A tear.

Once I cook my meal and sit down at the table, I look at the app I use to keep track of how much time has passed since I was hit. In this case, it has taken 993 days for the neurological connections that create tears to resume minimal production. My therapist and I had wondered if I might be crying inside, with my tear ducts physically damaged and unable to carry liquid. Now I know my right tear duct works.

I did not cry today for emotional reasons, but I did see a restart of the system that will allow me to produce emotional tears when I am able to cry. I sort of hope that, at that time, I cry out of just my right eye, the way only the right one produced a tear today. That anomaly would make for a good story.

Next up, I'll be writing to David A. Grant, my TBI mentor and contributor to Brainline.org, to ask if his friend who could not cry had intermittent episodes of watering eyes before he actually cried. I would like to know what awaits me.

My breakfast eaten, I sit and ponder what this tear really means. I examine my now-dry finger, knowing there is salty residue from my tear duct. I touch my cheek, wondering if there is an echo of the rivulet my tear produced. The biggest highlight prior to today was the day I could finally tolerate light well enough to shed my sunglasses, 21 months after the accident. I try not to think about the negatives: I still cannot follow a novel plot long enough to enjoy a book or even avoid headaches and great fatigue.

Yet I continue to write, to read a few pages when doing so won't prevent me from performing my teaching duties, and to remain hopeful that my recovery window has not closed. Today proves that my optimism is not misguided. I have shed a tear. Just one, and it was a histamine response or something like that. But the canal that leads to my tear duct was not broken by the impact. Today confirms that at least one tear duct behaves itself. The issues have been neurological.

I remember that I must be willing to accept that nothing else will improve, and that what I have been able to accomplish occurs in a way different from how it worked before my injury. Seán 2.0 continues to be a more competent creature, but there's no point in weeping for the features of Seán 1.0 that I cannot access.

Somewhere down the road there will be another moment of sadness or great joy, and perhaps by then the tears will be able to flow for the right reasons. The quest continues, but the end may be in sight.

Day 1,000 approaches. We'll see what happens after that. For now, I will sit at the table, drink coffee, and take several moments to thank my brain for reconnecting the tiny pathway that allowed me to shed a tear, and to encourage my brain to keep up all the exciting rediscoveries it has created for me. What a ride.

Part 4: Quest Dismissed.

Cardiff 2.0.
December 31, 2017

December is now the month when I visit Cardiff-by-the-Sea ritually. I intend to travel there every year now, because my children and granddaughter live in the Los Angeles area. I will fly down to visit them and make at least a day trip to the Meditation Gardens in Cardiff.

I am staying in Laguna Hills this time around. I have visited my granddaughter, and I will go back in a couple of days to see my son, his wife, and the baby again. I will also get to see my other two sons and meet the youngest one's fiancée. It is time now to make my way to Cardiff to enhance my memory of the landmarks and the atmosphere.

I remember starting a chapter for my novel the last time I was here. I was not able to finish the scene when I returned to Washington. Between school obligations and my inability to visualize fictional scenes, I couldn't make it work. I take my Surface and stroll two blocks to Besta-Wan Pizza, where the magic happened last year.

I sit at the same table where I wrote 12 months ago. It is right under the TV screen. Today they are showing sports, but the athletes are not horses. I order a large pizza, because I want leftovers to take back to my hotel room. I find the document I worked on, still dated December, 2016. I have not worked on anything related to the novel for more than a year. I am concerned that I might mess up the book if I start adding sections before I am completely ready to write vivid scenes. I cherish this novel. It is important to me that it be as good as I can possibly make it.

I look at the sequence I left unfinished a year ago. I read it and realize that I got off to a good start on this chapter. Reading it allows me to melt into the scene just a bit. I start typing.

I have thought of a subtle way to change the dynamic between my protagonist and a character I am introducing about halfway through the story line. This change adds a little bit of tension and perhaps more realism to the circumstances these two characters face. I manage to finish the scene this time, and I feel very comfortable with the tone I have achieved. As always, I need to be careful of how much I write in one day, so I box up my pizza and go to the gardens.

In 2016, a cold drizzle had settled over town. This year, the sun makes the ocean shimmer, and there are birds everywhere, birds who were hiding out in the cool, foggy afternoons last year. My photos this time are brighter and more appealing. I sit on a bench and look beyond some bushes to the ocean. Sitting on a bench far closer to the water is a woman who is either sketching or journaling. She is doing on paper what I am doing in my head. I will take the images I have internalized back to my room and write notes, so I can include this experience in my memoir.

It's time to get back to Laguna Hills before traffic gets rough. It's a short, easy drive if you make the journey at the right time of day. Before I leave, I make arrangements to have dinner with one of my fellow writers, a woman who is crafting her own memoir and was in my memoir class with Cami Ostman.

Renee DeMont has led one of the most eventful lives I have ever encountered. I met her face to face when she attended one of Cami's gatherings for writers in Bellingham. Renee and I were in Cami's class at the same time, but in different critique groups. For the second year of class, we were in the same group. I got to read chapters of her memoir then. Titled *A Careless Man's Careful Daughter*, it is the story of how Renee and her siblings wound up homeless in part because of her father's gambling addiction. Each time I read her rendering of one of her experiences, I am more convinced that her story is going to touch the lives of many people. I can only hope that my words are half as effective as hers.

Renee and I eat at a little Irish restaurant halfway between her house and my hotel. I have never seen her in her element before. She tends to be reserved when she comes to Bellingham, but she knows the owners of this restaurant and clearly is highly regarded here. We talk about her children and about her progress on her memoir. I encourage her to write it as quickly as possible, because I want a copy of it, and because of its potential for encouraging others who have had difficult childhoods.

I drive back to my hotel and meditate on my day. I did some writing, I connected with a writer I respect, and I communed with nature in a stunning setting. It has been a beautiful way to wrap up a year that has involved considerable progress in healing my brain, though reading and crying will wait till 2018, at least.

August Rush in January.
January 1, 2018

A new year brings good intentions and optimism. In 2016 and 2017, I vowed that I would grind my way through reading a novel. I succeeded early in 2016, but just once, and I was unable to repeat the feat in 2017. Once again, I tell myself that I will read a novel in 2018. I should start with another short, light mystery, or at least I should choose a novel I will find captivating. This year, as suggested by Cami Ostman, I will read a chapter a day, upping the daily quota once I feel stronger. But I won't try to read until my next break from school. I will teach three courses from January to late March, and there is no point in setting myself up for frustration.

I return from a delicious breakfast downstairs at my hotel in Laguna Hills. I splurged a bit on my room, because New Year's Eve in a budget motel would probably be a noisy experience. I make coffee, crawl back into my king-size bed, prop myself up with fluffy pillows, and open my Surface. An early-morning email from a TBI Survivor and ally, Donna LeClair, catches my interest. Her son, Shawn, suffered a brain aneurysm five years ago, and she has been a source of energy, hope, and useful information about the brain. I have been able to answer a few questions for her from the perspective of someone who understands her son's injury. Today, she tells me about a movie she discovered four days ago: *August Rush*.

She has watched this 2007 movie six times in four days, she says. Each time, the beauty of the story has made her cry. Maybe it will make *me* cry.

We'll see about that.

Since the day I produced my first tear as a result of choking on water, my eyes have stayed dry. I have tried to cry at emotionally loaded movies since that first tear, and even when I get choked up enough to feel physical pain, the emotions haven't led my brain to fire the neurons that turn on the waterworks.

Hence my skepticism this morning. I've tried interacting with many sad events and memories to push on my tear ducts. I may as well give this movie a shot.

August Rush, which features Robin Williams as one of his more sinister characters, is available on Netflix. I pull it up on my Surface. I read the synopsis of the movie to see what is so tear-worthy about it.

A boy named Evan Taylor lives in an orphanage in New York, where he is bullied for believing that his parents will someday find him. He knows they are alive because he hears them through the music of his surroundings, like wind chimes and the whine of tires.

I sip my coffee. I drink it black, but I wish it were stronger, so it would remove from my mouth the bad taste I sense when the other boys at the home bully Evan. They make me angry, not sad. I'm relieved when Evan runs away to New York City, because I know he, as the protagonist, won't get killed there. I'm not so sure about the fate of his parents, who split after one night together. The mother is injured in an auto accident and gives birth prematurely. Her father signs the preemie over to the State without her permission, and she believes the baby died.

My reaction to the movie surprises me. When I was two years old, I was so insistent on listening to records as my main source of entertainment that my parents taught me to use their record player. Without being able to read, I could find a record I wanted to play by my visual memory of the label. My fine motor skills developed well enough for me to place the tonearm, which was not automatic, on the 45s. I was easy to care for—I didn't get into trouble as long as I had my records.

When I was three, my parents started supplying me with toy musical instruments, including plastic horns to blow, a small xylophone, and, a year later, an electric organ that had to be warmed up before it would play. I remember my impatience when I wanted to play something, especially if I had an idea for a song in my mind.

That year, I experimented with intervals, and eventually I wrote a short piece that involved a suspended fourth that resolved to the root and third of a C chord. I say I wrote this piece because I could, and still can, reproduce the notes from memory.

The first song written by someone else that I learned to play was "Hark! The Herald Angels Sing." I heard it on the inaugural showing of *A Charlie Brown Christmas* in December, 1965, and after hearing the song at the end of the TV special, I taught it to myself by ear, from memory. When I played it for my mom, she asked me if I wanted to take formal music lessons. I said I did, and I chose the drums.

In the movie, Evan Taylor is a musical prodigy at 11 who, from the first moment that he touches a guitar, is able to play it far better than I can play guitar now. He goes on to play a church organ, as well as write complex sheet music with only minimal guidance in how music notation works.

I was no prodigy, but I have had an abiding interest in composition and performance throughout my life. I lost my chance to become a proficient drummer when my mom became ill when I was seven. We all lost a lot of our sense of joy in life and hunkered down in survival mode until, and really for years after, she died. And yet, the two sources of comfort that remained to me were my records and my books.

I know why I identify with this little boy. We have the same love for music, and we both lost our mother. His loss is reversible, and I want very badly for him to reunite with his parents. As the movie reaches its conclusion, I feel the tightness in my chest that is my main reaction to emotional impacts. Then, my throat tightens. I begin to push my eyes from behind them with my eye muscles, willing the emotions welling up inside my heart and head to spill over into tears.

But nothing happens.

And then something does happen! My eyes blur, both of them, and when I squeeze my eyelids, the inner corner of both eyes produces enough liquid that a tear runs down each side of the bridge of my nose. I wipe carefully and taste the water. Salt. I have cried.

I lie back against my pillows and savor the sensation. The catharsis is incomplete, because I know I have a lot of crying to do. The logjam did not break just now.

But I can check tears of emotion off my list of milestones. Now, to learn to read and write fiction again.

The "What-Ifs" (III).
January, 2018

I'm sitting at my desk at home, the blinds down as usual, soft music in my earphones. I'm drinking coffee and crunching budget numbers in the sluggish way I've grown used to moving. When the numbers begin to do the backstroke, I switch windows from the spreadsheet to the folder I have named "Bye Bye Civic," the collection of photos of my accident. I am supposed to scrutinize the photo Maureen took from the passenger's side of my crushed Civic, so my lawyer understands everything that went on during the collision. Three years later, we are still trying to get a fair settlement.

I have examined this photo ad nauseam, because I still cannot believe that this little metal rectangle held up under the force of the impact. After all this studying, though, I learn something new today. I see that my headrest bent backwards when my head slammed into it. I stare at the headrest, at the twin steel prongs that my head bent and wrenched partially from their mooring in my seat.

When my seat snapped flat and the back seat surged under it and slammed me toward the sky, my head whipped forward on my neck, my chin cracking into my sternum. Hitting that hard against the headrest on the way down and the way up, what was to keep me from breaking my neck? From shattering my skull? From bleeding to death internally? What if any one of those scenarios had played out?

I shiver. I look away. Rather than go back to my budget, which doesn't seem too important at the moment, I distract myself with Facebook. Clicking on cat videos and writing a couple of birthday wishes will clear my head.

A new post pops up from an author friend. She is doing a survey for a plot point.

The question is, "Do you know how to drive a stick?"

I write without thinking, "Yes, and it saved my life."

I reply to a message from another friend, and then I return to my budget work. I'm sorting the utility bills when I freeze.

It saved my life. Why did I just write that driving a stick saved my life? I look back at the photo of my totaled car. Somewhere inside me I know why I believe what I wrote, but I can't follow my thoughts beginning to end. As I strain to push through the logjam, my frontal lobe tingles. My cognition slows, and so does the flow of oxygen. My temples ache. My neck tenses up, and my eyes begin to burn despite the low light.

My jaw slackens, and I start to wheeze.

I sustained three whiplashes in three seconds? No wonder my neck still hurts three years later. Another sinister "what-if" begins to coalesce. I could be a quadriplegic now, unable to type these thoughts. I could be too damaged to think them at all. Much of my thinking over these three years has been haunted with the "what-ifs" I build in my own mind every time I look at this picture (not to mention the nightmares supplied by other people who think of scenarios that would never occur to me).

I gaze at the photo, still trying to remember why I think driving a stick that day saved my life. This steadfast little Civic never failed to start in seven Minnesota winters. It never had to be pushed out of snow. The engine was still purring quietly when I reached forward and turned it off for the last time. I had been sure we would get past our 227,000 miles together, up to 300,000.

But it wasn't to be.

Suddenly all the "what-ifs" I've ever entertained swirl through my mind like the ghosts outside Scrooge's window. Like those phantasms, some of them carry heavy chains, mountains of baggage. The combined weight on my soul leaves me staring at the photo, no longer seeing the image, but seeing through it to another multiverse where the "what-ifs" are realities.

What if I hadn't stopped?

Those pedestrians were waiting patiently. They didn't step out to block me. On such a dangerous road, they had no intention of darting into the crosswalk. In this scenario, I would still be the person I was. I don't know if I would be better off that way, because Seán 2.0 is more aware of the need to use every day to its fullest. I realize that in the three-plus years since I was hit at the crosswalk on the Boulevard, I have driven through that crosswalk more than 300 times, and I have never seen another pedestrian waiting to cross.

Even so, I'm sorry-not-sorry (today) that I put my foot on the brake.

What if the SUV that hit me had been going just a little faster than it was?

The summer after the accident, I happened to meet a personal-injury attorney, and she told me she had litigated a scenario similar to mine: her client was stopped at a light on a four-lane highway. The car behind his saw the red light and began to slow from 55, the speed limit. The third car in line was driven by an intoxicated driver. He became impatient when the car in front of him slowed, so he buzzed around it. He had no idea the light was red, and he plowed into the stopped car at sixty miles per hour, no brakes.

I asked the attorney how her client was doing after being hit at sixty. I was hoping to be comforted by the knowledge that he was well and had no brain injury.

"He's dead," she said. I detected a lilt of surprise in her voice, as if I should have realized on my own that being rear-ended at sixty was a death sentence.

Then, at last, my mind circles back to the question of how driving a stick saved my life. The answer hits me with as much force as the Land Cruiser did.

What if I had been driving an automatic?

My Civic rolled 136 feet. My head drops into the palms of my hands, their heels pressing against my cheekbones.

A wave of understanding washes over me, and I know why I wrote that the manual transmission saved my life. When I stopped the Civic, I put it in neutral and took my foot off the clutch. The young men stepped into the cross-walk, then backed away. All this time, the SUV was bearing down on me.

The bumper of the Land Cruiser plowed into me and through my trunk, hard enough to roll me 136 feet. If I had been driving an automatic, or if I'd had my car in first gear, the transmission would have locked the wheels in place, and the rubber of my tires would have resisted the asphalt. I would have skidded forward a few feet, with the Land Cruiser grinding farther into my rear end the whole time. The trunk and back seat would have encroached more on my seat, and the upward catapult would have been far stronger.

I look online and find a calculator that estimates the delta force that hit me: 29,000 pounds. I'm not sure what delta force means, but I don't need to understand the physics to know I was hit hard. That long, slow roll, most of which I spent lying unconscious, absorbed much of the force.

The disengaged transmission was the key to my survival. I have no idea why it took me so long to realize it. I stare at my screen, trying to comprehend how significant one tiny fork taken in the path of my life has turned out to be.

If my car had not rolled, the result would have been paralysis or death. There's no way to deny it.

A decision I made in May, 2003 to buy a five-speed Civic saved my life on January 29, 2015 at 3:42pm. I wonder what strings are being pulled, what future has been set up for me.

I think about time paradoxes, and visitors from the future, and parallel universes described in theories of quantum physics. I bought my Civic because a friend bought one, and I liked her car better than the Chevy Cavalier I had at the time. I nearly bought a green automatic Civic, but the salesman said he could get me a better financing deal on a black five-speed Civic. Did a version of my friend come from the future to buy her car, so I would buy one just like it to save myself from death? Did a merciful God put the salesman in my path so I would survive this accident twelve years later?

I don't know, of course, but if so, did I "survive for a reason"? I hate to think that way, as it strikes me as arrogant. I don't mind repaying the cosmos for keeping me alive, even with this awful cognitive slowness that frustrates me daily, but I don't think I can live up to the pressure of figuring out the reason I survived. All I can do is ask for guidance, so I understand my role in the world.

Starting with the nightmares about the accident having worse consequences, I have often consoled myself with an internal "at least" comment in an attempt to undermine any tendency toward self-pity. I know my situation could be worse.

Every time I hear "well, at least . . . " about the pedestrians, or my fragile but not broken neck, or my relatively good cognitive progress, those thoughts have already crossed my mind. Maybe I don't mind hearing those words because I *want* my accident to be diminished; I want it to be a little bump on the bumper, a bump on the noggin, and a transitory pain in my neck. If that's the case, I'll be better in a few days and ready to rock my second life as Seán 2.0.

But dang, three years have passed, and I keep re-enacting scenarios of events that didn't even actually happen. I want to scream, *"When will this end?"* I want to break down in tears and let go of nightmares of things that might have happened but didn't. What if I could do that? What if I could let go of what happened and what didn't happen?

What if I could cry, really shed tears and sob?

I don't know. I can't even remember what catharsis is like.

A Career in Music?
January 2, 2018

Fresh off my moving experience with *August Rush*, I encounter a National Public Radio program called *Hidden Brain*. Today's episode is a repeat of a broadcast that tells the story of Derek Amato, a fellow TBI Survivor.

Derek Amato hit his head on the bottom of a swimming pool, and he suffered a TBI that gave him significant hearing loss. But he gained something in return: Out of nowhere, he became able to play the piano at an awe-inspiring level. He had played some guitar prior to the accident, but now he composes complex pieces for the piano.

His "condition" is called "acquired savant syndrome." Just as the fictional character August Rush could pick up an instrument and play it with no prior training, Derek Amato acquired this skill as an adult. He says doctors have offered him medication to make the syndrome go away, but he has no desire to lose his piano skills.

I have a very small bit of piano training, so I figure I should sit down at my keyboard and see if there is some sudden flow of talent brought on by my own TBI. Shortly after I get home from my trip, I sit and place my hands on the keys. Can I create something from nothing?

Nope. Oh, well. On to the next adventure.

Finally Understood.
January 15, 2018

There are many types of intelligence. There are also many types of brain function. A sad fact I have learned since my accident is that many neuropsychologists cannot, or refuse to, detect the difference between intelligence and brain health.

I am a good test-taker. The first time I was tested for IQ was when I was three, and Dr. Weiner ran me through some age-appropriate tasks. He pegged me at just shy of the threshold for genius. Subsequent testing has shown the same results. I am better at some areas of such testing, but overall I am pretty solid. Among my strengths are vocabulary and the ability to do somewhat complex math story problems in my head.

My full neuropsych evaluations involved neurological testing, followed by memory checks and intelligence measures. The final step was a classic personality test with about 300 multiple-choice statements. Many of these statements resemble others, to suss out misinterpretations or inconsistencies.

I had a basic baseline exam with Dr. Judd in February of 2015, but it wasn't a full workup. My attorney asked a neuropsychologist in the area to test me. As always, I challenged myself to do my best work. In order to improve my results, I wore my dark glasses. I did well on the math and the verbal parts. Really well.

This neuropsychologist reported to my attorney that I am extremely intelligent and show no loss of ability to do math or listen to stories and recall the important details. I'm fine, she says.

The defendant's attorney requested that I go to Seattle for evaluation by their neuropsychologist of choice. Same process. She accommodated my sensitivity to the lighting by moving us for part of the testing to a room lit with daylight rather than fluorescent bulbs.

Her report states that she has had no more than two

or three clients who have done as well on the verbal and math areas as I did. My work was in the 99th percentile much of the time. I am fine. She does note that my executive function is terrible.

I tell my attorney that, if they are going to focus entirely on intelligence, those two doctors would have to give Stephen Hawking a clean bill of brain health. I made both of these doctors aware of my light sensitivity and my fatigue after doing cognitive work, but they ignored my complaints about issues that stem directly from brain damage.

My attorney sent me out of town for an opinion from yet another neuropsychologist. This one agreed that my intelligence is a problem, because it masks my injuries. But he looks deeper. We do my evaluation over two days, back to back, and by the middle of the second day, my cognition begins to wobble. Unlike the other two exams, one done over two days a week apart, and one done in a single day, my system now displays the cognitive fatigue of which I complain so much.

He also asks very specific questions about how my brain responds to certain stimuli. My answers satisfy him, and he reports that I am highly intelligent, with compromised cognitive processes stemming from damage to my visual cortex. Like the other two, he states that I have done my best possible work. Unlike the other two, he has noted my fatigue and given it its due recognition as a possibly permanent medical issue.

Finally, vindication. Just as when a forensic neurologist asked me if I had a sense of smell, as concussion victims often lose theirs because of damage to the olfactory bulb, this neuropsychologist knew what to look for and how to describe it in his report. Knowledge is power, and by getting a full estimation of my strengths and weaknesses, I will be able to stay on a course that will continue to heal the parts of my brain that are able to recover.

Dream Team.
March 4, 2018

It's a dream. I know it's a dream, because no architect would construct a building with as many entrances, hallways, and access roads as the one I'm circling. I'm on a narrow path, mostly damp, packed dirt with a thin layer of embedded gravel. I'm riding a dream-bicycle, certainly a dream because I've been forbidden to ride a bike on bumpy ground, a sure path to further neck injury.

I have visited this building before. In all my visits, the building looms tall, utilitarian, a poured-concrete complexity whose walls form an unpainted gray fortress. The monolith creates its own urban skyline, some sections low-slung and others rising several stories above the rest. If I find the right entrance, I enter a maze of narrow, dim hallways lit by greenish fluorescent bulbs encased in thick plastic covers that have trapped countless generations of insects. The hallways branch off into square lobbies of the same gray color, ceilings three stories above the smooth gray concrete floor beneath my feet.

I am here to meet what I now think of as my Dream Team: A black-haired woman, her skin olive, wrinkled from the years that have given her the wisdom I need. A man with a receding hairline, furrows in his forehead, his hair still brown. I do not know their names. They are TBI professionals with differing skill sets. I don't know which of them offers which bit of expertise, so sometimes I make my way through the building to one of them, only to be referred to the other.

I find the right person on the first try part of the time. Sometimes the woman sends me to the man, and I spend so much time trying to find his gray cell that I give up and go back outside, where I can circle the building until I find an entrance that might lead me to him. Other times, the man refers me to the woman. The person to whom I'm referred always has wisdom to offer, if I manage to find the proper mentor. When I do, I gain insights into my healing process and my next steps.

I'm having trouble getting into the building today. The sky is cloudy, but I don't sense a threat of rain. Sunshine would help me find my path, but the day is as gray as the building. In front of the tallest part of the complex runs a slight downgrade, so I use my brakes to avoid overshooting the proper entrance. The path swings to the left along an outcropping, leading me twenty feet farther from the building. The building takes advantage of the contours of the hillside by jutting out toward the edge. Around the corner I find an entrance I haven't seen before. It's unlit, darker than the other entrances I have crept into in earlier dreams.

I dismount and walk my bike up to the cave-like rectangle of darkness. My tires crunch on gravel, the only sound I hear now that my chain is no longer rolling through the sprockets. No birds, no breeze, somewhat like the silence in my brain shortly after my accident.

The path grows darker as I step deeper into the tunnel. The gray walls reflect very little light, but now they echo both the squeak of my rubber tires and the thuds of my footsteps. I'm less certain as I move forward that I've actually found a new entrance. It could lead to nothing more than a trash compactor. I'll walk until the light behind me fades completely.

I detect finally a pale rectangle on the right wall. I prepare to turn right, but the light is shining on that wall from an opening to the left. At the 90-degree angle in the wall I turn left, and the light grows. A jog to the right, and I have found the hallway that leads to the large cell where one of my therapists is working today. I enter a spacious warehouse with a rollup door broad enough to accommodate a tank. My woman TBI guide is sitting at a desk that resembles the information booth at a mall.

"Hi, Seán."

I've talked with her several times over several dreams, and since she knows my name, I'm ashamed to ask hers. Her dark-brown eyes are set deep under her black brows, and they gaze at me with more friendliness than concern.

"I'm glad I found you," I say, trying to avoid the name issue. "Am I supposed to see you this time?"

"James would have sent you to me," she replies. "By the way, I'm Ellen. I know you didn't know my name. You didn't need it before."

"Do I need it now?"

"You will find the path to me more easily if you check the building directory and come straight here." She holds up a paper with eight names listed on it. "Of course, I may send you to James."

"There are other people here?"

"One specialist in reading, one in creative writing. Four others you won't talk to anytime soon."

She must see concern on my face, because she continues, "The healing process involves scaffolding, building on healed areas to work on tender spots. You'll meet these others later. Probably."

I take a deep breath and sigh. She shakes her head.

"You can be patient. And determined. Don't think I'm pessimistic." She turns in her seat and grabs a sheaf of paper that lies on the desk behind her. "Now, let's talk about tears."

My eyes widen. Is my quest ended or continuing? She motions to a seat. I lean my bicycle against her desk, taking care not to scratch the wood with the handlebar or the pedal. I step into her work area and sit in a soft, blue-suede chair.

"I wanted to give you an update on your emotions." I give her one slow nod. I don't know if I should feel excited or worried, so I do what I mostly do, which is feel nothing.

"You're going to cry soon."

"Is that a good thing?"

The right corner of her mouth turns up in a slight grin. "It will put an unambiguous end to your quest. The only potential downside is that you may stop fighting for more brain repair once you can cry regularly."

"That's not really the only thing I still want to get back."

"I wanted to hear you say that. Rewiring your tear ducts is just a symbol of healing. The more important facets of your recovery are regaining the ability to enjoy reading and to write well again."

"You understand that?"

"It's my job. You keep returning to see us because we have the best insights into your healing. Better than any of your doctors. James and I have the map to your lobes, and we are consulting with the rehab team to make sure the work gets done the right way at the right time."

I sit back and look up at the gray concrete ceiling. I can barely detect it, because there is no overhead light, and the light entering through the warehouse door is just bright enough to mask the upper third of the room. After a few seconds I look back down, because my neck tightens when I move it more than a few degrees in any direction.

"Will these tears come from tragedy?" I think of my trip to see my aunt when I learned she had cancer.

"I don't see the future. I know that a bridge is almost built in the circuitry that will enable you to cry. It's the same team that rebuilt your ability to process light somewhat better. They are creating a detour, a new path, as with the light, but most of the reconstruction is a maze of detours. You can never go back to Seán 1.0."

"You know about Seán 2.0?"

"We invented you. Sorry the process is so slow."

"I've been taught to be patient. Thanks for your hard work."

James walks into the room. He puts a strong hand on my shoulder.

"Ellen has given you the update on your recovery, I see."

Her eyes fill with tears. "I told him."

He holds out a fist, and she lifts hers to bump his. I

sense that the meeting has ended, so I thank them and walk my bike out of the building.

I also know we will meet again.

A Blow to the Ego.
March 4, 2018

A new perspective, perhaps a result of visiting my Dream Team, perhaps the culmination of my therapy with Nancy, has taken hold of me as I navigate life. I have realized that there is absolutely no value in taking time to persuade people that I am not who I am.

As soon as I returned to school, I released the mythos of the professor who is completely in command of his brain. I did assure my students that practice classes as therapy for returning to school had shown my command of Spanish grammar to be intact. But I also remember a day when I struggled for a seeming eternity to find a word. My students finally decided it was OK to help me, and they supplied "concert."

I had to release my mortification at being outed constantly in the classroom because of my brain glitches. Over the course of the first year, I learned that my students were far more forgiving of my deficiencies than I was. I had to learn to be as kind to Seán 2.0's brain as my students were. I believe firmly that the student body at Western is better equipped to accept professorial frailty than the general population is.

My first interactions with other TBI Survivors comforted me, because most of us feel the need to tell our stories and explain that we weren't always "this way." I get constant reassurances, after I over-explain myself, that I seem normal. After pondering this dynamic I have released two perspectives I had clung to in order to feel better about myself.

First, I accept that people don't care if I was different before my accident. They might not even believe me, in the same way no one believes a guy who is stumbling around with a beer in his hand when he mumbles, "I'm not drunk." Second, I let go of my fear that I'm no longer socially adequate. My inner understanding that my brain works a *lot* harder to present me as average, rather than cognitively delayed, means nothing to most people. Talking about my past accomplishments almost never gains me more respect.

In other words, I had to release my ego and give up my unwillingness to accept my new reality. Nancy, who is very Zen, said it would be a triumph to get to a point where I can be happy with my new self, rather than rail against my losses. I am often in that happy place.

In more concrete, measurable areas of life, I have experienced the involuntary release of numerous cherished aspects of myself. I have chosen to view my deficits in reading, writing, organizing, and crying as features of Seán 2.0 that pale in comparison to losing the ability to talk, walk, or feed myself.

Releasing my pride about my cognitive skills allows me to move through my world with less stress and more appreciation of beautiful moments. My life is no longer a competition with myself or with anyone else. This lesson may help my construction crew work efficiently. It may allow gains in many areas of my life.

The most valuable impact of this perspective is that it brings me peace.

Deposition.
March 6, 2018

A high-stress day has arrived. The attorney for the other insurance company has scheduled today for a deposition in the personal-injury case. I have had my hair cut to a court-friendly length. (I have also received many compliments on this haircut, so I'll probably keep it this way for a while.) I am dressed in business-casual attire. I have my sunglasses handy, because this conference room has always fatigued me.

The attorney and the adjuster for the insurance company arrive and take their seats. The attorney has hired a court stenographer to type the event. There will be no video. I mention that I will be wearing my sunglasses for comfort.

My attorney has told me to expect the deposition to last a couple of hours. We start out at 10 o'clock with my description of the accident. From there, we go into my physical and cognitive complaints. The attorney, a white-haired man with a no-nonsense haircut, focuses carefully on my words. For that reason, I follow my attorney's advice and answer simply: yes, no, I don't remember.

We are still going at noon, so we break for lunch. Two attorneys who are sharing my case, Matt Conner and Dave Brown, take me to lunch at a Hawaiian poké place around the corner from their office. I get Spam musubi, a meal I discovered on Molokai, a true comfort food for me. Matt says we'll go no more than another hour.

But after lunch, the adjuster does not return, and the lawyer digs in. He pulls out a foot-tall stack of photocopied documents with sticky notes that protrude in all directions, in all colors. He hands me a similar stack.

He goes from one note to the next. "Do you see, Mr. Dwyer, on page 17, where you state that your pain level that day was a 4?"

"Yes."

"Do you see on page 21 where you state that you got

an estimated one headache per month prior to your accident?"

"Yes."

And so on. For four hours. By the end, I am as fatigued as I have been in a long time. He finally gets through all his sticky notes and releases me to return to my life.

I go to bed at five that afternoon. The next day, I struggle in the classroom.

It's the lawyer's job to find ways to help the insurance company enhance its profits while denying me a settlement that will make me feel that there is some positive result from my injury.

Thanks, legal system.

My Future's So Bright...
August 18, 2018

Maureen is in Seattle at a weekend seminar. I get a text from her: "Send me your SPECT scans!"

No need to ask why. I find them and shoot her an email. Then I go back to work.

I have been toiling on my memoir manuscript a lot lately. I am giving myself a tight deadline to finish writing it. I will get the work done more quickly if I create a self-imposed reason to push myself.

A couple of days ago I made a discovery I should have figured out even before my accident. I often see people use the microphone icon on their phones to send text messages. I have used it to send myself emails with bits of text for this book. But the biggest connection I could have made never clicked until this week.

Why, I asked myself, do I not use that microphone icon to write directly into Microsoft Word? I have the app on my phone. I try it out. I can speak coherent sentences straight into a Word document on my phone. There's no need to open an email and later copy the text into Word. The process is so simple, I can't believe I haven't yet done it. Maureen had suggested that I try it, but I kept forgetting. Finally, I'm going to use this procedure.

I'm sitting at my computer, but not yet dictating, when Maureen calls. She tells me she was talking to another person at the seminar, and he said he read SPECT scans for a Seattle doctor. He looked at mine and said immediately, "No wonder he can't read."

A little while later, he told Maureen that my visual cortex is so compromised that my brain uses all its energy to allow me to see. Basically, I can see—or think. I can see—or listen to music. Tasks that involve seeing for cognition to be accomplished—reading, watching movies, writing—will continue to be activities I can do only in limited doses.

I feel as if my visual cortex were an anchor chained to

my ankle. My writing suffers because I look at the screen while I write. Cami Ostman had previously suggested that I try typing with my eyes closed. I can do it, but I am not a perfect touch typist, so I'm not particularly fast.

It's a new day, and I am at the Rustic, writing with Dawn Groves, an incredible Web designer and Microsoft instructor who happens to write great fiction. I tell Dawn about the revelation I received from the scan reader. Suddenly, I decide I may as well try closing my eyes to see if I can visualize the scenes from my novel in 3-D, as I could before my accident. I shut my eyes and think of my protagonists, standing in an art-supply store.

And there they are. Vivid again, accessible to me again. My mouth drops open in surprise. It feels like I'm wearing virtual-reality goggles.

This experience persuades me that I must dictate to finish this memoir and attempt long fiction again. I'll close my eyes, commune with my characters, and report orally what I witness. My heart races with the joy this future workaround brings.

The day of my big experiment, I dictate 9,937 words. That's 36 pages when I print it out. I am back, sort of. I was prolific before my accident, and now I am even more so, though I don't know if I can form long fiction as well as I can tell a mini-story. I'll find out later.

For now, what I know is that I still can't enjoy reading a printed book. At our monthly brain group meeting this week, we were talking about reading, and when I visualized the idea of picking up a novel, I got sick to my stomach. My brain shuts down the reading area instantly and makes me dizzy. I can't tell you how much that response challenges my sense of well-being.

But the day will come, if I am fortunate, when I can read novels again. If not, I will learn to love audiobooks. I am struggling with the pain of losing this aspect of who I am for now, but I will persist, and as in so many other situations related to this accident, I will show myself to be the Survivor I am known to be. And I'll do all my work without crying, for now. Every day brings me closer to the completion of repairs that the Dream Team promises. They will remove the DETOUR signs, and I will cry.

Epilogue: Meditation on Mediation.
August 15, 2018

If your TBI did not result from some sort of negligence on the part of another person, this chapter may not apply to you. You are more than welcome, however, to stay with me through this other type of trauma. The info could come in handy someday if you ever do have your life changed by someone else's mistake.

As of this date, three and one-half years after I was hit, I still have nausea-inducing pain from neck spasms. I still take gabapentin to prevent the knife-stab headaches I otherwise get in the top of my head.

As for my brain function, I still cannot read fiction for more than a few minutes at a time. I cannot track a novel-length tale for more than thirty pages without having to go back and start again. I am the Sisyphus of novel-readers. I still have a student to mark the wrong answers on my students' exams. I still go to bed at 7pm because of fatigue, and I sleep until 7am. I cannot write fiction at a reasonable pace, though I have improved my ability to write cleaner first drafts for this memoir.

I also continue to have problems with short-term memory, which are related to my executive-function issues, including disorganization, forgetting important appointments, and becoming distracted easily. Those without a TBI may say that I'm describing your typical day with a healthy brain, but I assure you that we are not talking about the same phenomenon. You're in a hurry, and my life is blurry.

That's where I am when I stroll into a building to engage in mediation with the insurance company that is protecting the defendant from me. It's 9am, and Maureen has come along to provide both emotional support and thoughts I may not think to include in my statements.

The other legal team called mine to ask if we would attend mediation. They have realized that this case is not trivial. They have seen the medical reports, and they know I am injured. Now, they want to see if they will need to go to trial and attempt to trash my integrity, as well as that of my witnesses. Because this process is not one of ensuring that I get a fair shake after their client was negligent. It is about finding ways to do what would be just in the eyes of anyone related to a TBI Survivor.

My attorneys, Matt and Paula, are here, and they are a source of comfort to me because of their expertise and their calm demeanor. Matt has been on my case (literally and figuratively) since the beginning, and Paula, a partner in the firm, has mentored Matt, who became a partner a couple of months ago.

Our mediator, Jack, is personable and affable. His job is to bring us offers from the other team and take our counter-offers to them. He tells us what they plan to say in court, and he asks us questions to round out our case, so he can push on the other team to get their offer closer to our demand.

In this process, I learn that they plan to attribute my brain malfunction to a short period when my doctor thought I was developing some insulin resistance. They would fail to mention that I no longer face that problem. It is their job to cast doubt on my claim to a jury that will have little or no medical expertise.

When I tell Jack about my need for sleep, he finds that fact significant, and he shares it with the other team. Another fact that somehow never made its way into my team's knowledge (because I have a TBI, duh) is that although the substitute doctor I saw the morning after my accident did not diagnose a concussion immediately, I did see a noted TBI expert that same afternoon. He told me I was concussed, and that I needed to do a full concussion protocol immediately.

Those bits of information shake the other team, it seems, because the adjuster calls the company to ask for the authority to up the offer to meet what we are willing to accept. Jack returns with an offer of half of the liability insurance my negligent driver carries, and we sign off on the deal.

I feel an immediate sense of relief. I feared that their offer would remain so low that we would need to go to trial to get meaningful financial recognition of my travails. But now, the legal aspect of this nightmare has ended with the stroke of a pen. Do I feel vindicated? To some extent, yes. I refuse to think about the money that goes back into the pockets of the insurance company.

During our down time while Jack is talking to the other team, Matt and I discuss how much he has studied the TBI world. I can tell from his presentations that he learned far more than the minimum necessary to build a case. We make plans to grab a beer after work sometime soon.

A few months into the case, I mentioned to Paula that I had written a book about one Pablo Neruda poem. I invited her to read it, so she could see that I am a serious writer. Her response at the time touched me and made me long for the day when I can move that book into the publishing pipeline.

Now, Paula asks me if I have bought the new book of Pablo Neruda's lost poems. I say I have not, though I can enjoy poems more than fiction, because they do not involve a plot.

When we finish the mediation process, she pulls out the new Neruda book and tells me she got it for me as a gift. It's a beautiful hardback, full of "new" poems by my favorite poet. My chest tightens up, I get a lump in my throat, the muscles around my eyes clench . . .

And I do not cry, because the three tears I shed between October, 2017 and January 1, 2018 are still Seán 2.0's only tears. But I have this amazing new book, and the legal process is at an end. For today, that will suffice.

A Brief Appendix of Medical Resources

www.the-brain-initiative.com

Post-Concussion Syndrome.

According to the Mayo Clinic's website: Post-concussion syndrome is a complex disorder in which various symptoms—such as headaches and dizziness—last for weeks and sometimes months after the injury that caused the concussion.

Concussion is a mild traumatic brain injury that usually happens after a blow to the head. It can also occur with violent shaking and movement of the head or body. You don't have to lose consciousness to get a concussion or post-concussion syndrome. In fact, the risk of post-concussion syndrome doesn't appear to be associated with the severity of the initial injury.

In most people, symptoms occur within the first seven to 10 days and go away within three months. Sometimes, they can persist for a year or more.

The goal of treatment after concussion is to effectively manage your symptoms.

Symptoms

Post-concussion symptoms include:
- Headaches
- Dizziness
- Fatigue
- Irritability
- Anxiety
- Insomnia
- Concentration and memory loss
- Ringing in the ears
- Blurry vision

- Noise and light sensitivity
- Rarely, decreases in taste & smell

Post-concussion headaches can vary and may feel like tension-type headaches or migraines. Most often, they are tension-type headaches. These may be associated with a neck injury that happened at the same time as the head injury.

Family and Medical Leave Act (FMLA).

When a company is large enough, it must provide benefits under the Family and Medical Leave Act. But you must advocate for yourself, because you could fall through the cracks and not be notified of your rights under this law. If you are a Survivor or a caregiver, have a look at your rights here: www.dol.gov/whd/fmla/
Be sure to check your state regulations as well.

If you live outside the United States, you will have other options for care while you or your loved one need time off work.

Crying.

As Wikipedia so aptly states it, "The parasympathetic branch of the autonomic nervous system controls the lacrimal glands via the neurotransmitter acetylcholine through both the nicotinic and muscarinic receptors. When these receptors are activated, the lacrimal gland is stimulated to produce tears."

Sounds simple, doesn't it? And yet, something along the line didn't work in my brain for nearly three years. And it hasn't worked since that day. My quest may be over in a technical sense, but I still miss many opportunities to cry.

Acknowledgments

Fake It Till You Make It.
March 28, 2019

It takes a village to write a book, no one writes a book in a vacuum, blah, blah, blah. I agree with those sentiments. But there is far more truth to those statements when it comes to writing a memoir that is penned by someone with brain damage.

My wife, Maureen, tended to my physical, legal, and emotional needs during my crisis, and continues to do so as needed. There would be no book, no Seán 2.0, without her support.

My legal team: Matt Conner, Paula McCandlis, David Brown, and Lauren Kwiatkowski made many positive aspects of this memoir happen.

My university colleagues: Paqui Paredes advocated for my safe return to the classroom. Shannon Dubenion-Smith, Petra Fiero, and Cornelius Partsch filled in for me in the Winter 2015 quarter. Sarah Rowan filled in for my Spring 2015 courses. Holly Childs and Sara Helms kept me pointed in the right direction.

Driving Mister Seán 2.0: Tele Aadsen, Laura Rink, Dick Little, and Kiffer Brown. (I'm sure I was too foggy to recall every ride I got to an appointment, so let me know if I missed you, and I'll acknowledge you on my website.)

My medical team: Dr. Milan Banjanin, Dr. Brian Patterson, Dr. David Schmidt, Helen Lee, (and their support personnel, Cindy and Laurie), Dr. Sasha Blaskovich, Michele Siemion, Karen Russell, Dr. Michael Fraas, Lesley Stephens, the WWU C3D grad students, Dr. Tedd Judd, Dr. Glenn Goodwin, Dr. John Jefferson, Cindy

Maxwell. (Likewise on the brain glitches.)

My writer tribe: Much support, generally and specifically related to my writing, came from this crowd. I know I will miss names: Donna LeClair, Susan Chase-Foster, Mary Jane Fraser, Jolene Hanson, Laura Kalpakian, Peggy Johnson, Victoria Doerper, Jessica H. Stone, Lish Jamtaas, Jennifer Mueller, Mary Gillilan, Norman Green, Janet Oakley, Dawn Groves, Diane Wood, MaryAnn Faubion Kohl, Betty Scott, Renee DeMont, Andrew Shattuck McBride, Anneliese Kamola, Priscilla Sharrow, April Brown, Barbara Allen Clarke, Betsy Burnam, Susan Conrad, Laurel Leigh, Caitlin Upshall, Carol McMillan, Margie Manzoni, Catherine York, James Wells, Twist Phelan, CJ Prince, Rebecca Mabanglo-Mayor, David A. Grant, Angélica Gutiérrez, Janet Shawgo, Sharon Anderson, Sara Stamey, Meagan McGovern, Diana Dodds, Priscilla Long, Sandra Parshall, Gail Siler, Teddy Tedaloo, Kathy Murphy, Mitzi Szereto, Paul Hanson, Pamela Beason, Virginia Herrick, Heath Alberts, Kathleen Kaska, Jenny Milchman, Réanne Hemingway-Douglass, Sabine Sloley, Victoria Peters, Lala Corriere, Isabel Castro, Margaret Bikman, Marla Bronstein, Lisa Dailey, Jennifer Karchmer, Rob Slater, Molly Cochran, Lora Hein, Kathie Tupper, Lorinda Boyer, Kristy Lyn Reddy, Jennifer Wilke, Becky Burns, Jacquie Rogers, Diane Rhodes Garland, Jesikah Sundin, and Wendy Delaney.

Students who made my life richer and easier: Tosia Ruvalcaba, Andy Venegas, Aaron Olsen, Chris Lovgreen, Nick Iaconetti, Kellie Ketchum, and Emily Chesterfield.

My local TBI support team: Mary Hughes, Janet Mott, Adam Beatty, Ellen Winger, Melissa Challender, Amy Biondi, Meril Davenport, and Morgan Hendricks.

More general friend support: Tom Gruber, Steve Robinson, Jerry Herzog, Walli Ann Wisniewski, Margaret Adams, Shelly Lyon, Ray Wensits, Bridget and Mike M., Cassie Hernández and Molly Plamann, Barb Thomas and Cate McCarthy, Chris McQuillin, Racheal Sliter, Dr. Carol Tyler, Allie Drennan, Teri Bryant and Alex, Stephanie Oppelaar and John Oppelaar, Rick Iadonisi and Laura Fox, Anna Carey, Nat Whitman, Trude Sowada, Charis Weathers, Bill Rink, Emily Rose Mowrey and Katherine Bates, Bobbi Rypka, Robert Dodd, Mercedes Christesen, Valerie Ann Bargewell, Nancy Hiller, Deb Meijer, Carissa Bane, Laura Weigand, Lori Kamyk, Soula Christopoulos, Jeff Lowry, Rochelle Parry, Marianne Vere, Laura Adams, Jody Markgraf, Christina Keppie, Octavio Ávalos Ceballos, Kristi Thomas, Donna Goodin and Sam Goodin, Joan Acklin, Jeane Chelich, and Joan Hoffman.

My family: Special shout-out to Cindy Dwyer and to my children, John and Vanessa Dwyer, Tom Dwyer, Stevo Dwyer and Sarey Martin.

Animal guides: Sophie Kane-Dwyer, Luna Dwyer-Kane, Bob Colton-Carson.

Nancy Welch led me through four years of therapy to deal with the PTSD, the physical pain, the emotional challenges, and the perspective-building of coming back from this accident and TBI. Nancy died on March 11, 2019 from ovarian cancer. I was able to tell her that this book was written, but I wanted very much to hand her a copy. Thank you, Nancy, for your immeasurable contribution to my well-being.

There are no words to describe how important Cami Ostman has been to my writing career since I arrived in Bellingham. I did not meet her for two years, or I certainly would have gotten my novel published before my accident. Cami and I share the trait of being fervent in our support of other writers as they craft their stories, memoir or fiction. Cami already has published two successful books, *Second Wind: One Woman's Midlife Quest to Run 7 Marathons on 7 Continents* (2010) and *Beyond Belief: The Secret Lives of Women in Extreme Religions* (2013). She continues to write prolifically, but she has embarked on a new endeavor, and I got to be part of it.

Cami now runs a nine-month program that she calls the Narrative Project. A small group of writers who have personal stories to tell gather by videoconference twice a month. Each time they meet, they talk about strengths and bumps found in the submissions of two members of the group.

Cami encouraged me to join this program because she knew I was trying unsuccessfully on my own to write the book you are now reading. What I want to say here is that I could not have written this book without a group of the type Cami put together for me to lean on, and to push me.

Throughout this writing process, Cami worked to come up with ways for me to get around the difficulties my brain put in its own way. She suggested writing with my eyes closed, and because I am a tolerable touch typist, I found the project moved faster when I followed her advice. Cami also made me feel that my memoir has a place in the world, a reason for existing.

I hope you can see that as my mentor, Cami is largely responsible for my having gotten these words on paper. She is not responsible for the quality of the initial writing. She is responsible for invisible improvements over my original text.

Thank you, Cami. And you, readers, I hope you will consider using the Narrative Project to write out your own thoughts on the life journey you have undertaken, voluntarily or not. If I can help you in any way with such a project, contact me.

sean@seandwyerauthor.com

SEÁN DWYER

Seán Dwyer has published ten short stories. He is a strong advocate for new writers, and he hosts both English- and Spanish-language open mics at Village Books in Bellingham, Washington. A native of Gary, Indiana, he now resides in Bellingham with his wife, Maureen, his hairless cat, Luna, and his goat, Bob.

CPSIA information can be obtained
at www.ICGtesting.com
Printed in the USA
LVHW091511011019
632802LV00008B/50/P

9 780972 496063